Annotations to Geoffrey Hill's *Speech! Speech!*

Annotations to
Geoffrey Hill's *Speech! Speech!*

Ann Hassan

Glossator Special Editions

ANNOTATIONS TO GEOFFREY HILL'S *SPEECH! SPEECH!*
© Ann Hassan, 2012.

This work is licensed under the Creative Commons Attribution-NonCommerical-NoDerivs 3.0 Unported License. To view a copy of this license, visit: http://creativecommons.org/licenses/by-nc-nd/3.0, or send a letter to Creative Commons, 444 Castro Street, Suite 900, Mountain View, California, 94041, USA.

This work is 'Open Access,' which means that you are free to copy, distribute, display, and perform the work as long as you clearly attribute the work to the authors, that you do not use this work for commercial gain in any form whatsoever, and that you in no way alter, transform, or build upon the work outside of its normal use in academic scholarship without express permission of the author and the publisher of this volume. For any reuse or distribution, you must make clear to others the license terms of this work.

First published in 2012 by Glossator Special Editions, an imprint of punctum books (Brooklyn, NY) for *Glossator: Practice and Theory of the Commentary* (glossator.org).

Glossator publishes original commentaries, editions and translations of commentaries, and essays and articles relating to the theory and history of commentary, glossing, and marginalia. The journal aims to encourage the practice of commentary as a creative form of intellectual work and to provide a forum for dialogue and reflection on the past, present, and future of this ancient genre of writing. By aligning itself, not with any particular discipline, but with a particular mode of production, *Glossator* gives expression to the fact that praxis founds theory.

ISBN-13: 978-1468129847

Library of Congress Cataloging-in-Publication Data is available from the Library of Congress.

Cover image: Walters Ms. W.106, Bible pictures by William de Brailes (1250), fol. 4r. Printed with kind permission of The Walters Art Museum, Baltimore, MD.

TABLE OF CONTENTS

INTRODUCTION
   Geoffrey Hill's *Speech! Speech!*: "Footnotes / to
   explain"   1

A NOTE ON THE TEXT   46

ANNOTATIONS   47

BIBLIOGRAPHY   251

APPENDIX: IMAGES   268

INTRODUCTION

Geoffrey Hill's *Speech! Speech!*: "Footnotes / to explain"[1]

Geoffrey Hill's poetic career can be divided into two periods. The verse collections of his first period include *For the Unfallen* (1959), *King Log* (1968), *Mercian Hymns* (1971), *Tenebrae* (1978) and *The Mystery of the Charity of Charles Péguy* (1983) – the volumes reprinted in *New and Collected Poems* published by Penguin in 1994. After a hiatus of thirteen years, Hill published *Canaan* (1996), the volume that catalyzed the publications that constitute his second period: *The Triumph of Love* (1998), *Speech! Speech!* (2000), *The Orchards of Syon* (2002), *Scenes from Comus* (2005), *Without Title* (2006), the Clutag Press and Penguin versions of *A Treatise of Civil Power* (2005 and 2007 respectively), *Selected Poems* (2006), and *Oraclau/Oracles* (2010).[2] The obvious difference between these two periods is prolific output: Hill produced only five full volumes during the first twenty-five years of his career (when he was "the most costive of poets"),[3] but seven in the next ten. He has provided his own explanation for this increased output, attributing it to the successful treatment with prescription medicines of the debilitating depression from which he had long suffered.[4]

---

[1] The title quotation is taken from stanza 96: "Footnotes / to explain BIRKENAU, BUCHENWALD, BURNHAM / BEECHES, DUMBARTON OAKS, HOLLYWOOD".
[2] Hill's verse volume, *Oraclau/Oracles* (published in October 2010) is not included in my discussion.
[3] Adam Kirsch, 'The Long-Cherished Anger of Geoffrey Hill', *New York Sun*, 28 Mar. 2007 (accessed 1 Apr. 2009) <http://www.nysun.com/arts/long-cherished-anger-of-geoffrey-hill/51347/>.
[4] In an interview with *The Paris Review*, Hill states that his recent "unlooked for creative release has a great deal to do" with what the interviewer, Carl Phillips, refers to as "the taking up of serotonin", and that the treatment of his depression with pharmaceutical medicines "completely transformed my life" ('The Art of Poetry LXXX: Geoffrey Hill', *The Paris Review* 42.154 [2000]: 288). See stanza 3 of *Speech! Speech!*, in which he refers to the pharmaceutical 'tuning' and 'untuning' of his neurological state (referred to as his "harp of nerves").

While *Canaan* is the most obvious pivot of the stylistic shift from the first to the second period, *Speech! Speech!* remains (even after the publication of subsequent volumes) the most extreme example of a later style typified by what Robert McFarlane terms "prosodic restlessness".[5] In Hill's later poems, after his "sudden and surprising transformation",[6] the austerity and relentless assiduousness of the earlier work is supplanted by new vigour, with humour and a sense of urgency alternately expressed in feats of lyricism, vitriol and linguistic slapstick.[7] *Speech! Speech!* sees Hill engaged with – in a kind of *fin de siècle* flourish – the dictions and icons of the late twentieth-century world; the monumental quality of the earlier poems ('Genesis', for instance, or the poems of *Tenebrae*) is absent. The sentiments of his earlier work, however, are not: Hill's stock preoccupations (in shorthand, the triumvirate of martyrdom, memory and responsibility) are still present, resulting in a peculiar admixture of canonical gravity (a poetry always steeped in tradition) and whipsmart comedy.

Speech! Speech! is a poem comprised of 120 twelve-line stanzas of unrhymed verse. Published in the year 2000, the poem is a ceremonial marker for the new millennium, an encapsulation of two thousand years' worth of utterances as a symbolic act of remembrance and – with its 120 stanzas, "As many as the days that were | of SODOM"[8] – as an expression of despair for the coming age, an age into which he and his readers will enter, as the back cover of *Speech! Speech!* notes, with "minds and ears relentlessly fouled by degraded public

---

Although Hill is not named, Don Paterson is surely referring to Hill's career when he writes: "One spare and brilliant book every eleven years; then they change his meds and he cannot stop writing. Worse, he thinks he has discovered a sense of humour" (*The Blind Eye* [London: Faber and Faber, 2007], 91).

[5] Robert MacFarlane, 'Gravity and Grace in Geoffrey Hill', *Essays in Criticism* 58.3 (2008): 241-242.

[6] 'The Long-Cherished Anger of Geoffrey Hill'.

[7] That this vigour comes later in Hill's life and career is of note, his recklessness and playfulness having emerged only in his old age: perhaps the most well-known quality of his first poems – published when he was 21 and written even earlier – is their gravity and maturity.

[8] Geoffrey Hill, *Speech! Speech!* (Washington, DC: Counterpoint, 2000), stanza 55.

INTRODUCTION

speech".[9] Travelling at a hurtling pace[10] and along a careening course, the poem has an unexpected sense of urgency: born in 1932, Hill in his later years writes with a vitality that is expressed alternately in invective and brio (a tonality somewhat at odds with an oeuvre known for staid austerity), a "tragic farce"[11] with a sense of experience that derives from more than seven decades of listening and speaking. The poem has received rave reviews ("a classic of English poetry")[12] but also damning criticism ("a freak show");[13] it is a compelling example of the difficulties inherent in the act of making public utterance in the contemporary age.

The title of the poem is the appeal of an audience for the performer (here, the poet) to come forward, to speak, to make an address. *Speech! Speech!* is Hill's answer to this appeal, a performance punctuated with the calls *"encore"* and *"speech! speech!"* from those who made the commission; Hill's address, as Robert Potts notes, is often "hostile", but "utterly committed ... to the public good".[14] In responding to this call for speech, Hill chooses to speak about the difficulty of speaking: the struggle to find one's own voice amongst the multitude of other voices; the difficulty of having that voice heard amidst the all-

---

[9] Publisher's note, *Speech! Speech!* (2003 Counterpoint paperback edition).
[10] Hill instructs that the poem should be read in the same way. See 'Geoffrey Hill', *Don't Ask Me What I Mean: Poets in their Own Words*, eds. Clare Brown and Don Paterson (London: Picador, 2003), 116: "*Speech! Speech!* is not a book to be slowly pondered; it is meant to be taken, at least on first reading, at a cracking pace" (Hill may be referring to silent reading; at a 2006 recital, he read stanzas 15, 20 and 88 at a steady pace; see *Poetry Reading, Oxford, 1st February* [2006], tracks 21, 22 and 23). David Bromwich notes that the poem "aims to be read as a single continuous gesture, though the idiom of the poem tends towards fragmentation" ('Muse of Brimstone', review of *Speech! Speech!*, *New York Times*, 11 Mar. 2001: 28).
[11] Hill describes "tragic farce" as a "fairly accurate suggestion" for the genre of *Speech! Speech!* (*Don't Ask Me What I Mean*, 116) and asks in stanza 69: "Whát was I thinking – / Bergmanesque tragic farce?"
[12] Robert Potts, 'Theatre of Voices', *The Guardian*, 30 Nov. 2001 (accessed 23 Jan. 2005) <http:// www.guardian.co.uk/ books/2001 /nov/30/bestbooksoftheyear.artsfeatures2>.
[13] William Logan, 'Author! Author!', review of *Speech! Speech!*, *The New Criterion* 19.4 (2000): 65.
[14] Robert Potts, 'A Change of Address', review of *Speech! Speech!*, *Times Literary Supplement*, 25 Jan. 2002: 25.

pervasive din; the impossibility of speaking on behalf of others; the problem of speaking in and of the condition of Original Sin; the challenge of writing poetry after Auschwitz; the apocalyptic decline into wilful incoherence which Hill calls "the debauch";[15] and the necessity of memorialising the past – of discovering (as opposed to *making*) history – without recourse to romanticization or fictionalization. We are, according to Hill, "existentially compromised".[16] The publisher's blurb (into which Hill presumably had input)[17] defines the poem as essentially a formal and oratorical answer to two questions: "how do we even begin to think and speak honestly?", and "how does the artist find ways to communicate truth and beauty?"[18] These questions are answered despite and because of frustrating circumstances which impose manifold difficulties; and they are answered, Hill claims, via a "simple" scenario: "an individual voice battles for its identity amid a turmoil of public speech and media noise, a crowded wilderness of acoustical din".[19] *Speech! Speech!* is Hill's attempt

---

[15] Steven Burt, 'Meaningful Speech', *Publishers Weekly*, 8 Apr. 2002: 198. For Hill, what is 'in the air' is foul and should be rejected: in his 2008 Ash Wednesday sermon, he urged the congregation to reject simple acceptance of our reality: "the answer, my friends, is *not* blowing in the wind. What is blowing in the wind is hazard, mischance, the instructions and demands of well-meaning buffoons and idiots, the cries of rage and hatred, and tyranny, the terrible interminglings, the characteristic inability of our previous and present government to distinguish true democracy from plutocratic anarchy, an anarchy which poisons and rots the entire body of political, ethical, and aesthetic thought" ('Trinity Sermon: Ash Wednesday 2008', Trinity College: Cambridge [accessed 12 Jan. 2010] <www.trin.cam.ac.uk/ show.php?dowid=520>).
[16] Geoffrey Hill, 'Trinity Sermon: Ash Wednesday 2008'.
[17] Hill has professed a particular interest in the appearance of his published work: "I have always taken part (when permitted) in the physical preparation and presentation of my books – an aspect of things which I also considered academically in my teaching for the Editorial Institute. Title pages and dust jacket design particularly attract my attention and I give much thought to the choice of illustration" ('Confessio Amantis', *The Record 2009*, Keble College: Oxford: 48-49 [accessed 5 May 2009] <www.keble.ox.ac.uk/alumni/ publications-2/Record09.pdf>).
[18] Publisher's note, *Speech! Speech!* (2003 Counterpoint paperback edition).
[19] *Don't Ask Me What I Mean*, 116.

INTRODUCTION

to negotiate these difficulties and sound his "individual voice"; it is also his statement – itself obfuscated by the poem's various rebarbative features – about the difficulty of doing so.

Each of the poem's 120 stanzas has a considerable measure of independence, so that while there are repeated motifs, refrains, and various linguistic and conceptual connections the experience of reading the poem is fractured and disjointed, with any impulse towards sustained fluidity thwarted by typographical or conceptual jolts. There are lyrical lines such as those in the first half of stanza 16 ("like oil of verdure where the rock shows through; / dark ochre patched more dark, with stubborn glaze"), but there are also lines, such as the poem's last, which defy sense, working instead as alliterative exercises, or by means of subconscious connections ("AMOR. MAN IN A COMA, MA'AM. NEMO. AMEN").[20] Such 'jolts' have been cited as symptomatic of Hill's "collage technique"[21] with allusion and reference said to be the "basic *unit*"[22] for the construction of the collage. While using the vocabulary of twentieth-century visual art to describe *Speech! Speech!* (and other later poems of Hill) is a fresh approach, Hill makes greater use of other more obvious connectors to link phrases, lines and stanzas. Motifs, even quasi-characters reappear (as in 92, 93, 94 and 95: the 'Rapmaster' stanzas); and phrases are repeated, giving a rarely glimpsed sense of continuity (as with the last line of stanza 57, repeated almost verbatim as the first line of stanza 58). It is revealing that among the forty-eight stanzas from *Speech! Speech!* (40% of the whole poem) which were chosen for inclusion in the 2006 *Selected Poems*,[23] there are nineteen examples of consecutive stanzas, a fact which demonstrates the prevalence of intra-textual connections and the interdependence of the stanzas.

---

[20] David Bromwich identifies these closing lines as "omens of a passage to oblivion where thoughts like [Hill's] will have become unnameable" ('Muse of Brimstone', 28).
[21] Jennifer Kilgore, 'Peace it Together: Collage in the Recent Work of Geoffrey Hill', *Cahiers Charles V*, 34 (2003): 167.
[22] Carole Birkan, 'Geoffrey Hill's "Collated" Poems and Criticism', *Cahiers Charles V*, 34 (2003): 149.
[23] Geoffrey Hill, *Selected Poems* (London: Penguin, 2006). The selected stanzas are: 1, 3, 6, 10, 11, 15, 16, 20, 22, 24, 26, 34, 35, 36, 37, 38, 44, 49, 52, 57, 59, 64, 65, 71, 74, 77, 79, 80, 81, 86, 88, 89, 92, 93, 94, 96, 98, 99, 102, 105, 106, 110, 114, 115, 116, 118, 119, 120.

Geoffrey Hill's *Speech! Speech!*

The most striking manifestation of unity is the regularity of its stanzaic form: each stanza is twelve lines; no line is more than thirteen syllables; the stanzas are numbered consecutively and printed two-per-page, justified to the left margin. The combination of the regularity of form and density of content gives the poem the air of a feat, an impressive achievement, and the poem is described in the publisher's note on the back cover as a "caustic, tragicomic tour de force".[24] The disjunction between its rigidity on the page and the lurching quality of its content gives the impression of a poet struggling to speak within the confines and parameters of a difficult discourse. The poet makes certain that the difficulty of his achievement is known, that his audience will appreciate the effort to which he has gone to make his reply to their call for speech.

Significantly, the call is to speak, rather than to write. In *Speech! Speech!*, Hill is preoccupied with the spoken utterance: with its multitude of dictions, aural ambiguities, potential mishearings, misplaced phonemes and other phenomena and impedimenta of speech. In the second stanza, Hill introduces an image of the poet (with a rare identification of "Í") sitting by the Aga at day's end and listening to radio broadcasts made by "agents of Marconi". These broadcasts are "sputtering"; it is as if static or interference prohibits sustained, unhindered listening. This sense of changing stations pervades the poem, as does the image of one struggling to hear amidst a multitude of competing voices, all 'broadcast' across the airwaves on their own frequencies. In the poem, listeners, speakers, and even minds are variously "tuned" and "untuned".[25] Sometimes the poet assumes the role of the emcee (i.e., MC, or master of ceremonies), or Rapmaster, introducing his audience to this or that performer and taking charge of proceedings; elsewhere, he appears as if a film director, cutting and splicing images to create (or destroy) narrative. At other times, Hill takes the role of the stage performer, engendering and responding to the cries from the audience (*"applause"*, *"cheers"*)[26] which appear sporadically throughout the poem. These are phrased sometimes as stage directions, sometimes scripted as the

---

[24] *Speech! Speech!*, Counterpoint (2003 paperback edition).
[25] See stanza 3, in which the poetic lyre becomes the synapses of the brain: "How is it tuned, how can it be un- / tuned, with lithium, this harp of nerves?"
[26] For *"applause"*, see stanza 6; for *"cheers"*, see stanzas 26 and 94.

INTRODUCTION

response of a 'live studio audience', sometimes proclaimed in the "antiphonal voice of the heckler"[27] (the "unseen interrogative interlocutor" whom Hill constantly acknowledges),[28] sometimes attributed explicitly to the mob (the "PEOPLE"), and at other times expressed as scored dynamics – the composer's call for *"lento"* or *"presto"*.[29] The overall sense is that of staged, public performance, utterances broadcast to and for a listening public.[30] What unites these metaphors and images of public performance is their focus on audibility – all require "a court of auditors" (see stanza 63), a listening audience like that in Daumier's etching 'On Dit Que Les Parisiens...' which graces the cover of the poem.

Much of Hill's 'speaking' takes the form of commemoration, and Hill mentions many individuals by name: Max Perutz; Diana, Princess of Wales; Honoré Daumier and Honoré de Balzac; Isaac Rosenberg; Henry Moore; David Bomberg; and many others. But Hill pays homage not only to those who achieved fame. He honours also those who are not named in the pages of history: those war dead who, "missing their stars" (see stanza 7) escaped renown; the women of the Resistance movement. Hill has described his motivation to recognize and praise as a response to the broadcasts for newly-made martyrs of the Biafran War:

> When I arrived in Nigeria in January '67, a month or two after the assassination of Fajuyi, the radio was broadcasting praise-songs for him. And I took very much to the idea, so certain sections of *Speech! Speech!* ... are praise songs. And I wouldn't say that I meant much more than that; but I do seem to seize on figures who seem exemplary to me, and what I

---

[27] Andrew Michael Roberts, *Geoffrey Hill* (Tavistock: Northcote House, 2004), 40.
[28] Christopher Orchard, 'Praxis not Gnosis: Geoffrey Hill and the Anxiety of Polity', *Poetry and Public Language*, eds. Tony Lopez and Anthony Caleshu (Exeter: Shearsman Books, 2007), 201.
[29] For *"lento"*, see stanza 52; for *"presto"*, see stanza 3.
[30] Writing specifically of *The Triumph of Love*, Jeffrey Wainwright notes that "to use poetry as Rhetoric in the classical sense depends upon the existence of a forum in which to be heard, and upon a mode of discourse sharing common ground. This is precisely what the poem cannot lay claim to." *Acceptable Words: Essays on the Poetry of Geoffrey Hill* (Manchester: Manchester University Press, 2005), 82.

believe I know of Fajuyi is worth a praise-song or two.... Everyone says how negative I am, and I don't think I am, I think I'm very positive, and I love to praise, I love to admire."[31]

The poem can be read as a record of these half-forgotten lives, and as a commitment to remember them through this performative utterance.[32]

But just as Hill uses *Speech! Speech!* to praise and laud, he also uses it to lambast. From railing against the mob (identified repeatedly as "the PEOPLE"), to caricaturing those individuals responsible for particular crimes (Tony Blair and Bill Clinton, for instance), Hill proposes plenty of nemeses to his martyrs. With this juxtaposition of good and bad, worthy and unworthy, the poem can be read as an exercise in the obsolete device *laus et vituperatio*, a form most often found in epic verse, which is defined by a "tendency to divide characters into the polar extremes of virtuous and vicious" and "the injunction to make moral discriminations by praise and blame".[33] Jeffrey Wainwright recommends *laus et vituperatio* as a mode for reading *Speech! Speech!* as well as other later verse of Hill:

> One dimension of Hill's work that has become more evident in the later work has been his self-conscious use of the rhetorical modes of laus et vituperatio – praise and vituperation. Both what he admires and deplores is especially marked throughout *Canaan, The Triumph of Love* and *Speech! Speech!*[34]

Hill refers explicitly to this mode in *The Triumph of Love*, paying tribute to "*Laus / et vituperatio*, the worst / remembered, least understood, of the modes".[35] In *Speech! Speech!*, he first refers to "praise-songs" in stanza 19 ("Faithfulness wrong-

---

[31] Robert Potts, 'The Praise Singer', *The Guardian*, 10 Aug. 2002 (accessed 20 Jan. 2003) <http:// www.guardian.co.uk/books/2002/aug/10/featuresreviews.guardianreview15>.

[32] See Robert Maximilian de Gaynesford, 'The Seriousness of Poetry', *Essays in Criticism* 59.1 (2009): 1-21.

[33] Wainwright, *Acceptable Words*, 81. Wainwright is quoting from Brian Vickers's *Defence of Rhetoric*.

[34] *Acceptable Words*, 16.

[35] *The Triumph of Love* (Boston: Houghton Mifflin, 1998), XXIII.

footed...asks and receives praise-songs in lieu"), then again in stanza 99: "What / do I meán by praise-songs? I could weep. / This is a praise-song. These are songs of praise."[36] Hill's sense of advocacy – his lyric testimonies for unsung heroes – and his willingness to lampoon and lay blame – recall Ben Jonson's description of the poet's "ability to render the one loved, the other hated, by his proper embattling of them."[37] The sense is of "tragic farce": Hill's threnodies to heroes stand alongside his satirizing of the foolish and reprehensible.

In using "tragic farce" as his method of expressing the mode of *laus et vituperatio*, Hill identifies three precursors to whom he is indebted, artists who worked in similar way. According to Hill, his own treatment of "the PEOPLE" comes "courtesy / Balzac",[38] whose detailed cataloguing of the foibles and sins of middle class life in the ultimate bourgeois medium – the novel – stands as a prime example of nuanced satire and subversion. Hill refers in stanza 12 to *La Peau de chagrin*, the story of a wish-giving but life-sapping talismanic pelt in which Balzac criticises the grasping greed of his subjects. Honoré Daumier, whose depictions of the nineteenth-century bourgeoisie (including that of the insensible, applauding audience in his 'On Dit Que Les Parisiens...') are known for their darkly satirical view of the public and its fickle opprobrium, is identified as the poet's "latest muse" (stanza 31), and is also offered his "courtesy" (stanza 100). A debt to Catullus is acknowledged in the poem's penultimate stanza, Hill referring to his "sure- / footed" manipulation of the scazon ('limping' verse). Catullus's competent, strident, confident use of a form that intimates disjointedness and the haphazard is suggested as a model for *Speech! Speech!* Hill identifies

---

[36] Compare *Canaan* (London: Penguin, 1996): "what do you mean / praise / lament / praise and lament / what do you mean / do you mean / beatitudes" (39), and "Praise-song for oil drums, / a psalm of slippage" in the same poem (57).
[37] *Acceptable Words*, 81.
[38] *Speech! Speech!*, stanza 100; Balzac is offered "Additional acknowledgements" in the same stanza. According to Hill, poetry and criticism offer possibilities for the formal acknowledgement of such courtesies and debts; he writes in "Sydney Keyes in Historical Perspective" that "I owe him [Keyes] an immense debt that I cannot repay, except, most inadequately, in this present tribute" (*The Oxford Handbook of British and Irish War Poetry*, ed. Tim Kendall [Oxford: Oxford University Press, 2007], 418).

Daumier, Balzac and Catullus as his antecedents, and *laus et vituperatio* is a mode of reading the poem; but the density of reference and allusion remains, and poses a serious difficulty to anyone attempting a close reading of the poem.

THE PRACTICE OF ANNOTATION

Why annotate?[39] If annotation is "always a testimony to alienation from a text",[40] then the annotator's role is to bring reader and text closer together, to form connecting links. The cause of this alienating distance between reader and text is usually temporal: the text requires decoding and expanding because its language is archaic, or its syntax impenetrable, or its form obsolete. *Speech! Speech!* was published in 2000; that it requires annotation is itself interesting. The difficulties it presents do not result from temporal distance, but rather from its thousands of particulars – these being part of the singular, idiosyncratic experience of the poet. For Hill, alienation is central to the poem: "Whatever strange relationship we have with the poem, it is not one of enjoyment. It is more like being brushed past, or aside, by an alien being."[41] The task of 'decoding', translating for the "alien being" in *Speech! Speech!* which voices Hill's allusive ciphers, is onerous, but, I argue, finally rewarding; the seemingly élitist inaccessibility of the poem is a veneer which can be stripped away with the right tools. For Hill, who argues that simplicity and (pseudo-)

---

[39] It should be noted that textual work is an occupation in which Hill is deeply interested and with which he has sympathy: "During my final period at Boston University, I co-founded, together with Professor Sir Christopher Ricks, the Editorial Institute.... We shared the view (I believe) that in the past quarter of a century too much emphasis has been placed on theoretical methods of approach, coupled – oxymoronically – with the cultivation of a wild subjectivity of interpretative animus.... Christopher and I envisaged a programme... in which graduate degree candidates would edit, with full textual and historical apparatus, a work chosen in consultation with the directors." ('Confessio Amantis', 47).

[40] Ralph Hanna III, 'Annotation as Social Practice', *Annotation and its Texts*, ed. Stephen A. Barney (New York; Oxford: Oxford University Press, 1991), 178.

[41] Geoffrey Hill, *Collected Critical Writings*, ed. Kenneth Haynes (Oxford: Oxford University Press, 2008), 566.

INTRODUCTION

straight-talking are manifestations of tyranny and subjugation,[42] such difficulty is no bad thing; readers, while they may accept Hill's intent as democratic and egalitarian, may (not unreasonably) crave assistance in the form of notes and other explication.

This study is an effort to determine, in Hill's own words, "the true nature / of this achievement" (stanza 92). The self-evident difficulty of the poem (the existence of which Hill accepts, "though with some reluctance")[43] means that it is tempting when considering it to slip into generalizations. In part to evade such generalization the greater part of this study takes the form of close analysis, a synthesis of the primary resource (the text of the poem) and various secondary resources (which are collected in the accompanying notes and inform the content of the commentaries). This synthesis – manifested in annotations to Hill's original text – has obviously an explanatory function, but also creates its own narrative, negotiating the text line-by-line and as it is read. Difficulty is easy to identify, but identification of its causes and manifestations is a more demanding task. Responding to a need to "say something definite"[44] about the poem, I have interrogated examples of difficulty as they appear rather than dismissing them as inexplicable or irreconcilable. In explaining particular difficulties, I have tried to find the reason for their inclusion, and to describe their effect on and role within the poem. In doing so, an implicit argument about reading is sustained: by negotiating each example of difficulty as it occurs, the immediate and cumulative effect of the difficulty of the poem as a whole is dissipated. Treatments of *Speech! Speech!* have tended to focus on its inaccessibility. In relentlessly and mechanically 'accessing' the poem, I make two claims: first, that the difficulty of the text is not insurmountable; and second, that the products of textual analysis – in this case, notes and commentaries – are useful diagnostic tools for looking beyond the difficulty of the text in the attempt to make

---

[42] Genuine straight-talking, however, is Hill's aim: he quotes Junius ("an author new to me"): "I speak to the plain understanding of the people, and appeal to their honest, liberal construction of me" (*Don't Ask Me What I Mean*, 117).
[43] *Don't Ask Me What I Mean: Poets in their Own Words*, 116.
[44] Thomas Day, 'Geoffrey Hill's Finishing-Lines', *Cahiers Charles V* 34 (2003): 162.

definite, specific statements about it, to determine its "achievement".

In making supplements to the text, it has been necessary continually to question whether a particular fact or elaboration contributes significantly to the understanding of the text, and whether a note, or turn of phrase in the commentary brings out the appropriate nuance within the poem. This is a matter of determining validity: for each detail within the poem which requires or begs explication, there is a sphere of knowledge which can contribute to its understanding; outside of this sphere is a plethora of information which may be fascinating, titillating, and even compelling in terms of its relatedness to this text, but which does not bring to bear upon the poem sufficient weight as to warrant its inclusion, or which is so commonplace as not to require explanation. The context of the phrase, the line, the stanza and the position of the stanza in the poem are all considered when making an addition. In stanza 55, for instance, "impeachment" suggests ex-US President Bill Clinton, because of this stanza's proximity to another (stanza 53) which refers to his affair with Monica Lewinsky; and the echo of George Bush Sr's "Read my lips" is heard in Hill's next phrase, "Watch my lips", and only because of this Clinton connection. The same method is used for exclusion: in stanza 60, for instance, it is tempting to read Hill's reference to Bucer's signing "for England" as an autobiographical comment about Hill's return to his home country, until it is remembered that this return took place in 2006, six years after the publication of *Speech! Speech!* For each note and in each commentary, delicate balances such as these are struck, with an economy of interpretive validity being always played out.

Furthermore, in making additions to the text I have been mindful of the impossibility of knowing the 'truth' of the poem. My interpretation of particular details and even whole stanzas is presented as the best hypothesis I could propose; it is my hope that further work on the poem will refine or replace these hypotheses with better versions. This sense of hypothesis is especially true when dealing with a poem as rich in reference and allusion as *Speech! Speech!* There are, however, occasions when I am quite certain of a particular interpretation of the text. In stanza 88, for instance, when Hill speaks of "Odette" and "Violette" in the context of World War II, I am confident he is writing of Resistance heroines Odette Sansom and Violette Szabo. Likewise, in stanza 80, where Hill uses the word

INTRODUCTION

"*augenblick*", in the context of the surrounding phrases, "four chordal horns", "mute powers", "pitched in disorder" and "nadir of your triumph", I am confident about my deduction that he is alluding to Beethoven's *Der Glorreiche Augenblick*, although Beethoven is nowhere named. Elsewhere, the import of the text and the identification of contributing knowledge is more difficult to determine. In stanza 90, for example, I am not entirely convinced of my note allying the "apostles' jets" with with the super-rich religious far Right: but it is at present my best hypothesis, and my notes, I believe, contribute to the elucidation of the text despite this uncertainty about their final accuracy.

Determining *what* to include in my annotations was one question; deciding *where* to include different kinds of detail was another. My supplements to the text appear in two forms. The first of these is the note, the textual annotation with direct allegiance to the text, and which cites, translates, defines, contextualizes, signals reiterations and marks the repetition of motifs. The notes tell much about sources and meanings, but little about why a detail is included; they are obviously products of research, but, as Hill notes, research "is not anamnesis".[45] With notes only, the explicated poem is akin to a completed cryptic crossword, its many cracked enigmas fitting together in a jigsaw-like formation but to no great end and with no particular sense, the finished puzzle an achievement rather than an answer.[46] The distinction is one of intent: the poem *appears* cryptic to the reader, but the poet's intent is not to write in code. Textual commentaries – the second adjunct to the text – perform the conceptual work that is beyond the scope of the note; in these, the poet's arguments and conceits are identified and the development of his themes is recorded. The two apparatuses perform different functions in terms of

---

[45] *The Triumph of Love*, LXVII.
[46] Hill resists descriptions of his work as cryptic: "I am baffled and saddened when readers, friendly as much as unfriendly, approach my poems as cryptograms to be decoded" (*Don't Ask Me What I Mean*, 116). The crossword features in *Speech! Speech!* in stanza 2, when Hill describes the Scott Expedition as being "frozen in time / before the first crossword"; in stanza 55, with the imperative "Hoick out another clue"; and in stanza 85, with the quasi-cryptic clue, "Ruin smell of cat's urine with a small gin" and the instruction to "Develop the anagram".

difficulty: notes signal the existence of a surface difficulty, able to be negotiated by the dedicated library patron or the experienced Internet user (whom Hill in *Speech! Speech!* terms the "world-surfing ... junk-maestro");[47] commentaries deal with those problems which remain after the 'decoding' of poetic detail, and these aim to find an answer not to each clue but to the puzzle as a whole.

RECEPTION AND THE ROLE OF THE ANNOTATOR

But does Hill want to be 'cracked', explained to a greater, wider readership? Geoffrey Hill is a well-known and lauded poet, but, as Adam Kirsch notes, although it is "now common to hear English critics call Mr. Hill the greatest poet alive; in America [...] it is hard even to find his books".[48] Hill writes in *Speech! Speech!* of the possibility of addressing "fresh auditors" (stanza 92), and has claimed that his favourite review of the poem was one published on a popular culture website:

> The very best review of *Speech! Speech!* that I got, and one of the very best reviews I've ever had, was in an online program called popmatters ... by a man called Andy Fogle.... Springing up from somewhere, some entirely unknown quarter, one gets this vivid and vital response. I find it enormously encouraging.[49]

The poet is pleased to have reached an audience to whom he has been unfamiliar hitherto. Asked in an interview with the *Oxonian* about how he envisages his readership, Hill betrayed a desire to reach not only a larger but also a broader audience, a more 'public' public:

> When I see my half-yearly royalty statements I seem not to have a readership at all. Yet in 2006 when I gave a reading in the Sheldonian the place was packed, chiefly with young people. And at poetry

---

[47] *Speech! Speech!*, stanza 47. Gregory Wolfe, however, notes that "Despite Wikipedia and Google Translate, [Hill's] foreign phrases and allusions are resented"; see 'Who's Afraid of Geoffrey Hill?', *Image* 66 (2010) (accessed 1 Oct. 2010) <http://imagejournal.org/page/journal/editorial-statements/whos-afraid-of-geoffrey-hill>.
[48] 'The Long-Cherished Anger of Geoffrey Hill'.
[49] 'Meaningful Speech', 198.

INTRODUCTION

readings I continually meet older people who bring for signing a copy of every book since *For the Unfallen* (1959). There are obviously devoted readers, but it's all rather subterranean, a bit like wartime resistance.[50]

It seems that Hill feels keenly the isolation that resulted from his "elevated and coldly austere" earlier verse.[51] And although he believes contemporary culture to be increasingly 'debauched',[52] in this second period he prefers to address the populace rather than to reject it. He makes clear this intention in *Without Title* when he writes: "Turning towards / the people is no worse, no better, say, / than chancre of exile.[53] This turn towards the people as a way out of exile is symptomatic of a major shift in Hill's verse.

Speech! Speech! occupies an uncomfortable position in Hill's oeuvre: it stands apart from the first period, and is the most dense, obtuse and difficult example of the second. Perhaps as a result of this difficulty, the poem is rarely given sustained attention. Some critics dismiss *Speech! Speech!* in a few words; others omit it altogether from their considerations of Hill's recent work. Michael O'Neill nowhere addresses *Speech! Speech!* in his *The All-Sustaining Air*, despite its pertinence to his discussion and his consideration of adjacent

---

[50] Alexandra Bell, Rebecca Rosen and Edmund White, 'Strongholds of the Imagination', *The Oxonian Review* 9.4, 18 May 2009 (accessed 19 Sept. 2009) <http://www.oxonianreview.org/ wp/geoffrey-hill/>.

[51] Elisabeth Knottenbelt, *Passionate Intelligence: The Poetry of Geoffrey Hill* (Amsterdam: Rodopi, 1990), 1. As Jeannine Johnson has noted, Hill appears not to notice that against the numbers who ignore or deride his poetry, there are "at least as many critics who never fail to laud his work: this positive fact, as well as the fact that he has more professional readers – critical and admiring – than almost any other living poet writing in English, seems lost on him". *Why Write Poetry: Modern Poets Defending Their Art* (Madison, NJ: Fairleigh Dickinson University Press, 2007), 258.

[52] In an interview, Hill explained that one aim of *Speech! Speech!* was to ask "how to make speech meaningful when the world has done all it can to debauch and trivialize it.... I am almost bound not to believe that any particular age in human society was a golden age, when everything was right and everything was good." But Hill adds that in recent decades, "the tempo of the degradation, the intensity of the debauch, have certainly increased" ('Meaningful Speech', 198).

[53] Geoffrey Hill, *Without Title* (London: Penguin, 2006), 39.

volumes *The Triumph of Love* and *The Orchards of Syon*.[54] Jennifer Kilgore, in a passage determining 'Pound as Persona in *The Triumph of Love* and *Speech! Speech!*', cites lines from *Speech! Speech!* only once.[55] After making an argument for understanding the first and second periods of Hill's career as the "epoch of gravity and the epoch of grace" respectively, Robert McFarlane mentions *Speech! Speech!* only to signal its exclusion from further discussion: "With the exception of *Speech! Speech!*, all these volumes meditate on graceful experience".[56] Obviously, any derisions and omissions must be weighed up against examples of great praise – descriptions of the poem as "magisterial" and claims for its place as "a classic of English poetry",[57] for instance – but their existence points to a difficulty that is worthy of attention.

For many devoted readers of Hill, the new style of his later work, and in particular its manifestation in *Speech! Speech!*,

---

[54] Michael O'Neill, *The All-Sustaining Air: Romantic Legacies and Renewals in British, American, and Irish Poetry since 1900* (Oxford: Oxford University Press, 2007). O'Neill argues for a reading of poetry as a form of literary criticism.

[55] Jennifer Kilgore, 'Seeking "The Root in Justice": Geoffrey Hill on Ezra Pound', *Ezra Pound and Referentiality*, ed. Hélène Aji (Paris: Presses Paris Sorbonne, 2003), 100.

[56] 'Gravity and Grace in Geoffrey Hill', 241-242.

[57] As claimed by Robert Potts in 'Theatre of Voices': his sense that the poem "will, I suspect, become a classic of English poetry" and his final enunciation, "Magisterial", are conflated in the publisher's note on the back cover of the Counterpoint paperback edition of *Speech! Speech!* in the following, distinctly unequivocal iteration: "the London *Guardian*, naming it the poetry book of the year, called it "magisterial – a classic of English poetry." John Lyon draws attention to the fact that positive criticism of Hill's later work is often reluctant: writing of *The Triumph of Love*, he notes that positive reviews "present the fact of Hill's major standing as a chilly concession rather than a celebration, and proceed to unearth or reveal or expose the 'real' Geoffrey Hill beneath the implicitly unnecessary clutter of his difficulty" ('"Pardon?": Our Problem with Difficulty [and Geoffrey Hill]', *Thumbscrew* 19 [1999]: 11). William Logan ventures beyond the "chilly" when he writes that "Geoffrey Hill stands by his words by standing apart from everything else, proud of an authority no one wishes to dispute because no one cares to be lord of such limited wasteground" ('The Absolute Unreasonableness of Geoffrey Hill', *Conversant Essays: Contemporary Poets on Poetry* [Detroit, MI; Wayne State University Press, 1990], 47).

INTRODUCTION

was difficult to digest. Critical responses to the poem have been largely ambivalent. William Logan considered *Speech! Speech!* a "brute monologue" which alienated readers by refusing to identify its references and allusions.[58] Reacting to what he perceived as Hill's wilful obfuscation, Logan described Hill's assertion that the stanzas number "As many as the days that were | of SODOM"[59] as "perhaps the only time the poem is helpful".[60] Kevin Hart considers this 'unhelpfulness' to be a symptom of Hill's laziness and inattention; his image of Hill is of a septuagenarian who waxes on banalities because he is "drained of verbal and intellectual energy".[61] On no page of the poem, Hart claims, is Hill "writing with full attention"; rather, he projects "a shadow play of learning while not freshly responding to the mystery of why we live, love, suffer and die."[62] Hart yearns for the Hill of the first period – in comparison with earlier verse, *Speech! Speech!* is simply "unworthy of such an impressive poet";[63] summarizing Hill's career, he writes that: "Not all of Hill's book-length sequences are successful: *Speech! Speech!* (2000), 120 twelve-liners, remains clotted and inert".[64] Hart is, finally, entirely unequivocal: when he compares *Speech! Speech!* with earlier Hill, he finds it to be essentially "a failure, the weakest book by far in the poet's work".[65]

In acknowledging the need for further and closer attention to be given to *Speech! Speech!*, some critics have made explicit requests for an annotative study. Online reviewer Rachel Barenblat wrote that she "Again and again" found herself "wanting an annotated version of *Speech! Speech!*, a guidebook to lead [her] through these seemingly-unconnected words".[66]

---

[58] 'Author! Author!', 65.
[59] *Speech! Speech!*, stanza 55.
[60] 'Author! Author!', 65.
[61] 'Up and Dówn the | Hill', review of *Speech! Speech!* and *The Orchards of Syon*, *Notre Dame Review* 17 (2004): 161.
[62] 'Up and Dówn the | Hill', 161.
[63] 'Up and Dówn the | Hill', 161.
[64] Kevin Hart, 'Varieties of Poetic Sequence', *Cambridge Companion to Twentieth-Century English Poetry*, ed. Neil Corcoran (Cambridge: Cambridge University Press, 2007), 194.
[65] 'Up and Dówn the | Hill', 158.
[66] Rachel Barenblat, 'Review of *Speech! Speech!*', *Pifmagazine*, 1 Mar. 2001 (accessed 12 Jul. 2005) <http://www.pifmagazine.com/SID/662/>.

Andy Fogle, a regular reviewer at the pop-culture site *PopMatters* (and of whose review Hill's own grateful mention has been noted earlier), claimed that "with the right tool or two" he could come to believe Harold Bloom's declaration that Hill is the "greatest poet living".[67] These statements come from outside the academic discourse of Hill criticism, but the desire for closer textual analysis is reiterated by established critics in various literary journals. Thomas Day writes that definitive notation of the poem is required and that "it is not enough to speak of difficulty in Hill by playing on his words and citing irreconcilables" because doing so "ignores the urgent need to say something definite".[68] Andrew Michael Roberts notes that "No brief account can do justice to the poem's range, nor interpret more than a fraction of its lines".[69] Reviewing *Speech! Speech!* in *The New York Times*, David Bromwich wrote of stanza 19 that "Annotation will be needed before such a passage can sort itself into coherence in a second mind".[70] John Lyon simply assumes the existence – and so points to the necessity – of "future editors and annotators of Hill's work".[71]

Requests for closer textual analysis of *Speech! Speech!* – and the sometimes specific request for an annotated edition – come not as a result of temporal distance from the text (what Ralph Hanna identifies as the "response to a prior culture"),[72] but from its textual difficulty. There is a perceived imbalance between the cerebral range of the poet – which spans the many

---

[67] Andy Fogle, 'This Canon Fires', review of *Speech! Speech!*, *Popmatters* (accessed 10. Oct. 2008) <http://www.popmatters.com/pm/review/speech-speech>).
[68] 'Geoffrey Hill's Finishing-Lines', 162.
[69] *Geoffrey Hill*, 41.
[70] 'Muse of Brimstone', 28.
[71] '"What are you incinerating?": Geoffrey Hill and Popular Culture', *English* 43 (2005): 89.
[72] For Hanna, the practice of annotation mirrors the simultaneous nearness and distance which societies feel with the past: "annotation is always a testimony to alienation from a text, always represents a response to a prior culture from which one believes oneself (and consequently, nearly everyone else) distanced. Yet simultaneously... annotation also testifies to inclusion: one usually assumes that only canonical texts deserve annotation, and such canonicity depends on the acceptance of the text by some critical community, a community of which the annotator is the designated representative ('Annotation as Social Practice', 178).

INTRODUCTION

references and allusions within the poem – and his reader. This imbalance engenders a kind of guilt: readers consider themselves simply not up to the job of reading the poem. Nicholas Lezard described the sense of inferiority that he suffers from while reading the poem, and he craves assistance: "As so often with Hill, one guiltily yearns for extensive explanatory notes; only now more than ever".[73] For David Rogers, the imbalance between reader and poet is the prime cause of alienation in *Speech! Speech!*: "The difficulty of this book for the ordinary reader attracted to poetry is a detail of reference beyond the experience of most readers".[74] For Michael Schmidt, Hill's later poems will "eventually require footnotes or explication ... for many readers unequal to the coherent past worlds he draws together in all their otherness."[75] The image is that of Hill as a taskmaster making unreasonable demands on his struggling readers; many of those struggling readers would welcome the assistance offered by detailed annotations to the text.

There is acceptance, too, of the principle that cataloguing the "detail of reference" is a long-term project: Peter McDonald writes that *Speech! Speech!* is "Hill's most difficult volume of poetry to date, and it is likely that critical approaches to it ... will be slow to take its true measure, just as they will have long work in weighing up its different registers and fields of reference."[76] John Lyon attests that the reader of later Hill "knows from past and continuing experience" that understanding will be a "slow and painstaking" (but ultimately "worthwhile") process.[77] William Logan's responses to *Speech! Speech!* can be seen as a manifestation of this slowness to take the poem's "true measure". Reviewing *Speech! Speech!* for *The New Criterion* in December 2000, Logan was scathing: its stance is described as "lazy", its development a "descent circle by

---

[73] 'Hill Starts', *The Guardian*, 17 Nov. 2001 (accessed 10 Jan. 2008) <http:// www.guardian.co.uk/books/ 2001/ nov/ 17 /poetry.tseliotprizeforpoetry2001>.
[74] 'Review of *Speech! Speech!*', *World Literature Today* 76:1 (2002): 152.
[75] Michael Schmidt, *Lives of the Poets* (London: Weidenfeld and Nicolson, 1998), 875.
[76] *Serious Poetry: Form and Authority from Yeats to Hill* (Oxford: Oxford University Press, 2002), 198.
[77] '"Pardon?": Our Problem with Difficulty (and Geoffrey Hill)', 11.

circle into an Inferno of blitherings".[78] Of the four poets with whose work Logan reviewed the poem – John Ashbery, Yusef Komunyakaa, Gjertrud Schnackenberg and Michael Longley – Hill and *Speech! Speech!* received the worst assessment. By June 2002, however, Logan had revised his opinion. Reviewing *The Orchards of Syon*, he reported: "I was not kind to *Speech! Speech!* when I reviewed it, and I must now eat my words, or some of them."[79] According to Logan, close textual analysis encouraged him to make this revaluation: "If there are critics to labour over these poems as they have over Eliot and Pound, the deep shafts of footnotes will gradually mine their subliminal hurts and sublime graces."[80] It is my contention that Logan's response is typical and thus a model: readers' first responses to the poem (the amalgam of bewilderment, guilt, and hostility frequently described) can be transformed via "deep shafts of footnotes" and other explicatory work into appreciative understanding.

The Politics of Difficulty

The difficulty of *Speech! Speech!* means that – unlike Logan – many readers do not persist and return for reappraisal, but instead reject the poem, perhaps for political reasons. The concepts of 'difficulty' and 'élitism' are closely linked and remain very much in the foreground of discussions around twentieth-century literature; the modernist long poem, in particular, is notorious for such difficulty. The density of Pound's *Cantos* correlates to its élitism (even, according to many, to its fascism); similarly, Eliot's *The Waste Land* with its myriad invocations is emblematic of a high modernist ethic of difficulty which sees works embedded in the literary tradition to such an extent that they can be inaccessible to those outside it. Hill writes from within this and other traditions: the traditions, for instance, of the church and theology.[81] Responses

---

[78] 'Author! Author!', 65.
[79] 'Falls the Shadow', review of *The Orchards of Syon*, *The New Criterion* 20 (2002): 75.
[80] 'Falls the Shadow', 75. "[T]hese poems" are what Hill describes as his "tetralogy", *Canaan*, *The Triumph of Love*, *Speech! Speech!* and *The Orchards of Syon* (see 'Meaningful Speech', 198).
[81] David C. Mahan provides an account of the relationship between Hill's poetry and the Christian tradition in *An Unexpected Light: Theology and Witness in the Poetry and Thought of Charles Williams,*

to *Speech! Speech!* have included accusations of élitism and wilful obscurantism. In his first assessment, Logan reasoned: "Refusing to lower yourself to the mob is one thing, sneering at your readers is another – it's not a matter of finding the fit though few when there *are* no fit and no few".[82] Even after his reassessment of the poem, Logan claims that "Hill would be delusional not to realize his poetry is beyond the reach of the common reader, or even most uncommon ones."[83] Likewise, Laurie Smith believes the poem to be "accessible only to the educated few", and hence fundamentally "fascist".[84] Rowland, on the other hand, acknowledges the poem's difficulty but argues that "Hill does not loathe his readers" but rather expects them "to think harder than some of them want to".[85] Hill himself echoes this sentiment: "I am happy to make my work as generally accessible as I honestly can. But this is less often than many professional and amateur readers consider right and proper."[86] For Christopher Orchard, the source of Hill's difficulty is "the physical distance between him and those who should be the subject of his praxis".[87] Hill himself acknowledges the difficulty of his poetry and the work required to make sense of it; after a cryptic reference to Dante in *The Orchards of Syon*, he issues the instruction "Don't look it up this time", urging readers instead to rely on their "sub- / conscious" to assist understanding.[88]

Michael O'Siadhail, and Geoffrey Hill (Eugene, OR: Pickwick Publications, 2009).
[82] 'Author! Author!', 65.
[83] William Logan, 'Falls the Shadow', 75.
[84] 'Subduing the Reader', review of *Speech! Speech!*, *Magma* 23 (2002) (accessed 12 May 2007) <http:// www.poetrymagazines.org.uk/ magazine/ record.asp?id=14974>.
[85] Antony Rowland, *Holocaust Poetry: Awkward Poetics in the Work of Sylvia Plath, Geoffrey Hill, Tony Harrison and Ted Hughes* (Edinburgh: Edinburgh University Press, 2005), 71.
[86] *Don't Ask Me What I Mean*, 117.
[87] Christopher Orchard, 'Praxis not Gnosis: Geoffrey Hill and the Anxiety of Polity', 200.
[88] The passage is from XXI: "Can you stand -- / cleft – but in the spirit, as a tree / by lightning, close to the shored heart? / I believe this has been done. Dante / describes it somewhere – I may be mistaken. Don't look it up this time; the sub- / conscious does well by us; leave well alone."

Geoffrey Hill's *Speech! Speech!*

And yet Hill's direction to not "look it up this time", his championing of the sub-conscious over the encyclopaedia, is somewhat disingenuous. He argues for a complex, difficult consciousness and a complex, difficult poetry to match – both mind and poem rejecting simplification and requiring decoding, whether by ourselves or by others:

> We are difficult. Human beings are difficult. We're difficult to ourselves, we are mysteries to each other. One encounters in any ordinary day far more real difficulty than one confronts in the most 'intellectual' piece of work. Why is it believed that poetry, prose, painting, music should be less than we are? Why does music, why does poetry have to address us in simplified terms, when, if such simplification were applied to a description of our own inner selves, we would find it demeaning?[89]

Describing *Speech! Speech!*, Hill reiterates this mirroring of everyday difficulty in poetry: "The difficulties of daily living get in the way and my poems, unavoidably it seems, collide with the densities of common existence".[90] To produce deliberately 'simple' poetry is, then, to demean one's readers. The converse is for Hill equally true: delivering complex poetry flatters, even democratizes the reader. According to Hill, difficulty and complexity liberate readers from the threat of tyranny:

> I would argue that genuinely difficult art is truly democratic. And that tyranny requires simplification.... And any complexity of language, any ambiguity, any ambivalence implies intelligence. Maybe an intelligence under threat, maybe an intelligence that is afraid of consequences, but nonetheless an intelligence working in qualifications and revelations ... resisting, therefore, tyrannical simplification.[91]

---

[89] 'The Art of Poetry LXXX', 277
[90] *Don't Ask Me What I Mean*, 116.
[91] 'The Art of Poetry LXXX', 277.

INTRODUCTION

More recently, Hill has identified difficulty as "the greatest safeguard that democracy possesses".[92] For Hill, then, difficulty is not a poetic construction, but rather an extension of the difficulty human beings face in every aspect of their lives. To write and provide these same people with a simplified art would be to suggest that their lives are also simple, thereby denying the multitude of genuine complexities with which they regularly cope. As Hill writes in 'Isaac Rosenberg, 1890-1918', the "true common reader is a natural aristocrat of the spirit".[93]

Modernist poetry, in which tradition Hill writes, is a difficult discourse. Typically, poems do not function as independent, discrete units of verse, but rather as *contributions* to poetry, continually referring to themselves, the work of other poets, and – perhaps most commonly and significantly – to the act of writing poetry. Hill writes in a similarly intertextually-rich style, and the texts to which he refers and which contribute to and are present (in quotations, or images or vocabulary)[94] in *Speech! Speech!* are (largely) those (canonical) texts which contributed to the (now canonical) modernists: Yeats, Eliot, Pound and others. In *True Friendship*, Christopher Ricks discusses the effect of this iteration and reiteration within the highly-referential discourse of twentieth-century poetry, in particular Hill's complex relationship with Eliot, whom he admires but resents: "In Hill's art, though not always in his argumentations, resentment at Eliot becomes something altogether other by being exactly placed and by being nourished by so much more than resentment."[95] A mixture of awe, gratitude and resentment typifies *Speech! Speech!*: it is not easy to determine when the poet is mocking, and when he is sincere.

This understanding of poetic difficulty places Hill firmly within the tradition of modernist difficulty, a tradition which has been variously interpreted as an expression of élitism and homage. For Laurie Smith, Hill's preoccupations are

---

[92] 'Civil Polity and the Confessing State', *Warwick Review* 2.2 (2008): 16.
[93] *Collected Critical Writings*, 459.
[94] See, for instance, the note on "haruspicate" in stanza 28, which identifies the word as having come to Hill via Eliot.
[95] Christopher Ricks, *True Friendship* (New Haven and London: Yale University Press, 2010), 69-70.

exclusionist and alienating. Like Pound, Hill makes "the same appeal to the culture of the past as infinitely better than the present"; he demonstrates "the same wide range of learning displayed for a few like-minded readers"; and he exhibits "the same contempt for accessibility".[96] According to Smith, the root of this inaccessibility is the lack of the confessional:

> Both Pound and Hill show what happens when poetry loses touch with the need to speak to the individual. A poem that addresses a person, rather than a culture, a class or other abstraction, can never be fascist, as the poems of Eliot and Yeats, despite their authors' reactionary tendencies, almost always show. In their work there is the humility of self-exposure: 'These fragments I have shored against my ruins' is a confession, as is 'the foul rag-and-bone shop of the heart'. For Pound and Hill, the fragments are ammunition and the heart is unmentionable.

Hill's work has never warranted the description 'confessional', and yet there is arguably more 'Hill' in *Speech! Speech!* than in any other of his poems, and there are certainly moments of autobiography as the older poet looks back on his age (in both senses of that word). As Adam Kirsch notes, in the later poetry Hill is "still intricate and ambiguous", but "much more personal";[97] John Drexel writes that the older Hill adopts a "determinedly personal tone".[98] Indeed, Hill has spent much of his later criticism arguing against Eliot's ethic of authorial absence, and has described his own experience of 'coming through' Eliot:

> Forty or fifty years ago, nothing would have induced me to say that there is anything resembling self-therapy or exorcism in the art of poetry or the art of writing. I had been trained, by the Eliot essay 'Tradition and the Individual Talent,' to deny this.

---

[96] Laurie Smith, 'Subduing the Reader'.
[97] 'The Long-Cherished Anger of Geoffrey Hill'.
[98] John Drexel, 'Geoffrey Hill: The Poet in Winter', review of *The Orchards of Syon*, Contemporary Poetry Review, 7 Apr. 2003 (accessed 9 Aug. 2007) <http://www.cprw.com/geoffrey-hill-the-poet-in-winter/>.

Introduction

> And because I was not quick enough to understand the qualifications that Eliot himself would have entered, I acquired a far too extremist view of what seemed then a total incompatibility of the objective and the subjective, and I would have said the poem is achieved by the fullest possible objectification of individual subjectivity. Obviously I no longer think so.[99]

Hill is contemplatively confessional in stanza 11 (when the poet describes how he "clown-paints" his pyjamas with red pen while reflecting that he would like to "shuffle off alive"), and stanza 70 (when he describes approaching the town of Groton by train, looking out the window for a loved one but "without desire"). These are moments at least as autobiographical as Eliot's 'confession' of his shored fragments, and they show that in *Speech! Speech!* the heart is by no means "unmentionable".

As Smith points out, arguments about individual voice are political as well as poetical. Movements in the middle of last century focussing on egalitarian issues associated difficulty not only with literary élitism, but also with the rarefied atmosphere of universities in the days before general admittance. Antony Rowland relates an exchange between poets Philip Larkin and Tony Harrison to illustrate the gulf between Larkin's assertion that "a good poem should be understood immediately"[100] and Hill's inaccessibility: "when Harrison asks the reader in one of his early poems to look at one of Goya's paintings in the Prado, Larkin retorts in a letter, 'WHY THE FUCKING HELL SHOULD I?'"[101] This effort required – the consultation of sources outside the poem – for Rowland defines the two poets' different interpretations of democracy: "Larkin and Hill's versions of democratic art clearly diverge: for Hill, it requires the reader's perseverance; for Larkin, it must be accessible, acceptable, and

---

[99] 'The Art of Poetry LXXX', 282-283. Hill's one-time commitment to Eliot's ethic of impersonality was evident in a 1981 interview with John Haffenden, where he explains that he sees "no reason to quarrel with the celebrated passage from Eliot's 'Tradition and the Individual Talent'" (Haffenden, *Viewpoints: Poets in Conversation* [London: Faber and Faber, 1981], 86).
[100] Antony Rowland, *Holocaust Poetry*, 71.
[101] *Holocaust Poetry*, 71.

widely read."[102] Hill, on the other hand, in making his case, quotes Theodor Hacker's dictum: "Tyrants always want a language and literature that is easily understood",[103] and states that he "will not stoop to the defensive innuendo that learning is anti-pathetic to 'true' intellect".[104] The trouble here is that 'immediate understanding' and 'accessibility' are taken to be one and the same thing; there is no place for the text which is difficult but in which the difficulties are negotiable.

Hill's distrust of populism finds its way into *Speech! Speech!* In stanza 37, he describes *The Sun* as a newspaper which "condescends ... daily" to its readers, while in stanza 99 the "AUTHENTIC SELF" – the locus of the faux-egalitarian artistic voice – is dismissed as "a stinker". Hill is at his most explicit in the final stanzas of the poem when he writes that the public endures the "ACCESSIBLE / traded as DEMOCRATIC" (stanza 118). These are forthright expositions; he also makes other, more subtle arguments. Hill's repeated interrogation in *Speech! Speech!* of demotic utterances serves two purposes: first, indicating current *abuse* of the language, reducing it to an excess of the hackneyed and clichéd; second, indicating that responsible *use* of such language can have a redemptive quality, that it can discover truths and rescue language from "the debauch".[105] Hill champions the responsible use of language, and attention to semantic, syntactic and lexical detail. He aims to produce a language and a "fine-edged discourse",[106] capable of reproducing the complexity of everyday life in the written word. In a sermon for Ash Wednesday, Hill provided an antecedent as an example of how to negotiate complexity in literature: "What I brought away from my study of Tudor and early Stuart English was the realization that our language at that time could sustain nuance and fine distinction in ways not now sustainable or understood".[107] Language for Hill has always the potential for nuance and fine distinction; it is the sustenance of these qualities that is required of those who use it.

---

[102] *Holocaust Poetry*, 71.
[103] *Don't Ask Me What I Mean*, 118.
[104] *Collected Critical Writings*, 174.
[105] 'Meaningful Speech', 198.
[106] 'Trinity Sermon: Ash Wednesday 2008'.
[107] 'Trinity Sermon: Ash Wednesday 2008'.

INTRODUCTION

This idea of the lexicon as a powerful, redemptive force is attractive, and yet even those sympathetic to Hill's theory of democratic difficulty struggle with its practical application. For some critics, the satisfaction of 'decoding' the poem does not warrant the effort required. For William Logan, "The labor of decoding comes at a price higher than the likely benefit";[108] for *The Economist* reviewer, "Mr Hill has always been difficult, but the beauty of his writing helped readers persevere. In *Speech! Speech!* there is less to draw you in".[109] For others, Hill's "learning" does not appear "real". Thomas Day notes that although:

> Hill might give the impression of having read his way through the whole of literature ... the procedure is more like that of a *flâneur* in a world of books ... taking a phrase from here, a word from there – which is perhaps not so difficult as it looks, and which, since it may be relatively easy to counterfeit, implies the sensuous intelligence might be espoused as a way of shirking the labour of real learning.[110]

Here, close textual analysis can be useful not only as an explicatory tool but also as a means of assessment. Notes identify the poet's references, allusions, and translate unknowns; commentaries lay bare his method, the conceits and linguistic tricks employed. Readers are then able to judge for themselves whether or not Hill's references are "particularly obscure",[111] or pose a surface difficulty only.

THE PROBLEM OF 'SPEAKING'

Despite the inherent difficulties of speaking, the poet is burdened with a responsibility to answer the call for speech. *Speech! Speech!* is a set of utterances in which the poet is "continually questioning his own impulse to public

---

[108] 'Author! Author!', 65.
[109] Anonymous, 'Books and Arts: Trust in Words', review of *Speech! Speech!*, *The Economist* 21 June 2001: 81.
[110] 'Sensuous Intelligence: T.S. Eliot and Geoffrey Hill', *Cambridge Quarterly*, 25.3 (2006): 267.
[111] According to Logan they are not: it is "not the allusions but the arguments that have fallen into mystery" ('Author! Author!', 65).

utterance."[112] The opening stanza, with its obscure staccato dictum, "Erudition. Pain. Light.", provides a great deal of information about the reasons for the poet's need to speak. *Speech! Speech!* is described as a "great" and "unavoidable work"; to speak is unavoidable despite the recognition that "heroic verse" – epic narratives (such as *Speech! Speech!*) commemorating legendary figures – in the current age (dominated as it is by the "PEOPLE") is "a non-starter". Despite the general "confusion" of the modern world, with its focus on instant gratification and "rapid exposure", the poet must sound his "music". In doing so, he impedes the march of history and prevents its many narratives – here condensed in one word: "Archaic" – from being forgotten, "pillaged", and "erased" in the space of only "one generation". *Speech! Speech!* is Hill's effort to rescue the heroes (Diana, Princess of Wales, or David Bomberg, or Isaac Rosenberg, or Charles Ives) and the "innocent bystanders" of history (those unnamed, "speechless dead"[113] who, "missing their stars", are forgotten, such as the women of the Resistance movement) from the potential product of the "distance" between us and them, of being reduced to nothingness by the great "auto-da-fé" of time which destroys any trace of their existence.

There are other perils, too. The poet can speak *about* the heroes and bystanders of history, and he can also speak *to* them in a formal address of homage, but he cannot hope to speak *for* them:[114] to do so would be an act of reckless irresponsibility

---

[112] Andrew Michael Roberts, *Geoffrey Hill*, 40.

[113] See Hill's poem from *King Log* (1968), 'History as Poetry': "Poetry / Unearths from among the speechless dead // Lazarus mystified, common man / Of death."

[114] Michael Schmidt describes Hill's position as based around the question of how far, "with the Bergsonian past in mind, can a voice speak, speak of, speak to (it cannot hope to speak for); how far can it contain and judge the unspeakable and counter-weigh Adorno's notorious dictum that there can be no poems after Auschwitz?" (*Lives of the Poets*, 986). Adorno's assertion was that "To write poetry after Auschwitz is barbaric, and this corrodes even the knowledge of why it has become impossible to write poetry today". See *Can One Live after Auschwitz?*, ed. Rolf Tiedemann (Stanford: Stanford University Press, 2003), 162. In "'it / is true'", Kevin Hart notes that in 'September Song', Hill "recoils from the very possibility" of beginning to "talk *for*" the subject of the poem, a child victim of the Holocaust (*Words of Life:*

INTRODUCTION

and inauthenticity. As Gareth Reeves rightly notes: "Hill's poetry would give voice to the silent dead, but is all the time conscious that in doing so it relives and resurrects the atrocity buried with them." [115] In writing about the Holocaust, for instance, Hill (and any other contemporary poet) enters a realm of perils. Born in 1932, Hill was a child when World War II began and an adolescent when it ended; any mention of the pain and suffering caused by this catastrophic event, or even of the heroism of those allied soldiers who fought against it, risks the pitfalls of voyeurism, hollow righteousness, or – perhaps worst of all – of self-styling as a prophet, one somehow possessed of especial vantage from which to make pronouncements. As Tim Kendall notes, "having 'not been there', Hill must ceaselessly invoke an imperfect act of witness". [116] Hill speaks in *Speech! Speech!* of his "childish anger" at the injustices of the twentieth century. He claims that "At twenty, ignorance was my judgement", indicating his willingness to accept the limitations of his own life, and the subjectivity that these parameters impose. [117]

In responding to claims of 'propheteering' by making art from the misfortunes of the dead, Hill argues that:

> They say that Hill claims for himself the status of the prophet, and nobody has a right to make such a claim in the late twentieth century, and that there is something disgusting in seeing a writer describe on the same level the Shoah, the First and Second World Wars, and his petty resentments. No such claim is made by the author. The author is perfectly aware of the grotesque difference between his own resentments and the plight of millions, between the claims that he makes for himself and the several holocausts of his age. [118]

New Theological Turns in French Phenomenology, ed. Bruce Benson and Norman Wirzba [New York: Fordham University Press, 2010], 78.
[115] Gareth Reeves, 'This is Plenty. This is More than Enough', *Oxford Handbook of British and Irish War Poetry*, ed. Tim Kendall (Oxford: Oxford University Press, 2007), 584.
[116] Tim Kendall, 'Geoffrey Hill's Debts', *Modern English War Poetry* (Oxford: Oxford University Press, 2006), 224.
[117] *Speech! Speech!*, stanza 83.
[118] 'The Art of Poetry LXXX', 284-285.

In memorializing history, Hill must be careful (especially as he has "nothing about which he can decently complain")[119] lest panegyric spill over into faux-autobiography; he must ensure that he bears witness to his own experience. The act of looking into the dead, as he notes in stanza 113, is both "destructive" and "vital"; destructive in that the act of 'autopsy' – seeing for oneself, eye-witnessing – requires the dissection of the dead, but "vital" in that it brings the dead to life, pulls them "back into being" by the authentic act of bearing witness. But to bring the dead "back into being" without falling into the trap of speaking on their behalf, or idealizing or romanticizing them, or unintentionally reinventing them, is a delicate feat of responsibility and sustained attention, and the poet must be constantly alert to its many dangers. Moreover, the voices of the dead compete with one another: the poet must balance all these voices.

As R. K. Meiners rightly points out, Hill's efforts to continue speaking despite the mitigating circumstances constitute for him a dedication to a kind of linguistic heroism. Writing in response to the title of Hill's essay collection *The Enemy's Country*, he notes that, for Hill, it "may be the enemy's country and the enemy's language, but that doesn't mean you don't walk through it and keep on speaking and writing."[120] This call to speech is the prime compulsion of *Speech! Speech!*; the heroism derives from Hill's commitment to engaging with that with which he battles: with a language, a diction, an environment which evades rather than embraces the burdens of memory and responsibility. This engagement with 'the enemy' is not to the liking of all. For Kevin Hart, Hill's attempt to employ contemporary diction with which he is only newly familiar is a failure, with the poet vainly trying "to incorporate demotic speech, which sometimes turns to glue in his hands"[121] and including "alien influences" which "have not been properly digested".[122] The resulting verse is, for Hart, "slack";[123]

---

[119] Kevin Hart, "'it / is true'", 85.
[120] R. K. Meiners, '"Upon the Slippery Place"; or, In the Shit: Geoffrey Hill's Writing and the Failures of Postmodern Memory', *Contemporary British Poetry: Essays in Theory and Criticism*, ed. James Acheson and Romana Huk (Albany: State University of New York Press, 1996), 238.
[121] Kevin Hart, 'Up and Dówn the | Hill', 161
[122] Kevin Hart, 'Poetics and Power', *First Things: A Monthly Journal of Religion and Public Life* (1 April 2008): 46-47.

INTRODUCTION

the contending voices seem not so much an imagistic babble as a mess of confusion.

For Hill, the compulsion is to speak, and to speak responsibly, accurately, fully cognizant of the language he uses. More than any of his poems, *Speech! Speech!* carries this philosophy through to its logical conclusion: the resulting verse – 120 stanzas of juxtaposed fragments – is difficult. Its difficulty arises not only from the arguments within (memory, responsibility, and speech are all profoundly difficult) but also lexically, syntactically and typographically. The devices which cause this difficulty and engender a sense of reader-alienation, the symptoms which appear on the page as diacritics, capitals and other devices, represent Hill's efforts (not always successful, nor yet always failures) to speak to his audience with their own language and to use it with the utmost responsibility. I am not sure that Wainwright is right in assuming the existence of an 'I' (the poet's "true", distinctive voice) somewhere at the bottom of the poem, but his comments about the locus of the poem's true difficulty are wholly accurate:

> To maintain a distinctive voice, sometimes by jabbing the reader with diacritics to be sure we hear it right, is the great struggle of the poem. Moreover, to achieve such a voice is to ... maintain an ethical responsibility, albeit one that is never transcendent but always beset by our creaturely being. Which is why this work is rough, crude, 'ugly'.[124]

Voices from across the spectrum appear and are themselves variously rough, crude and ugly (John Lyon provides an excellent account of the preponderance in the poem of scatological jokes and other 'dirty' humour);[125] no one voice is given any especial primacy, nor any position suggestive of a hierarchy of credence.

It is easy to read Hill's dirty jokes and undermining of clichés as implicitly self-critical, yet there is no real reason to do so. It is far more likely that readers are unwilling to believe that Hill – whose work is loved by the present Archbishop of

---

[123] 'Poetics and Power', 47.
[124] *Acceptable Words*, 107.
[125] John Lyon, 'What are you incinerating?', 89-95.

Canterbury, Dr Rowan Williams[126] – makes scatological jokes, threnodies for Diana and music-hall comedy *in earnest*; it is tempting to see such utterances as incompatible with the refined, highbrow content elsewhere in the poem. And so – conveniently and erroneously – such passages are read as satirical, or are deemed to be evidence of the poet's poor taste: as Michael Schmidt notes: "One [poetry prize] judge declared that Hill had put himself beyond the pale when he dedicated a poem to Princess Diana."[127] There is of course an element of satire in the poem, but it is not limited to the lowbrow: the scholars, "Masters of arts toiling as they are bent / to Saturn's justice in praetorian bunkers" (stanza 96) and the new breed of academic, the "junk-maestro" (whose work merits no more than a dismissive slur, "quote research / unquote") are as worthy of lampooning as anyone else. For Hill, the apparent disjunction between the serious and the comic passages is wholly intentional:

> The whole structure of the sequence, particularly the way phrases are shaped, the way certain allusions are made to Laurel and Hardy, and comic papers is an acknowledgement of this monstrous inequality; and to read it in any other way seems to me to reveal humourlessness and an inability to listen.[128]

When Hill states that he has "learnt as much from Daumier, Hylda Baker and Frankie Howerd" as from "John Donne and Gerard Manley Hopkins",[129] there is no compelling reason to doubt him. Humour is part of the problem of speaking: Hill's jokes are sometimes foul and often terrible; they offer a necessary escape from the burden of responsibility, while demonstrating the potential for language to embody any

---

[126] The Archbishop's support for Geoffrey Hill is quoted on the cover of *Scenes for Comus*: "Hill remains for me the supreme voice of the last few decades. The recent work, telegraphic, angry and unconsoled, at once assertive and self-dispossessing, is extraordinary".
[127] Michael Schmidt, 'Editorial', *PN Review* 32.4 (2006) (accessed 1 May 2010) <http:// gateway.proquest.com/>.
[128] 'The Art of Poetry LXXX', 285.
[129] Geoffrey Hill, 'A Matter of Timing', *The Guardian*, 21 Sep. 2002 (accessed 13 July 2003) <http://www.guardian.co.uk/books/2002/sep/21/featuresreviews.guardianreview28>.

INTRODUCTION

sentiment, and the implication of "nuance" and "fine distinction" in the lighter (as well as the darker) side of life.

A MULTITUDE OF VOICES

The problem of speaking is made manifest in *Speech! Speech!* by the preponderance within it of multiple – sometimes competing – voices and the difficulty of separating from these the 'I' of the poet. The authorial voice – the 'I' in poetry – is a locus fraught with difficulty in twentieth-century work. After Adorno's "notorious dictum"[130] that there can be no poems after Auschwitz, those who continue to communicate in verse have had to address how far a voice can "speak", "speak of", and "speak to"[131] in a climate which must "contain and judge the unspeakable".[132] Readers have learned not to trust, at least not entirely, any 'I' they encounter; in Hill's oeuvre this 'I' is often altogether absent. His work has been characterized by a kind of voicelessness, a suspicion of the authorial 'I' so deep and so profound that it is almost entirely ignored. The result is verse which some perceive as cold, lifeless and so impersonal as to be impenetrable. Critics perceive in *Speech! Speech!* this same inaccessibility, but as a result of too many voices rather than too few.

Whether these voices are, as William Logan suggests, the "the divided dictions of one voice"[133] or, as Jeffrey Wainwright argues, are instead a "cacophony of different voices",[134] is a point of contention: critics are at odds as to whether the authorial 'I' speaks, or does so only in fragments, or whether the poet at all times utters an adopted voice, making the poem a "modified form of montage".[135] For Hart, the poet's voice has been "untuned" and is as such "incapable of harmony".[136] The difficulty which these voices pose lies in their number: without

---

[130] William Logan, 'Falls the Shadow', 75.
[131] As already noted, according to Hill, "it cannot hope to speak for".
[132] Michael Schmidt, *Lives of the Poets*, 986.
[133] 'Author! Author!', 65.
[134] Jeffrey Wainwright, *Acceptable Words*, 97.
[135] Andrew Duncan, *The Failure of Conservatism in Modern British Poetry* (Cambridge: Salt, 2003), 73: "At this point he breaks with the canons laid down by the academic taste of the 1950s, to use prose form and a modified form of montage. It seems that the share of fear in his make-up has led to a certain conformism and vacillation, alongside so many positive qualities."
[136] Kevin Hart, 'Up and Dówn the | Hill', 158.

character, narrative, and the authorial 'I', it is often difficult to determine who, if anyone, is speaking: the sense is more often of snippets of broadcast material than any individual voice. In *Speech! Speech!*, what replaces the 'I' is a cacophony; a multitude of voices competing for space on the page, some 'shouting' via capitals, others cooing in italicized French or German. The resulting text is difficult, confusing; it is for Logan no more cohesive than the babbling of "a man receiving radio broadcasts through his fillings":[137] the pervading sense is of the poet's own "doubt about whether he can represent the dissenting poet's voice".[138]

The authorial 'I' is notably absent throughout Hill's oeuvre, but particularly so in *Speech! Speech!*. Romana Huk has commented:

> Any conventional performance of lyric expressivism becomes all but impossible in Hill's poems, which are much more frequently spoken in a strangely choral voice, even when the personal pronoun is present – as though culture itself were speaking, or an "I/We" whose choices of form and response are so heavily overdetermined by cultural possibilities that volition becomes the nonissue at issue, flickering in the gaps opened by contradictions and conventionalities. The "true commitment" of the poet, as Hill puts it, sounding like Adorno, is to the "vertical richness" of his or her medium – to "mak[ing] history and politics and religion speak for themselves through the strata of language.[139]

This lack of a unified – however fragmented – authorial 'I', no trace of "that transcendent poetic self"[140] to which readers are accustomed, has its own politics. According to Meiners:

---

[137] William Logan, 'Author! Author!', 65.
[138] 'Praxis not Gnosis: Geoffrey Hill and the Anxiety of Polity', 203.
[139] Romana Huk, 'Poetry of the Committed Individual: Jon Silkin, Tony Harrison, Geoffrey Hill, and the Poets of Postwar Leeds', *Contemporary British Poetry: Essays in Theory and Criticism*, ed. James Acheson and Romana Huk (Albany: State University of New York Press, 1996), 190.
[140] R. K. Meiners, 'Geoffrey Hill's Writing and the Failures of Postmodern Memory', 228.

INTRODUCTION

> Geoffrey Hill's distrust of the notion of a poetic "voice" is nearly as deep as his suspicion of commonplace notions concerning the poet's mastery of language. Although Hill has nowhere taken notice of the flood of postmodernist theoretical argument engaged in the deconstruction of the romantic-modernist poetic self and its deflected "voices" assigned to textual personalities ... there is a powerful way in which he is coeval with such argument and simultaneously, in ways theoreticians have yet to grasp, makes much of the argument obsolete, irrelevant, and even naive.[141]

As Meiners acknowledges, Hill, while not contributing to contemporary debates about the deconstruction of the self, has in his criticism argued that "[w]hat we call the writer's 'distinctive voice' is a registering of different voices".[142] In *Speech! Speech!*, it is not a question of the authorial voice disappearing, but rather of more voices entering the mêlée so that a clamorous noise is created.

As Wainwright notes, even when Hill appears to be writing autobiographically, he instructs us to mistrust his authorial authority:

> We might see the Nigerian sections as in part at least authenticated by the poet's autobiographical involvement. But 'AUTHENTIC SELF a stinker' says the headlines, and the gossip is passed on in the manner of schoolboys' snide whispering.[143]

If speaking in one's own voice is agreed to be so problematic as to be "a stinker", and if one is always contending with a hundred, a thousand other voices in a din of noise, then the poem's title, *Speech! Speech!* – the call for one voice to speak out – is surely ironic. And yet, with Hill, such a call is not entirely ironic: just as his politics of language dictate that his difficulty be not élitist but democratic, so his politics of heroism dictate that – although he knows that speaking in a

---

[141] R. K. Meiners, 'Geoffrey Hill's Writing and the Failures of Postmodern Memory', 227.
[142] Geoffrey Hill, *Collected Critical Writings*, 190.
[143] *Acceptable Words*, 97.

'debauched' environment, speaking after Auschwitz, speaking of and for others is fundamentally impossible – he must nevertheless continue, aiming to use language responsibly, to appeal to a contemporary audience with the authenticity of "pitch" rather than the vacuity and trickery of "tone".[144] For Hill, his efforts to negotiate what Wainwright describes as the "individual poet's relationship to language and to poetic form and structure" and for the poet to endure the many "external, contingent pressures" of the contemporary world, is to undertake a "particular kind of heroism."[145]

Clearly, the prevalence of demotic, idiomatic and contemporary speech contained within *Speech! Speech!* is at least in part the result of the poet's efforts to engage meaningfully with his audience in its own language, even if the meaningful engagement is of an essentially satirical or derisive kind. Although Hill's other work has included little demotic speech (it is at odds, for instance, with the austerity of 'September Song' or even the sometimes playful poetics of *The Mystery of the Charity of Charles Péguy*) – it seems that Hill has for a long time felt it necessary to engage with the language and the voice of his peers. Expressing his admiration for the art of seventeenth-century disputation, Hill writes in 'The Eloquence of Sober Truth' that its practitioners were "not monolinguists, nor are they determinists or mechanistic dialecticians; they engage with the (hostile) other as a contending voice among others."[146] If a man "belongs to his age and culture by virtue of language, institutions, objects, landscapes", and if "to understand him well enough to use his voice is the poet's tact, a tact he will use, too, in constructing his own voice",[147] then these contending voices must also be of the poet's own time. According to Hill, to sound his "own voice" and engage with other voices, the poet must accept that self-interrogation is a pre-requisite for self-expression, for finding one's "own voice":

---

[144] See stanza 90 for an indication of Hill's understanding of 'pitch' ("Animus / is what I home on, even as to pitch"), and his essay 'Dividing Legacies' (*Collected Critical Writings*, 375-391) for a full explication of his differentiation between the terms 'pitch' and 'tone'.
[145] *Acceptable Words*, 106.
[146] *Collected Critical Writings*, 329.
[147] *Lives of the Poets*, 982.

INTRODUCTION

> A great deal of the work of the last forty years seems to me to spring from inadequate knowledge and self-knowledge, a naive trust in the unchallengeable authority of the authentic self. But I no longer think that the answer to this lies in the suppression of self; it requires a degree of self-knowledge and self-criticism, which is finally semantic rather than philosophical. The instrument of expression and the instrument of self-knowledge and self-correction is the same.[148]

In addressing a hostile other and expressing (rather than "suppressing") his "self", Hill employs a language which is sometimes a hostile instrument of expression: perhaps unsurprisingly, the resulting verse often takes the form of a "hostile address".[149] For Hill, engaging successfully, and simultaneously, with the lexicon of popular culture and its sometimes disconnected public does not require a "suppression of self", a subjugation of the 'I', but rather an 'I' which is so self-aware, self-interrogating, and self-editing as to be almost unrecognisable as itself, its "self".

TYPOGRAPHICAL ECCENTRICITIES

The poem's "idiosyncratic punctuation" is its "most obviously rebarbative feature";[150] the various supra-segmentals and diacritics which litter the text are a constant interruption and distraction, and urge the reader to take the text word-by-word, phrase-by-phrase. The use of such techniques is neither accidental nor incidental. Thomas Day – referring to a passage in Hill's criticism in which the presence of "howlers" and grammatical errors in literary work is listed with other (more serious) crimes – notes that for Hill:

> amongst the list of rather trifling sins for which he says one must atone testifies to his conviction that language, and grammar in particular, is implicated in the Fall. The title *Speech! Speech!* makes the connection by gesturing towards a pair of speech

---

[148] 'The Art of Poetry LXXX', 282-283.
[149] Robert Potts, 'A Change of Address', 25.
[150] Jeremy Noel-Tod, 'Curious and Furious', review of *Speech! Speech!*, *The Observer*, 20 Jan. 2002: R.16.

marks. These debar hermeneutic innocence by bringing an ironic pressure to bear on the whole poem and by suggesting the words they contain are in a peculiar way hollow or void.[151]

Hill's use of "radically rhetorical punctuation"[152] to be emphatic and suggestive threatens to compromise any lyric beauty he achieves, but I am arguing that such use is intended to 'annotate' the text, foreground a particular meaning, or signal an ambiguity. The various typographical elements serve different purposes; in stanza 117 Hill offers some insight into the exact nature of these purposes:

> CAPITALS | STAGE DIRECTIONS AND OTHER
> FORMS OF SUBPOENA. *Italics* | words
> with which Í – *sometimes* – surprise myself.

These lines are plainly disingenuous: offering such an explanation at the poem's close only adds to the obfuscation; moreover, capitalization (the other-voiced interjections which Hill terms "STAGE DIRECTIONS") and italicization are by no means the full extent of the oddities. I will demonstrate (here and in the annotations) that, in the final assessment, these oddities provide necessary information about how to read the poem, bringing the reader close to the poet's intent.

Several typographical features contribute to the physical denseness of the poem and give it the 'barbed' surface that many readers struggle to penetrate. While Jeremy Noel-Tod is right to assert that "capitalised words serve, roughly, as the

---

[151] 'Geoffrey Hill's Finishing Lines', 160. Day refers to a passage in 'Poetry as "Menace" and "Atonement"' (*The Lords of Limit*), when Hill writes: "Under scrutiny, this is the essence to which my term 'empirical guilt' is reduced: to an anxiety about *faux pas*, the perpetration of 'howlers', grammatical solecisms, misstatements of fact, misquotations, improper attributions. It is an anxiety only transiently appeased by the thought that misquotation may be a form of re-creation" (*Collected Critical Writings*, 9).

[152] R. K. Meiners, 'Geoffrey Hill's Writing and the Failures of Postmodern Memory', 236. Meiners identifies four "characteristic structures" in Hill's writing: "paratactic nominative phrases, obsessive paronomasia, radically rhetorical punctuation" and "the entire stubborn texture of his writing".

INTRODUCTION

typographical equivalent of shouting at the deaf",[153] Hill also uses capitalization more variously and specifically in *Speech! Speech!*[154] Capitalization can indicate the presence of direct quotation, as from the Bible (stanzas 23 and 116), or from Charles Williams (stanza 107), where it draws attention to the quoted words by marking them as distinct from the surrounding verse, giving the impression of these words having been lifted from another text and dropped into the poem – a poetic shorthand for acknowledging source material. Hill also uses capitalization to signify the titular; in stanza 38, for instance, of Caravaggio's 'Flagellation'. This technique gives a stuttering quality, what Wainwright describes in *Acceptable Words* as "a performance that can sound like static, or the product of the frantic, irritated twiddling of a radio-tuner".[155] It may also mark the interjection of an editorial voice, although this voice is not (as it is in *The Triumph of Love*) explicitly identified, but instead (and for obscure reasons) appears within square brackets in stanzas 104 and 114, but without them elsewhere. This metatextual 'editor' offers comment to the poet: "GO ON" in 68, "MAKE ANSWER" in 32; or comments on the poet's performance (e.g. "HE'S GOT A NERVE" in stanza 44). Elsewhere, capitals mark the iteration of the clichéd, the hackneyed, and the overtly demotic (such as "EITHER WAY THEY GET YOU" in stanza 63, or "HE'S GOT A NERVE" [again] in stanza 44); they may draw attention to etymological connections (emphasized by capitalizing two words within a stanza; see "CHARADE" and "CHIE" in 31, "REDUCE" and "LEAD BACK" [its definition] in 24, "POMEGRANATE" and "GRENADE" in 19); or they may signify the weighty and conceptual by means of literally 'big words' scattered throughout the poem – e.g., "BEHOLDEN" in stanza 18 or "TETRAGRAMMATON" in stanza 62. Tetragrammaton –

---

[153] 'Curious and Furious', R.16.
[154] It should be noted that, as well as the standard capital font which is used for the usual purposes, Hill and his printers employ the 'small caps' version of the Monotype Spectrum MT (the font in which the poem is printed) for the kinds of uses here discussed. The effect of these 'small caps' is less jarring than standard capitals, with all letters being of a standard size and sitting no higher than those of the lower case. This effect is not represented in the font used for the commentaries and for this Introduction (Helvetica, chosen for its marked difference from the font of the poem).
[155] *Acceptable Words*, 97.

properly the name for the unpronounceable four-letter rendering (YHWH) of the name of God – also alerts us to the typographical resemblance between *Speech! Speech!* and the English Old Testament in which YHWH is translated 'LORD' (as distinct from the Hebrew *Adonai*, translated 'Lord'). In other words, the capitalization gives the poem a rather seventeenth-century *and* Biblical appearance.

Likewise, Hill uses the italic to mark vocabulary borrowed from other languages, to denote coinages, to insert quasi-stage directions and literary instructions, and to draw attention to a repeated refrain. The italic is used for 'dog' French (5, 46); coinages (25, 40, 39); and, though rarely, for its conventional use of emphasis (59, 106, 117, 120); to imitate the scripted response of a 'live studio audience' (stanzas 26 and 94); or to indicate musical tempo ("presto", "lento"), stage directions (74), and literary instructions (see stanzas 8, 13, 44, 84, 104). There is potential confusion with capitalization: the title *De Regno Christi* is italicized throughout, but Holst's *Jupiter*, for instance, is not. The Martin aria 'Mein Ariel...' is repeated in variations (see stanzas 54, 65, 79, 91, 115) and italicized to indicate the title. Such treatments of capitalization and italicization are relatively conventional; while they add to the surface difficulty of the text they are familiar to readers and their functions are not difficult to discern. However, two other typographical devices – the verticule and the accentual mark – require further explication.

Hill's vertical mark is separated by spaces from the text that surrounds it. Following William Logan, I have termed this mark the "verticule". As Logan rightly recognizes in his review 'Author! Author!',[156] the verticule performs two functions. First, the mark is used to indicate multiple readings or point to the possibilities implicit in an ambiguous phrase; rather than leave to chance the discovery of less obvious readings, Hill manipulates punctuation to bring to the fore particular interpretations. A good example can be found in the opening stanza, where the verticule indicates that the phrase "archaic | means" can be read as both 'archaic methods' and '[the word] archaic signifies'. In stanza 18, the verticule points to the ambiguity of the phrase "Write whát | I ask", which can be read

---

[156] Although he does so disparagingly: "vertical slants (call them verticules) ... sometimes mark an ambiguity but otherwise serve as little more than fancy pauses" (65).

Introduction

as 'write what I instruct you to write' or 'I ask you what I should write'; there are many other examples. At other times, the mark is used as an explicit articulation of caesura; examples can be found in stanza 110 ("unfixable fell-gusts | ratching") and stanza 83 ("Even so | childish anger at the injustice of it"). Hill's use of the verticule, therefore, reduces the potential for unintended readings: ambiguities are made explicit and have their existence formally sanctioned, as it were, by the poet; likewise, caesurae do not wait to be acknowledged by the attentive reader but are instead printed on the page.

The accents used as stress marks throughout the poem have been widely interpreted as a kind of typographical homage to Gerard Manley Hopkins: Thomas Day calls them the "accentual marks of Sprung Rhythm",[157] while Peter McDonald describes them as the "printed cues that recall those employed by Hopkins".[158] There is little of Hopkins about their use in *Speech! Speech!*; rather, the accents are used as stress marks and in contrary purpose to the verticule. Hill employs the verticule to indicate multiple possible readings and to draw attention to ambiguous phrasing; the stress marks, on the other hand, dictate a specific reading, explicitly marking the diction of lines or phrases to eliminate undesired or accidental stresses, or to indicate an unexpected stress pattern. The use of stress marks to eliminate ambiguities is most evident in the instances in which phrases are repeated, but with shifted accents, as in stanzas 57-58, when "better than thát I should hope" is repeated as "Better | than that I should hópe". In some cases, the exact weighting of a clichéd exclamation can be identified only by the placement of the stresses, as in the disingenuous – rather than placatory – "THÁT'S ALL RÍGHT THEN" in stanza 48. Likewise, an unusual or unexpected diction is sometimes specified, as in the phrase "whoever you are / or máy be" in stanza 70, which denies natural phrasing.

Narrative or Not?

Discussions of the impact of its typography address the material difficulty of *Speech! Speech!*. Its stylistic, technical difficulty is more troublesome to diagnose, and more open to interpretation. One reading of *Speech! Speech!* frames it a

---

[157] 'Geoffrey Hill's Finishing Lines', 157.
[158] *Serious Poetry*, 198.

directionless collection of abbreviated sonnets united only by their apocalyptic tendencies and the (often oblique) recurrence of images and references, located around an ill-defined topos of Sodom. Even its opening, the staccato dictum, "Erudition. Pain. Light.", is more revelatory than its final line: "AMOR. MAN IN A COMA. MA'AM. NEMO. AMEN." I contend that while it is true that the poem suggests more a "Shambles of peripeteia" (stanza 119) than a linear narrative, and more a "self-centre of anomie" (stanza 87) than an example of thematic development, its author has nevertheless taken care to build into it the beginning, middle and end which hint at conventional narrative development. This framework is manifested in the poem through a series of flagged milestones, utterances that are delivered most often in the voice of, or in imagined response to, a reader frustrated with the palpable lack of evolution in the poem. These milestones – the poet's metatextual narrative regarding a lack of narrative – I contend, become the narrative structure of the poem.

Stanza 1 is a self-conscious opening, with the poet beginning his "great unavoidable work" and identifying his mandate. "Although" heroic verse is in this forgetting age, he claims, "a non-starter", the poet must nevertheless speak – as its title requires. Still in introductory mode, Hill in stanza 12 informs the reader that he has "the instructions" for the poem, and in stanza 13, perhaps acknowledging the first stirrings of frustration and discontent, admits that he may be "failing" his reader. He at this point provides an image of Original Sin, presumably as some form of penance. By stanza 32, these stirrings have taken a definite shape and assumed a legitimacy which Hill acknowledges with an instruction to himself and a promise to his reader to "Take issue"; it is, in this second quarter of the poem, "About time" he does so.

Throughout its middle sections, Hill draws attention to the shape and shapelessness of his poem. In stanza 55, the reader is reminded that *Speech! Speech!* comprises 120 stanzas ("As many as the days that were | of Sodom"), perhaps as an assurance that it will, eventually, come to a close. The poet gives voice to the reader's dismay and frustration with the capitalized response: "THE LENGTH OF THE THING"; he is at pains to mimic the reader's sense of travelling through the poem, but progressing nowhere. Five stanzas later and at the halfway point, the poet asserts that he thinks he "shall get thróugh" to the poem's conclusion but that he will spend the rest of stanza 60 having "a bit of a breather", imagining himself as Bunyan's Christian pilgrim stopping for lunch. By stanza 78, an exasperated reader decries disingenuous, congratulatory surprise at having "come thís far"; and the sense of treading water is reiterated in stanza 86 via the image of the poet as an endurance swimmer doing laps in a pool: "He voids each twelve-line blóck | a head / solemnly breaking water". Like the swimmer, the poet is making progress; however, this is qualified by a prediction that the final lap – excepting the exhaustion, ennui, and sense of futility, and at least to the untrained, naked eye – will closely resemble the first. The problem, it seems, is the poet's inability to resist the tangential: if only he could, he claims in stanza 87, "once focus" on but a "single factor", he would avoid the "plainly disordered" argument he is here submitting. But this wish for direction remains unfulfilled. In stanza 99 Hill's exasperated cry is heard: "Hów many móre times?"; Christopher Orchard notes that although Hill "frequently refers to endurance [...] there is also extreme fatigue here, as if he barely has enough energy to push through".[159] Significantly, while the poet admits to his directionlessness, he does not lack drive: he claims in stanza 100 (in characteristically poor taste) that he can, irrespective of his frustration at his own lack of progress, "keep this úp all night".

The closing stages of the poem are also signposted. The first mark of the close of the poem is found in stanza 113, where Hill informs readers that the remaining stanzas are to be an "Eight block coda" dedicated to the "City of God" (the realised achievement, at the end of the poem, of the 'Jerusalem' promised or hinted at earlier). However, in keeping with the meandering which characterizes the bulk of the poem, no sooner is this directive pronounced than the poet formally acknowledges his inability to follow through: he has been "stuck" in one of Dante's "bolge", unable to approach his destination. It comes as no surprise, then, that in stanza 115 Hill asks – either rhetorically or in the voice of the reader – "Where CODA to the CITY OF GOD?" The final stanzas serve not to further any argument, but rather to confirm the chaos which has typified their predecessors. The final line of the poem is the confused cry of a voice desperate to be heard amidst the din of confusion, but (importantly) what this voice

---

[159] 'Praxis not Gnosis: Geoffrey Hill and the Anxiety of Polity', 202.

utters is a muddle of quasi-anagrammatic mock-profundity, a nonsense: "AMOR. MAN IN A COMA. MA'AM. NEMO. AMEN." In this final moment of the poem, the literal 'last gasp' of its fissured voice, an implicit comparison is made between the experience of the reader (whose journey has ended, but who has not arrived) and that of the poet (who has finished his poem, but who finds chaos in place of epiphany).

As well as this directorial signposting, the poem features several recurring themes and images. These recurrences fit together in a kind of jigsaw, and although when complete the puzzle offers a picture of abstraction, it is an abstract picture featuring recurring motifs. Such recurrences provide a thread of continuity through the poem and serve as a form of narrative, just as the repetition of motifs in the visual arts can take the place of a prominent subject. Such recurrences are of three kinds: direct repetition, as with the refrain from Frank Martin's *Der Sturm*; thematic repetition, as with the appearance and reappearance of Diana, Princess of Wales, or that of ancient and modern martyrs; and lexical repetition, as with the preponderance of legal and judicial language and the incessant deployment (and interrogation) of clichés. Direct repetition is explicit and obvious, while thematic and lexical repetitions are often more subtle and not immediately apparent on first reading. Such recurrences are signalled in the textual notes through cross-referencing and in the commentaries by the tracing and signalling of thematic lines.

Conclusion

By continually emphasizing the difficulty and inacessibility of the poem, and in favouring discussion about its highbrow rather than lowbrow references and allusions, the academic readership is as responsible as Hill is for readers' perception of the poem as élitist. No reader, as Logan recognizes, wishes to be sneered at, and critics encourage the image of a sneering Hill when they interpret the poem's density as the product of Hill's wilful obscurity, or its demotic elements as proof of a scathing and supercilious conception of the contemporary world. Such a reading is reductionist: notes and commentaries, with their line-by-line and stanza-by-stanza focus on the text and its explication, offer one way of evading such an oversimplification. If each utterance is addressed in turn, then no voice is unduly privileged, nor any of the poet's preoccupations unwittingly favoured over any other.

INTRODUCTION

As with any work which focuses on particulars as opposed to generalizations, mistakes are inevitable. Attempts at certainty – identifying a source, for instance, or the poet's intention in a particular stanza – are bound on occasion to miss their mark. But I agree with Day's assertion that there is "an urgent need to say something definite", for the very density of the poem invites and encourages analysis. My textual commentaries, though necessarily imperfect, shorten the gap between reader and poet by cataloguing Hill's lauding and lambasting, by identifying his humour and his seriousness, and by tracking the development of the poem. They also make an implicit argument about the democracy of difficult poetry: if Hill's poem flatters rather than insults its readers with its detail of reference, if its difficulty is sited in its myriad references and rebarbative surface but not in any fundamental inaccessibility, if the text itself is not made up of disconnected fragments but forms rather a sequence of verses (albeit one which leads "NEMO" to "A COMA"), then Hill has succeeded in his effort to make democratic poetry, or, equally, poetry democratic.

Geoffrey Hill's *Speech! Speech!*

A NOTE ON THE TEXT

Section or stanza numbers are used when quoting from *Speech! Speech!*, *The Triumph of Love*, *Scenes from Comus* and *The Orchards of Syon*. Page numbers are used when quoting from *Canaan* and *Without Title*; when quoting from Hill's earlier verse, I refer to the titles of individual poems.

Notes are consecutive on the page and do not correspond to line numbers. Cross references within a stanza are made using the note number; cross references from one stanza to another are made using the stanza number.

References to Hill's criticism are to the *Collected Critical Writings* (2008) if they are included therein; where pertinent, I have included the title of the original piece or collection.

In the commentaries, the terms 'Hill', 'the poet' and 'the author' are used interchangeably to describe the first person position; while aware of the problematic nature of the 'authorial "I"' in Hill's – as in most twentieth-century – work, I have interchanged these terms in the interests of fluidity and ease of reading.

Double quotation marks are used to indicate direct quotation, whether from *Speech! Speech!* or another source. Single quotation marks are used to indicate that a word or phrase is slang, jargon, or is being discussed (rather than used) within the sentence. To preserve this distinction, single quotation marks are used to refer to the titles of articles, chapters etc. when they are quoted in the footnotes and commentaries; in the interests of continuity, I have maintained this style for the introduction and bibliography.

In writing the annotations, I have made extensive use of material in the common domain, in particular *The Oxford English Dictionary (Second Edition)* and *The Oxford Dictionary of National Biography*. Unless stated otherwise, biblical quotations are from the *King James Version*.

ANNOTATIONS

I. In memoriam David Wright.
I. David Wright Wright was born in Johannesburg, South Africa, in 1920 and died of throat cancer in 1994 (see stanza 25). When in his teens, Wright and his family relocated to England, where he attended Northampton School for the Deaf and (in 1942) graduated from Oriel College, Oxford. After working as a freelance writer for *The Sunday Times*, he co-founded and co-edited, with Patrick Swift, the quarterly literary review *X* from 1959-1962. He also wrote, with Swift, three books about Portugal. Wright's tenure as Gregory Fellow of Poetry at the University of Leeds (1965-1967) coincided with Hill's period in its English Department (1954-1981), and with his directorship of the Poetry Room (1962-1968). Wright edited *Longer Contemporary Poems* (1966), the *Penguin Book of English Romantic Verse* (1968) and the *Penguin Book of Everyday Verse* (1976). He is best- known for his volumes of verse, which include: *Moral Stories* (1954), *Monologue of a Deaf Man* (1958), *Adam at Evening* (1965), *Deafness: A Personal Account* (1969), *Roy Campbell* (1961), *To the Gods the Shades: New and Collected Poems* (1976), *Metrical Observations* (1980), *Selected Poems* (1988) and *Elegies* (1990). Hill's brief essay on Wright, 'What Hymn is the Band Playing', was included in a 1980 special issue of *PN Review* (6.6) marking Wright's sixtieth birthday. See also stanza 25.

II. Epigraphs: Ennius; Günter Grass.
II.i. Ennius Ennius Quintus (239-169? BC), "But the trumpet sounded its terrible taratantara" or "And then the bugle with a fearful cry blew taratantara", from his masterpiece, the epic *Annales* ('Lesser Fragments of the Annals') of which about 600 lines survive (see *The Annals of Quintus Ennius*, ed. Otto Skutsch, line 451); the quotation comes from the first of the fragments, which describes the fall of Troy. Regarded by the Romans as the father of Latin poetry, Ennius learned to speak the three languages of his birthplace, Calabria (Oscan, Greek and Latin); as a poet, he styled himself after Homer and was

responsible for many innovations in Latin poetry. He moved to Rome after serving in Sardinia under Cato the Elder, and there spent the rest of his life teaching and writing; he was granted citizenship of the city in 184 BC.
II.ii. *Grass* Günter Grass (1927-) is a German novelist, lyricist, artist and playwright, born in Danzig (now Gdansk, Poland). This is the last line of 'The School for Tenors' [Die Schule der Tenöre]: "The high C, the many tributaries of the Mississippi, / the glorious breath / that invented cupolas and applause. / Curtain, curtain, curtain. / Quick before the candelabrum refuses to jungle, before the galleries droop / and silk becomes cheap. / Curtain; before you understand the applause" (*Selected Poems of Günter Grass*, tr. Michael Hamburger and Christopher Middleton, Penguin, 1980, p. 21). Grass was awarded the Nobel Prize for Literature in 1999.

III. Title.

III.i. *Speech! Speech!* As at a party or after a performance: the call (in this case ironic, yet mingled with respect) by those present (the PEOPLE) to the poet to respond, to 'say a few words'. From this simple image the complex themes of the poem arise: the problem of what to say, and how to say it (what Eliot in 'East Coker' calls "the intolerable wrestle / With words and meanings"); the poet siting himself (at times citing himself) in relation to his society, his tradition, his audience; and, finally, the intractable mystery of the logos itself.

1. The opening three words of the poem echo the 'Lights! Camera! Action!' of the film director, and testify to the learning and agony that is inseparable from poetic enlightenment. This allusion to film is the first of many within the poem to affirm something at which the title – *Speech! Speech!* – hints: the poem as public performance, *directed* by the poet. Further emphasizing this element is the contrast between music produced for public performance and private 'practise': music simply for demonstrating virtuosity ("crossed / hands"); simple to play but entertaining ('Chopsticks', scored "for two fingers"); music to numb the senses ('Muzak'), such as that played before the take-off of aeroplanes and at cremations. The equivocal "Archaic means" indicates that history ("files") has been obliterated ("erased") in only "one generation", but also that the definition of 'archaic' has been reduced to a single generation: in this degraded democratic age ("PEOPLE"), history is lost; heroic verse is no longer an option. The stanza ends with the poet/director "judging the distance" – finding the perfect point from which to consider his subject matter in this, the poem's début. The detachment of the cinematic 'take' is the primary image of the stanza: as the poem taxis "to take-off", music sets the scene, as in a film score; extras, "bystanders on standby" (a neat chiasmus), wait until required. There are witnesses to the "auto-da-fé" of Hill's heretic, as there are to this poem; self-immolation is a painful process to behold.

1.1 Erudition In The Triumph of Love, the poet defends himself from the charge of 'erudition': "Shameless old man, bent on committing / more public nuisance. Incontinent / fury wetting the air. Impotently / bereft satire. Charged with erudition, put up by the defence to be / his own accuser" (XXXVII).

1.2 unavoidable work Cf. the epigraph to *The Triumph of Love*, Nehemiah 6:3: "AND I SENT MESSENGERS UNTO THEM, SAYING, I AM DOING A GREAT WORKE, SO THAT I CAN NOT COME DOWN: WHY SHOULD THE WORKE CEASE, WHILEST I LEAVE IT, AND COME DOWN TO YOU."

1.3 heroic / verse Various verse forms used in epic or narrative poetry on heroic subjects, such as the ancient Greek and Latin hexameter, the iambic pentameter or alexandrine; specifically, in the English tradition, the outmoded 'heroic couplet', two lines of rhymed iambic pentameter.

1.4 non-starter With heroic verse, like a scratched horse, a "non-starter" in the poetic race, David Rogers notes in his *World Literature Review* of *Speech! Speech!* that Hill's "commitment *was* to heroic verse from his first great poem, *Genesis*, so his suffering is great" (p. 152).

1.5 PEOPLE The *vox publica*, in the guise of a popular magazine, for which the model may be *People* (in full: *People Weekly*), an American celebrity and human interest magazine, published by *Time*; first appearing in 1974 and still popular. For Hill's use of capitals, see Introduction, pp. 39-40.

1.6 Some believe / we The use of the majestic plural offers a sense of the grandiose, and reinforces the image of the poet beginning his "great" and "heroic" work.

1.7 self-emulation In the sense of self-imitation or repetition, but audibly suggesting *self-immolation*, the destruction of the self.

Geoffrey Hill's *Speech! Speech!*

1.8 means / files The virgule/verticule usually works as an agent of double articulation (see Introduction, pp. 40-1). Here, the phrase can be read as either a) 'the definition of archaic is pillaged files' or b) 'the archaic method of pillaging and erasing files'.

1.9 auto-da-fé Portuguese: 'act of faith'. Widely used at the Inquisition to refer to the procedure whereby heretics, condemned to die at the stake, were called to make an act of faith to redeem their lost souls. With time, the words acquired the meaning of 'persecution' and 'disaster'. The phrase gained new currency in 1933 Germany, when used to describe Nazi book-burning and the torching of the Reichstag. Within this stanza, "auto-da-fé" recalls the lines "History is adorned / with bookish fires" in Hill's *Canaan* (p. 21).

2. The poet interposes a "fire-curtain": that is, he withdraws from public acclaim, although he is troubled by the epigraph, the overt, perhaps arrogant assertion of his link to Grass (was the epigraph chosen before the poem was written?). The key conceit of this stanza is that of cries for help heard on the radio. Human tragedy is communicated to the poet through emergency radio calls, but the poet is unsure exactly how to proceed: the applause must be cut out while he listens keenly to the human voices which "sputter" from his radio. But merely *hearing* the 'cries' from the past is not enough, and Hill struggles to know how to act, what use to make of all the information available to him ("Help him, someone"), how to respond to Nagy's and Scott's historical cries for help, the cries of human tragedy. Like the crossword, the information is cryptic; Hill's radio transmits only clues, yet to be deciphered. Hill issues his own "cries": imperatives ("Interpose"), questions ("do you") and pleas ("Help him, someone"); here, as throughout the poem, he demands complicity and cooperation from his readers. Listening, but wondering how to proceed, the poet, not unlike Böll and Grass, may be in a state resembling the post-Auschwitz condition (as defined by Adorno) where all expression is gratuitous and decadent.

2.1 fire-curtain The fire-curtain of a theatre (recalling the Grass epigraph and continuing the imagery of performance), a barrier to both flames and sound.

2.2 unromantically linked As opposed to 'romantically linked', a tabloid-style phrase that insinuates a sexual relationship.

ANNOTATIONS

2.3 going spáre Double articulation: a) redundant, waiting to be used; b) going mad. Likewise, "dó you" is both a rhetorical question and a direct challenge to the reader. Hill uses the same technique to articulate "going spare" in *Without Title*: "I would not have you say / I speak ungratefully; or that there's self / going spare in our unsparing tribute" (p. 25). For Hill's use of accents and stresses, see Introduction, p. 40.

2.4 Aga Two appliances: 1) a Swedish-made AGA radio set; and 2) the Aga cooker (originally Swedish- and now British-made), a stored-heat oven typical of English country houses ("sitting by the fire").

2.5 Marconi Guglielmo Marconi (1874–1937), Italian physicist celebrated for his development of wireless telegraphy, and so the radio; shared winner (with Karl Ferdinand Braun) of the 1909 Nobel Prize for Physics.

2.6 Imre Nagy Nagy (1896–1958) was a Hungarian political leader and symbol of the 1956 revolt against the Soviet Union, for which he was convicted of treason and executed.

2.7 Scott of the Antarctic Robert Falcon Scott (1868-1912), British explorer and naval officer, the first to reach the South Polar plateau (1901-1904). A 1911 effort to reach the Pole was successful (Scott and his party arrived on 17 January 1912) but disappointing (the Norwegian Roald Amundsen had reached it five weeks earlier) and tragic (all five members of Scott's party died on the return journey); hence, the equivocal "frozen in time". See also stanza 101, in which a photograph captures the Scott team "frozen in time".

2.8 crossword The first crossword puzzle, invented by Arthur Wynne, a native of Liverpool working in New York, appeared in the *New York World* of 21 December 1913, almost two years after the death of Scott (see Tony Augarde's *Oxford Guide to Word Games*, p. 12).

2.9 Böll Heinrich Theodor Böll (1917-1985), German author of short stories, novels, radio plays and essays; noted critic of capitalist society and negative aspects of prosperity; winner of the 1972 Nobel Prize for Literature.

2.10 why not Günter? Böll is believed to have uttered these words upon receiving the news that he had been awarded the Nobel Prize; the German has been variously reported: "Was ich, und nicht Günter Grass?", "Was, ich allein, und nicht der Grass auch".

3. This (at first) more fluent, syntactically regular lyrical stanza moves from a tuned radio to an attuned body. Alternately "tuned" and "un-tuned" (note the disruptive effect of the hyphen) by psychiatry and pharmaceutical drugs, the poet's imagination – which should be responsive only to the heart's rhythm – either soars or stalls; the "daimon", or muse, thus fares well or is gone. Sometimes the poetic impulse is 'suspended', as for De Quincey by opiates or some contemporary equivalent, and is further compromised by the need for commercial guarantees. The poet, like other members of a mercantile society, cannot "persist without sureties"; his output, like any other item in a supermarket, bears a barcode and instructions for use ("cut here"). The impulse of the imagination may be to soar, but everyday necessity interrupts: the poet's "wings of suspension" are "cut here" (like the final line itself) as real life "contractual" obligations intervene.

3.1 Lithium Lithium bicarbonate is used to treat bipolar disorder, since unlike most mood-altering medications it counteracts both mania and depression. The active principle is the ion Li+, which interacts with the normal functions of sodium ions to induce changes in the neuro-transmitter activity of the brain. Lithium can be used to augment other antidepressants.

3.2 harp of nerves The harp is both the poetic lyre and the body tuned and untuned by pharmaceuticals. Hill claimed that part of the reason for his later prolificacy was the acquisition of better drugs: in 2000, responding to his interviewer's reference to "the taking up of serotonin", Hill stated: "I'm quite sure that this unlooked for creative release has a great deal to do with that.... And it wasn't until I came over here [America] that this began to be treated.... It's completely transformed my life" ('The Art of Poetry LXXX', p. 288). See also *The Triumph of Love*, in which Hill refers to his "taking up of serotonin" (CIX). In *The Orchards of Syon*, Hill requests his audience to "Tune him to GOSPEL" (VII).

3.3 Fare well A potential ambiguity: "Fare well" as both 'prosper' and 'goodbye' (here, to inspiration).

3.4 daimon An inner or attendant spirit or inspiring voice – a kind of internalized muse.

3.5 measures As in a) the quantity and potency of medication; and b) poetic rhythm. Hence the Hopkins-like use of 'stress' (both psychological and poetic) in the same line.

ANNOTATIONS

3.6 wings of suspension Thomas De Quincey's essay 'On the Knocking at the Gate in *Macbeth*' (1823) argues that the moment in which real life recommences after being 'earth-stalled' due to some major event (there, the murder of Duncan) is also the moment in which the import of that event is most keenly felt: "the most affecting moment in such a spectacle is that in which a sigh or a stirring announce the recommencement of suspended life".

3.7 sureties Double articulation: a) assurances; and b) assets of tangible value.

3.8 accommodation *Accommodation* (from the same root as 'commodity', line 8): willingness to put up with anything; but also money advanced by a financial institution (or publisher) as a favour before a formal credit arrangement is made.

3.9 Scattergood / Commodity A Bunyanesque personification suggesting the wasting of resources in an age of materialism. John Scattergood edited Skelton's *Complete English Poems* (1983). Cf. the address to William Cobbett in *Canaan*: "your labour that brought to pass / reborn Commodity with uplifted hands / awed by its own predation" (p. 9).

3.10 *presto* Meaning both 'swiftly' (as in direction of tempo) or as if by magic ('Hey Presto'); "by return" means to send back by the next post. For Hill's use of italics, see Introduction, pp. 37-38.

3.11 contractual retraction The phrase anticipates references to Luther and Galileo (see stanzas 20 and 92).

3.12 cut here – The poet's work reduced to a supermarket commodity, such as a box of cereal.

4. The principal image in this stanza is that of the breakdown in communication, and the stanza ends on a note of despair, or desperate belief. The simplicity of the Reformation woodcut, in which each speaker is literally attributed space for expression, has been replaced by the "communications breakdown" of contemporary culture. Indeed, what achieves expression is now "expressionless"; the spiritually-devoid fare dealt out by the disc jockey ("show-host") repeats itself endlessly and without development (on a "stuck track"). The "show-host" suggests the modern showman (Alice Cooper, perhaps, or the Master of Ceremonies in *Cabaret*): a blank-faced, self-created, gender-confusing ("say her") entertainer, a type that has "died many times" and which in a travesty of resurrection is reinvented (like the "fetish pig" of the following stanza) in each generation. The Christian message, fraught but still audible in Luther's time, is now drowned out by the din of popular culture. The 1960s (the era of Roy Orbison's song) were at least the years of protest, but even that impulse is gone. The sense is that of a lawless age ("Anomie") achieving its meaningless 'apotheosis' entirely at random ("pick any"); the liturgical "words / of welcome" also dismiss. The stanza closes with an expression of a desire to cling to belief in the midst of disbelief: but even God, implicit in the grand mystery of the Tetragrammaton, has been reduced to a small, anonymous 'g', and nobody will even care enough to protest.

4.1 Reformation woodcuts enscrolled such things / between the lips Reformation woodcuts frequently featured speech balloons attached to speakers' lips. See Appendix, fig.1, for an example, the engraved title page of Lewis Bayly's *The Practise of Pietie*, 9th ed. (1617). Here, Hill may be suggesting that the reader should compare a visual image and its accompanying written emblem, as an example of two messages presented in different modes of communication.

4.2 communications breakdown 'Communication Breakdown', a song recorded by popular singer Roy Orbison in 1966. Like many of Orbison's songs, it is ostensibly romantic, but the lyrics have a strong religious subtext: "we never walk, we never talk / we never find the time to be close again / communication breakdown". The recording ends with the repetitive 'communication breakdown' refrain, suggesting the "stuck track" of line 6.

4.3 (say her) A gesture towards political correctness whereby the unthinking use of the male pronoun is replaced by the ostentatious use of the female equivalent.

4.4 show-host has died many times The sense is of repeated resurrection; and of the performer, who is said to have "died" when his act fails on stage.

4.5 words / of welcome dismiss us The liturgical tone suggests the blessing of the congregation on both arrival and departure. See stanza 5: "Remind me: *bienvenue* – is that arrival or welcome?"

4.6 Anomie Lack of the usual social standards in a group or person; lawlessness. The term was popularized by French sociologist Émile Durkheim in his 1897 case study, *Suicide*. Hill has described the challenge of living in the contemporary age as to "Somehow ... encounter the Logos within the

ANNOTATIONS

lawlessness and inarticulacy of our daily being" ('Trinity Sermon: Ash Wednesday 2008').
4.7 who on earth A phrase meaning both a) literally on earth, as opposed to in heaven; and b) the clichéd expression 'whatsoever, at all'.
4.8 unnamed god Throughout the poem, the unnameable, anticipating the 'tetragrammaton' (see stanza 20: "the condition of Hebrew"). Compare Paul's speech regarding the worship of a supposedly 'unknown God' in Acts 17:22-23: "Then Paul stood in the midst of Mars' hill, and said, Ye men of Athens, I perceive that in all things ye are too superstitious. For as I passed by, and beheld your devotion, I found an altar with this inscription, TO THE UNKNOWN GOD. Whom therefore ye ignorantly worship, him declare I unto you".

5. The muse is split in two. One half – a dark lady called the "Enforcer" – is intent on murdering and torturing the other, a "guardian spirit" who cries out "under interrogation" and is ripped to shreds ("What intact part of her was found"). The "Enforcer" makes demands (answered "freely", because voluntary and invited) upon the poet. But the Enforcer is also the dominatrix ("perfected with some pain") and the Inquisition's torturer ("cry out under your interrogation"; "sate your inquiry"). The action is depicted as a *psychomachia*, a battle of disparate forces within the soul, or self. Hill's daimon (introduced in stanza 3, and now expressed as a "guardian spirit") resists any confession of heresy, but is nevertheless martyred and burned, identifiable only by dental records, the transcendental reduced to the dental (but does a daimon have teeth?). The linguistically identical (but politically disparate) *salaam* and *shalom* are mocked by the bastardized French of *"Napoo Finee"*, to express the ironic profundity, 'there is no more'; that is, in the Middle East, as in the Great War, the violence will go on, and there is finally nothing more to be said. The repetition of "Remind me" (from line 3) enforces the sardonic, deliberately disingenuous tone. Again, the "signal" of God (transmitted in stanza 1 on Hill's Aga radio) is being lost in the din; the cycle of futility is expressed in the ritual destruction of the *carnival* idol, and in the sinister ambiguity of *bienvenue*: here we go again.
5.1 Enforcer! The opening lines suggest the sadomasochism of the dominatrix torturing the muse. 'Enforcer' implies the

secular arm of the Inquisition (cf. "auto-da-fé" in stanza 1; "interrogation" and "inquiry" here) that meted out punishments for heresy and used torture to extract confessions. The term also refers to the Enforcer (or hitman) of the modern Mafia, the low-ranking 'Piccioto' of the family whose job is to 'persuade' debtors to pay.

5.2 What can I / freely give you According to Christopher Orchard, the voice we hear at this point is not that of an "haranguer/pugilist poet", but rather an "exasperated poet of despair, exhausted by the gift that he recognizes he has 'over-employed'" ('Praxis not Gnosis', p. 202).

5.3 perfected with some pain Cf. Eliot, 'Little Gidding' III: "Whatever we inherit from the fortunate / We have taken from the defeated / What they had to leave us—a symbol: / A symbol perfected in death"; see Hill's discussion of these lines in *Collected Critical Writings*, pp. 540-541.

5.4 guardian spirit Cf. 'daimon' in stanza 3.

5.5 intact Cf. 'intacta' in stanza 15.

5.6 *Salaam. Shalom.* Greetings, respectively, Arabic and Jewish. Cf. "*bienvenue*" in line 12.

5.7 *Napoo Finee* As Eric Partridge notes in *A Dictionary of Catch Phrases*: "No more—finished!: army: 1914-18. A tautological elab. of *napoo*, nothing more, and *finee*, finished: Fr. *Il n'y en a plus, fini*, lit., 'there's no more of it, finished'. The British soldier dealt no less heroically with foreign languages than he did with the enemy" (p. 320). Hill associates the phrase with Ivor Gurney (see stanza 111); see Hill's 'Gurney's "Hobby"': "'Na pooh fini' is a bit of the pidgin French that Gurney enjoyed'" (*Collected Critical Writings*, p. 446).

5.8 dental records Incinerated bodies are finally identifiable only by their teeth since dental enamel, the hardest form of bone, resists reduction.

5.9 gets to them Double articulation: a) irritates his readers; and b) reaches them, as a radio signal. Hill uses the poem as a metaphor for a broadcast radio signal throughout this poem, as well as in *The Orchards of Syon*, where he asks "Can you / receive me?" (VII).

5.10 fetish / pig made of terra cotta The practice – pagan, though incorporated into local Catholicism – in many Latin American countries of making earthenware idols to be ritually destroyed at *carnival* and then rebuilt to be destroyed again, thereby suggesting the birth-death cycle of life, as well as the Resurrection.

ANNOTATIONS

5.11 arrival or welcome 'Bienvenue' means both arrival *and* welcome, and is most commonly a greeting upon arrival; as in the opening song of the musical, *Cabaret* (1966), delivered by the Emcee: "Willkommen, bienvenue, welcome / Im Cabaret, au Cabaret, to Cabaret". Cf. the "show-host" in stanza 4.

6. Beginning with an equivocation implying self-correction ("They invested – were invested"), the poet in this stanza (which has the air of a speech reported in a newspaper, the interjections of the audience placed within parentheses) confronts his own tradition and revisits the question of how to act and react appropriately. "They" of the first line refers to those soldiers and civilians who were casualties of or survived the First World War. Hill struggles to find an appropriate reaction to their heroism and sacrifice, made for a questionable cause (where "cost" outweighed "reward") and for the "proprieties" (both social and commercial) of Georgian life. A later audience demands (and applauds) accountability, or at least an ironic critique (parody); but this Hill cannot offer; he can only "gape or grin / haplessly" at the tragicomic ("tying confession to parody") spectacle. Hill stage-directs his own response: he applauds their commitment to "decency" and "duty", but finds that, as a bystander considering a war resolved before his own birth, he cannot in this instance speak as "WE"; for the 'we' is his own generation, those who escaped service in either World War. The Great War, its futility now seen through distance, might seem to demand parodic laughter as a fitting response (as in the 1963 musical *Oh, What a Lovely War!*); but the "formal impromptus" that come to his mind are those of great British battles (Rorke's Drift, Jutland); these "have their own / grandeur", and urge him ("*speech! speech!*") both to acknowledge that "grandeur" and to make his own response to the past.

6.1 proprieties Both a) decencies; and b) commodities. Hill intimates sordid commercial activities underpinning "investment" in war, whatever the clichés of 'decency' and 'duty'.

6.2 I cannot / do more now Cf. Martin Luther's refusal to retract his teachings at the Diet of Worms (1521). Luther asserted that he had no choice but to refuse – 'I cannot do differently' – given the Scriptures and his conscience. In Mozart's *The Magic Flute*, Tamino, unable to free a chained Papageno, can merely look upon his suffering: "Ich kann nichts tun, als dich beklagen / Weil ich zu schwach zu helfen bin" [I can do nothing except lament you, because I am too weak to help]. The setting ("floorboards", "gape or grin") implies a spectacle, such as a musical or a music hall.

6.3 grin / haplessly Cf. *The Triumph of Love*: "The nerve required to keep standing, pedaling, / grinning inanely" (CXXXIII).

6.4 self-advisement The seeking of one's own counsel; see also "advisement" in stanza 50.

6.5 I / is a shade Shade: a) a little; and b) a ghost. Rimbaud wrote to Paul Demeny (5 May 1871), "Je est un autre" [I is another] (*Complete Works, Selected Letters*, p. 374); for Hill, however, self-scrutiny forces a recognition of his ties to shades of the past. Cf. his *The Mystery of the Charity of Charles Péguy*: "'Je est un autre', that fatal telegram"; and *Without Title*: "I can't say more as yet, the hurtling agent / fixed in mind's body, a last steadying beam: / *I* is an other" (p. 45). Hill likewise explores the potential ambiguity of 'shade' in *Canaan*: "you turn to speak / with someone standing deeper in the shade ... Formalities preserve us: / perhaps I too am a shade" (p. 52).

6.6 Rorke's Drift The Battle of Rorke's Drift, 22 January 1879, during the Boer War, in which some 4000 Zulus were opposed by 139 British troops, whose heroism made the battle one of the most famous in British military history. Eleven defenders were awarded the Victoria Cross, more than in any other engagement in history.

6.7 Jutland A peninsula in Northern Denmark, known for the Battle of Jutland (in Germany, the Battle of Skagerrak), 31 May 1916. This was the only major engagement between British and German fleets of WWI. The Germans, although heavily outnumbered, proved to be brilliant naval tacticians, while the British suffered heavy losses and were strategically inferior, the conflict ending only with the onset of fog and darkness. The poor British performance was one of the great controversies of WWI. See also stanza 86.

6.8 (*speech! speech!*) The title of the poem; the poet either 'taking a bow' (like an author called to front of stage), or being provoked into action.

7. The opening of the stanza is still focused on the First World War generation, and the metaphors of commodity.

Although the stanza then shifts from the Great War to the Second World War (Bletchley Park), Hill accentuates the need to acknowledge our debt to and our 'at-one-ness' with the earlier as well as the more immediate past. Hill uses an oratorical tone, but instead of the expected 'they did all that they could do' he delivers the more accommodating "Not all they coúld do they háve done". Although his ironic counterpoint debunks the tenor of grandiose post-war patriotic speeches, his thanks to his forebears are nevertheless sincere. For Hill, the ranks of war heroes are filled with "many true arbiters", those who escaped fame and laudation only through chance – those who simply "missed their stars". They, like failed astronauts, represent unexercised and unfulfilled heroism, but demand to be 'admitted' nonetheless. Hill's aim is to be truthful and accurate but still thankful: the stanza escapes satire of the futility of the Great War because Hill's primary concern is to bring "atonement beyond dispute". Our debt to the past is to be observed, regardless of the futility of past actions; the sins of the fathers are visited upon the sons and restated in commercial and legal jargon (as "breakages chargeable to all parties"). The second half of the stanza sees Hill imagining himself in a kind of 'poetry court', accused of obscurity (and broken verse) but escaping on a 'double jeopardy' clause ("they cannot / charge us again for that"). In the court, "Claimant / Fatality" appears and pleads his suit in an affected mannerist manner, as if in ironic dramatization of what Hill is himself doing (or perceived as doing). Where, then (goes the hypothetical question) is the evidence (the "Citations") to warrant his claims?

7.1 Not all they coúld do they háve done There is perhaps an echo of John 19:22: "What I have written I have written".

7.2 atonement Reparation for or expiation of sin; when capitalized, the reconciliation of God and humankind through Jesus Christ. For Hill, the etymology of 'at-one-ment' is symbolic of the disjuncture between language and that which we wish to describe with it; ultimately, language does not equate to, make sense of, or *atone for*, its subject: Hill writes in 'Poetry as "Menace" and "Atonement"' that "the technical perfecting of a poem is an act of atonement, in the radical etymological sense – an act of at-one-ment, a setting at one, a bringing into concord, a reconciling, a uniting in harmony" (*Collected Critical Writings*, p. 4). See also Christopher Ricks's assessment of Hill's use of the word in *The Force of Poetry* (pp. 319-55).

7.3 Beulah The land of Israel (Isaiah 62:4), from the Hebrew, 'married woman'. In the mythology of William Blake (1757-1827), a semi-paradise beyond the vale.

7.4 In Hut Eight the rotors Hut Eight: one of eleven Huts erected between 1939-40 at Bletchley Park, the site of a secret British military intelligence operation during WWII. Hut Eight's specific area of work was the cryptanalysis of naval communication; it housed some of the "stars" of codebreaking, such as Alan Turing, who were responsible for cracking the Enigma code. A 'rotor' was part of the mechanism of the Enigma machines. Hill refers to cryptanalysis in *The Triumph of Love* as "Britannia's own narrow / miracle of survival" (XV).

7.5 admit Meaning: a) let in; b) confess to; and c) acknowledge.

7.6 chargeable to all parties A commercial phrase indicating that all present will be responsible for paying, "breakages" echoing the code-breakers of the opening of the stanza, the logic of which turns on this pun.

7.7 ingemination Repeated utterance, reiteration, typically for emphasis; there is a mild irony in being charged "again" for something: both the legal double jeopardy and commercial over-charging are implied (see 7.8).

7.8 charge us again for that 'Charge', as in a) demand payment; b) arrest; c) accuse; and d) military attack, but suggestive too of the 'charging' of a heraldic device on a shield or banner. Hill uses the language of commerce to convey the notion of 'paying for' acts (of sin) and speaking (on behalf of others); see *The Orchards of Syon*, in which he requests that his readers "Nod / if you can't speak and let me charge it / to my own account" (X).

7.9 Claimant / Fatality Another Bunyanesque personification; cf. "Scattergood Commodity" (stanza 3) for a like "mannerist" conceit of the self on trial.

7.10 Citations please An examiner's request for a quotation from or reference to a book or author; a note of a praiseworthy act in an official report, especially during wartime; or a former utterance used in the trying of comparable cases or to support an argument in a summons.

8. This stanza is concerned firstly with the pitfalls of popularity for the artist, and secondly with the seminal dereliction of mankind. The setting is still the court of law, where Hill wonders whether his apparent ability to maintain a stiff upper lip in the face of his detractors is a symptom of inner strength ("stiffened by rectitude") or of being scared stiff ("rigid with indecision"). Hill observes that an author can write pot-boilers ("roulette set pieces") and make a significant income ("killings"), but that were he to do so it would require the sacrifice of his poetic talent ("exchange / my best gift"). The "killings" of "cameo actors" imply the recurrent bit parts of extras in thrillers, or the money to be made by unknown actors playing violent roles. The equivocations "even so" and "but for", which frame and introduce the discussion of original sin, indicate that while Hill, like Augustine, believes mankind to be burdened (in his legalese, "indicted") by original sin, there must nevertheless be some worth in our existence – he cannot believe humanity to be "absolutely struck off", like errant lawyers, however irrefutable the indictment. The ambiguity of Hill's address to Lilith suggests both the poet's strong affiliation with her, and a bar-room scene in which a socially compromised poet meets her, behaving disingenuously as if this were their first encounter.

8.1 spools of applause Canned laughter. The 'gift' is poetic creativity, as confirmed by the casual repetition of 'say', but compromised by popular success.

8.2 roulette set pieces As in a) luck at winning at roulette; and b) the 'sureties' of the court case. Although roulette is a game of chance, it is a game of *mechanical* luck; conventional tropes may lead to an eventual success.

8.3 cameo actors A cameo is a brief dramatic scene played by a well-known personality in a film or television play, for instance Hitchcock's celebrated brief appearances in his own films.

8.4 killings As murders on film, but also as easy money. The "legacies" are the record on film, but also the money gained.

8.5 dereliction Both a) decay, dilapidation; and b) abandonment of responsibilities and duties; it is "seminal" in the theological sense of being bred into Adam's first seed, as a consequence of the Fall.

8.6 zillionth Used colloquially since the 1940s for an extremely large but indeterminate number.

8.7 (*vide* Augustine) Saint Augustine of Hippo (354-430), philosopher and theologian, here called as an expert witness because of his knowledge of original sin and for his expression of the paradox: that unless there were some good in humanity, it could not be damned.

8.8 But for that / primal occasion "But for" here meaning both a) except ('were it not for the enormity'); and b) despite ('on account of the triviality'). The primal occasion is that of original sin, specifically, man's first disobedience in the Garden of Eden; but also the act of sex (as in Freud's "primal" scene). For Hill, this ancestral sin is essential to his faith: "If I am a Christian it is because the Church's teaching on Original Sin strikes me as being the most coherent grammar of tragic humanity that I have ever encountered" ('Trinity Sermon: Ash Wednesday 2008').

8.9 absolutely struck off Humanity struck off (from God's grace) as a consequence of original sin, like a lawyer disbarred.

8.10 Lilith In Jewish mythology, Adam's first wife: a vampire-like child-killing demon and symbol of sensual lust; here emblematic of the libido and unconscious impulses. She is both acknowledged ("we háve met") and denied ("and do I knów you"), the denial itself suggesting complicity. Cf. 'LILITH' in stanza 67.

9. Stanza 9 opens with the language and syntax of the auctioneer: the "Going | attrition" recalling 'going, going, gone...'; and the following two lines continue the auction scene. Hill is unwilling to attract the notice of the poetry-reading public by raising his hand to bid for their affections, or for objects ("tictac") not worthy of purchase. Cost, again, outweighs reward (see stanza 6). The changing of the millennium ("centennial") marks "some half- / heard plea"; the proclamation – the truth – is that all millennia, centennials, and indeed all New (Christian) Years are anniversaries of the Incarnation. Hill asserts that humanity is yet to gain significant insight into its situation, as (despite the counter-claims of "attrition" and "Eternal progress") "Most things are still in the dark". The poet is willing (though in no hurry) to debate the esoteric issues ("sometime this century") with the rabbi, and "in the dark" of the Jewish ritual he is willing to seek (in principle) profound illumination. Hill is engaging with a voice that hears all utterance as selling something; the final line of the stanza asks the significant question: "what kind of pitch is that?", which extends the auctioneer's lexicon, questions the marketing and attraction of his wares (the public's adoration), and asks how the poet can talk about the everyday in a manner that makes it in some way immortal. The contrast is between the (rabbi's) cabbalistic – the esoteric and mystical – reading and interpretation of a sacred text ("I AM AND HAVE NOTHING"), given the insistence of the commonplace and the ordinary.

9.1 put up That is, to put up one's hand to bid at auction.

9.2 tictac Bric-à-brac, tat, tatty, tack, tackiness, tic-tac-toe (the word's origins), possibly even Tic-Tacs (a popular brand of tiny breath mints).... Tictac is also the secret language of hand signals and codewords used by bookmakers and their runners to communicate odds without the knowledge or understanding of bettors.

9.3 I AM AND HAVE NOTHING From a devotional selection by the English mystic novelist Charles Williams (1886-1945), *The New Christian Year* (1941), p. 99. The source is the anonymous fourteenth-century text *Theologia Germanica* (XXXIII): "As though God in human nature were saying: 'I am pure, simple Goodness, and therefore I cannot will, or desire, or rejoice in, or do or give anything but goodness. If I am to reward thee for thy evil and wickedness, I must do it with goodness, for I am and have nothing else'". Cf. "I ám – this / also ís – broken" in stanza 13, and "THIS ALSO IS THOU, NEITHER IS THIS THOU", in stanza 107.

9.4 in the dark The setting is a séance, or a Jewish gathering in the dark, seeking illumination. Cf. the ancient jest: Q: 'Where was Moses when the light went out?'; A: 'In the dark'.

9.5 rabbi The leader of a Jewish congregation, or the chief religious official of a synagogue; a scholar qualified to teach or interpret Jewish law; here, the point of discussion might be the insistence of the Old Testament Jehovah in Exodus 3:14: "I AM THAT I AM".

9.6 *welch ein Gruss* German, 'What a greeting'. In Luke 1:29 of the Luther Bible (1534) a bemused Mary is greeted by the archangel Gabriel: "Da sie aber ihn sah, erschrak sie über seine Rede und gedachte: Welch ein Gruß ist das?" [And when she saw him, she was troubled at his saying, and cast in her mind what manner of salutation this should be].

9.7 pitch The word 'pitch' (here, as an auctioneer's urging) is of great import for Hill. He complains, in his essay-length review of the second edition of the *Oxford English Dictionary* (1989) that "The signification of the word *pitch*, in the same set of notes, remains undefined, nor is the sematology of 'Pitched past pitch of grief' (in the sonnet 'No worst, there is none') adduced at any point in the entries on *pitch* and *pitched*" ('Common Weal and Common Woe', *Collected Critical Writings*, p. 267). Writing of what he later terms "ordinary words raised to an extraordinary pitch of signification" (p. 273), Hill adds: "Hopkins, in his uses of *pitch* / *pitched*, has pitched its significations beyond the range of the *OED*'s reductive method … in his notes 'On Personality, Grace and Free Will', he has himself offered a model reduction: 'So also *pitch* is ultimately simple positiveness, that by which being differs from and is more than nothing and not-being'" (p. 267).

10. Almost as in a word-association game, Hill moves, through the implied "end" of the "beginning", from the drama of Christian revelation – the simultaneous creation of Heaven and Earth – to the sexual act, and by the phrase "any way", from the sexual act to democracy. The purpose of modern life in a shiftless age of democracy is called into question; a "final answer" is sought. The suffrage enjoyed by the contemporary citizen is no more than a "franchise" which is "free" to all comers, but which – significantly – is a freedom "of slavishness" (rather than 'from slavery'). In the modern world, the wisely-foolish ("butt-headed") Sothsegger will not be heard among the many Mums of the bar-room ("spilt beer"), where the punters engaged in the futile sport of arm-wrestling are given an inevitably clichéd voice ("TALK ABOUT LAUGH, TALK ABOUT / ANGRY"). But Hill does not "count" on a good outcome, as the paradox of democracy may well be governance by those who would formerly have been slaves, those "without distinction". Democracy, it seems, has not so much enabled the voice of *every man* in the crowd as disenfranchised all but that of the *everyman*.

10.1 Shiftless That is, without one's shift, or nightdress (suggested by the "sex / fantasies" had "any way" of the previous lines); but equally, lacking purpose, as in the paradox of 'working at it' when there is no 'shift'.

10.2 butt-headed Perhaps a reference to the MTV animated series *Beavis and Butt-head* (1993-1997), in which two apathetic Texan teenagers express their critical world-views.

10.3 Sothsegger *Mum and the Sothsegger*, a fifteenth-century anonymous English poem which debates the merits of holding one's tongue (keeping mum) or speaking out (soothsaying); an

ANNOTATIONS

"alliterative verse meditation on statecraft and an often satirical anatomy of contemporary institutions, especially the estates and courts of law" (*Richard the Redeless; and Mum and the Sothsegger*, p.i). The debate is one-sided: the scorned, derided Sothsegger is a figure of truth, a voice crying in the wilderness, whereas the popular, influential Mum is an exemplar of all that is wrong with the author's society. The goal is to determine which of these two ways of self-expression should, in the poem's words, "have / The maistrie". Although the poem is fragmentary, the clear victor (there, but not here) is the Sothsegger. William Logan in his review of *Speech! Speech!* for *The New Criterion* describes this reference to *Mum and the Sothsegger* as one of the poem's "bits of arcana" ('Author! Author!', p. 65).

10.4 who or what ends uppermost The image is of arm-wrestling (a pursuit on which viewers *do* bet) in the bar-room, the competitors' arms on wet tables, the victor's arm literally ending "uppermost".

10.5 franchise Both the vote, and freedom from slavery.

10.6 without distinction Both a) without exception; and b) lacking fine qualities.

11. The stanza begins with a scrupulous questioning (delivered with the academic philosopher's abstract, impersonal, conjectural tone used for ethical issues) of the must/ought paradigm, as the poet asks whether, because one *should* do something, it follows that one *must*. The author finds himself awake at night, fiddling with a red ballpoint pen (he "clown-paints" his pyjamas, no exit wound appearing on the back of his leg as his weapon is, after all, nothing keener than a "biro"). With his scrupulosity "unnerved" (*not* vigilant, impulses not tingling), a kind of placidity ("*gelassenheit*") takes over, an ironic "gift in faith" since its rewards are unattended, perhaps undeserved (*not* the product of an attuned sensibility) – which is "fair enough" as there is no reason to believe in universal fairness ("given injustice"). These late-night creative blocks are countered with the admission that each burst ("strafe") of poetical, intellectual activity produces both failures ("duds") and hits ("freak chances"); scrupulosity, both in the moral sense and with close reference to particulars, will necessarily produce the occasional misfire. There is an irony in Hill's pyjama-doodling and late-night prevaricating: the 'hit or miss' process is not the creative burst it might appear – in fact, creativity is noticeably absent from this scene. Hill muses on the eunuch's sexual desire; this and the word "terrible" invoke a Hopkins sonnet which describes the horror of the poet's inability to create, and rails against the injustice that allows the "sots and thralls of lust" (like the barflies of the previous stanza) to create with abandon. In a final burst of frustration, the stanza closes with the poet's wish not to shuffle off this mortal coil, as the Prince of inertia desired, but rather to "shuffle off alive". The tone is thus that of a deep *ennui*.

11.1 Is MUST a true imperative of OUGHT? Because Hill *ought to* do something, *must* he therefore do it? The complex nature of imperative moods and modal auxiliaries in English offers no easy answer.

11.2 biro The usual European or British word for what Americans call a ballpoint pen; "clown-paints" implies colouring his pyjamas with red dots.

11.3 exit-wound Where a bullet emerges on the other side of the body, often causing much greater damage than at the entrance.

11.4 Scrupulosity Inordinate attention to small details, here nervous impulses, essential for creativity.

11.5 *gelassenheit* German, a laissez-faire attitude in the sense of 'letting it drift', placid acceptance. See Hill's 'Trinity Sermon: Ash Wednesday 2008': "One is put to mind, by this melancholia ... of the morbid, masochistic *gelassenheit* of that peculiar people, the early 16th century anabaptists of St Gall."

11.6 heart's ease See *Romeo and Juliet*, IV.v: "*Peter*: Musicians, O, musicians, 'Heart's ease, Heart's ease'. O, and you will have me live, play 'Heart's ease'. *First Musician*: Why 'Heart's ease?' *Peter*: O, musicians, because my heart itself plays 'My heart is full of woe'. O, play me some merry dump, to comfort me."

11.7 gift in faith, / most difficult among freedoms Grace as hard to accept, since unmerited; the most difficult freedom is humility.

11.8 Each strafe / throws in some duds A strafe is an attack from low-flying aircraft with machine-gun fire; a 'dud' is a munition that fails to fire or explode.

11.9 libido of eunuchs, they say, is terrible 'Terrible' recalls the last poems of Gerard Manley Hopkins (1844-1889), written during his isolation in Dublin and named the "terrible sonnets" due to their intense melancholy. The desirous eunuch is found in 'Thou art indeed just, Lord, if I contend', which expresses the frustration of writer's block and the injustice of God allowing vitality to those who least deserve it, while an agonized Hopkins ("Time's eunuch") remains barren. There is an echo, too, of the ageing, impotent lover of John Gower's *Confessio Amantis*.

11.10 shuffle off alive Cf. Hamlet's: "Ay, there's the rub; / For in that sleep of death what dreams may come / When we have shuffled off this mortal coil, / Must give us pause" (III.i). Hamlet's scrupulosity prevented his embarking upon decisive action. See also Yeats's 'The Scholars', in which antiquated academics in the library edit passionate poetry: "All shuffle there; all cough in ink ... Lord, what would they say / Did their Catullus walk that way?". Hill wrote of the title of *The Enemy's Country* that "Yeats's contrast between young poets 'tossing' in lyric anguish and aged impotent scholars who 'edit and annotate' such gems of youthful suffering is a piece of sentimental cant" (*Collected Critical Writings*, 173). As in Eliot's 'The Hollow Men', the impulse to prayer at the end of this stanza trails off into an inarticulate frustration.

12. Despite the anxiety of the previous stanza, the poet – in a recurrence of legalese – has "the instructions", which read like the back of a medicine bottle. In keeping with the Christian tradition, these directions advise acceptance of the burden ("REMIT / NOTHING") and surrender to a higher judgement ("refer your pain"); for David Rogers, they are ironic, and "refer to his pain like an HMO [Health Maintenance Organization] number, indicating how little the modern world can do about it" (*World Literature Today*, p. 152). These rules "stand for our redemption", but this assurance is fatally compromised by the contemporary demotic equivocation, "Or whatever", a casual cliché deliberately at odds with the following statement, which implies that this poetic and theological agony is too easy, if the heart is not in it. You (being he) have to be *alert* to the moment (your heart "alive / to its own beating"), to the sense of the redemptive; an alertness that is often likened to the creative phase of the mind at the moment of intense being. But this analogy (Hill asserts) is a misconception: a confusing of the experience with the act of recording it. That is too easy: *chagrin*, in the sense of being clad in an ass's skin, is not true penitence, for *penance* (in this startling, horrific image) entails the debasement of drinking blood from the leper's dish, a eucharistic acceptance of humility, suffering and atonement.

12.1 instructions In the legal sense: from a judge to the jury, concerning how to deliberate in deciding the case at bar. Instructions contain statements of fact, and delimit the laws applicable to such facts.

12.2 REMIT In the legal sense: to send a case back to a lower court for further action to be taken; in the common sense, 'don't send the money yet'.

12.3 REFER In the legal sense: to direct somebody to something or somebody else for judgement; in the common sense, to accept higher judgement. Here, the instruction is to "REFER YOUR PAIN"; 'referred pain' is pain that has its source in one part of the body but is felt in another.

12.4 Your heart has to be in it Coming after the dismissive and equivocal "Or whatever" of the previous line, the assertion that "Your heart has to be in it" suggests that the poet's "heart" was not "in" the first four lines of the stanza, which are typified by a terse impersonality. The "it" may also refer to "redemption" in the previous line; the implication is that one cannot pay lipservice to redemption but must be entirely committed to it.

12.5 Balzac [...] the wild ass's skin Honoré de Balzac (1799-1850), French novelist (see also stanza 100). One of Balzac's early successes was *La Peau de chagrin* [*The Wild Ass's Skin*], his 1831 story of a talisman pelt which granted every wish, but contracted as each was delivered, the user doomed to die when the pelt shrank to nothing. Hence the implied pun on *chagrin*, as one form of penitence.

12.6 easy-over The American description of eggs cooked on one side, then flipped without breaking the yolk: 'over easy'; *chagrin* is easy, flippant, but penitence is not.

12.7 Penance A Christian sacrament in which the penitent confesses his sins and is given absolution, which permits participation in the mass and partaking of the Eucharist.

13. The "instructions" (legal) of the previous stanza return, but now as part of the image of a lawyer consulting with his client, informing him that the date for his case has not yet been specified ("blind / date"). Each stanza of the poem is a "mêlée", the milieu for what Eliot calls in 'East Coker' V "a raid on the inarticulate". The first line is ambiguous: the phrase can be read as both 'If I am failing, [then] you [shall] sense this'; and 'If

ANNOTATIONS

I am failing you, [then] sense this'; the poet's instructions are failing his audience just as the lawyer is failing his client. Hill is failing, weakening, but if he fails in this poetic endeavour, his contract with his audience is null and void. However, he dedicates this stanza, like a radio showhost ("This for") in a request session, to Max Perutz, as representative of the stellar individuals who should be observed, and lauded with the accolades ("honours", "titles" and "wreaths") proffered "in the name of the PEOPLE". Genius and nobility do exist and are applauded, but in name rather than with understanding. In reality, society (the "acclaimed chorus") too often remains conspicuously silent. In like manner, this poem, to which the reader is urged to "Listen", both "ís" and "ís – broken", like the Mosaic 'I AM', as is the very syntax in which it is expressed.

13.1 blind / date A romantic assignation between people who have not met before (as poet and reader); alternatively, a policy or contract that has no date specified.

13.2 exclusion An item or risk specifically not covered by an insurance policy or contract.

13.3 mêlée Literally, a commotion; here referring to each stanza of the poem.

13.4 Max Perutz Max Ferdinand Perutz (1914-2002), Vienna-born ("alien") biochemist who fled to England in 1936 to escape Nazism, and who discovered the structure of haemoglobin; with John Kendrew he was awarded the Nobel Prize for Chemistry in 1962. Here, Perutz is a "star" who observes (via the microscope), as opposed to a star which is observed.

13.5 Fates In Greek mythology, the goddesses who preside over human life. Destiny is a thread spun, measured and cut by the three Fates, Clotho, Lachesis and Atropos.

13.6 power among powers In medieval angelology, 'powers' are a member of one of the orders of angels. See, for instance, The Fifth Ecumenical Council, The Second Council of Constantinople AD 553, The Anathemas Against Origen, VII: "If anyone shall say that Christ, of whom it is said that he appeared in the form of God, and that he was united before all time with God the Word, and humbled himself in these last days even to humanity, had (according to their expression) pity upon the divers falls which had appeared in the spirits united in the same unity (of which he himself is part), and that to restore them he passed through divers classes, had different bodies and different names, became all to all, an Angel among Angels, a Power among Powers, has clothed himself in the different classes of reasonable beings with a form corresponding to that class, and finally has taken flesh and blood like ours and is become man for men; [if anyone says all this] and does not profess that God the Word humbled himself and became man: let him be anathema" (*A Select Library of Nicene and Post-Nicene Fathers of the Christian Church*, pp. 318-319). See also Eliot's 'Ash-Wednesday' for the sense of time and place as our "inheritance".

13.7 PEOPLE See stanza 1; the mob is invoked throughout the poem.

13.8 chorus In Ancient Greek tragedy, a group of performers (representing the common people) who comment on the main action, speaking and moving together.

13.9 I ám – this / also ís – broken Hill's ironic echo of the great 'I AM' imparts a sense of idols broken and implies the shattering of the old (Mosaic) dispensation. Cf. Exodus 3:14: "And God said unto Moses, I AM THAT I AM: and he said, Thus should thou say unto the children of Israel I AM hath sent me unto you". Cf. stanza 9: "I AM AND HAVE NOTHING".

13.10 *passim* Literary instruction used especially in footnotes to indicate that what is referred to is found throughout the text. Here, the instruction functions sardonically; the entire poem ("*passim*") is evidence of a broken venture. Compare *supra* in stanza 44.

14. Again in a self-reflective moment in front of the mirror, Hill searches for his self as an object, as in the accusative case; but the lapse between the object and its perception, between Hill and his reflection, means that a true "recollection in the act" is impossible (cf. stanza 12, with the like sense of the gap between experience and re-creation). This lapse is contextualized within the Christian mystery and its "axiomatic / redemption"; axiomatic in that it is unfolded *in time* with a sequential inevitability no more escapable than that of Hill's delayed perception of the moment. Past, present and future are determined, and must be played out; Christ's cross is "grafted" onto Adam's tree of knowledge. Abraham's mourning for Hagar is part of the plan, for it is followed by both the Christian story of redemption and the discrepancies of belief (in which faith contests with faith); whether Abraham can rightfully weep for both his wife and his mistress is the question. What Hill seeks is the one truth; what he finds (the instructions having been re-

ANNOTATIONS

read more carefully) is an implicit diversity that makes the Christian story (what he 'seeks') more complex. Predestination is at once affirmed and denied: the path of Abraham was "axiomatic", and yet – paradoxically – it ended in more than one destination. The problem of diversity of faiths (Islam, Judaism) may be reduced to a like problem of perception. What looks like many (destinations) is in fact one: the seeking of redemption for original sin, whatever different sects and theological panels might say. Just as Hill finds in the mirror that the moment of perception must follow the moment that is perceived, which in turn follows the act of perceiving, so in the Christian mystery did the Fall follow the Creation, and, inevitably, it must be followed by the Redemption.

14.1 accusative of recollection The 'accusative' is a grammatical case of nouns and pronouns that expresses the object of an action or the goal of a motion; here, recollection (an invented category of grammar), as in the lapsed, reflected image: 'It was me' (as opposed to 'It is I'). 'Accusative' also suggests the 'accused' of the courtroom (appearing before "juries" in line 11) whose misdemeanour is found out ("caught") in line 1.

14.2 VARIETY Like *People* in stanza 1, *Variety* is a popular American magazine, a glossy tabloid newspaper published weekly since 1905.

14.3 Sarah ánd Hagar's travail The story of Abraham (in Genesis) tells of the divergence of faiths: Sarah, wife of Abraham, could not bear children and urged her husband to take her servant-girl Hagar as a wife. Hagar bore Abraham a son, Ishmael. But God came to Abraham in his old age and promised him (in return for circumcision of the faithful) a son with Sarah. This son was Isaac, and is the continuation of the Judeao-Christian line, while Ishmael – driven away by Sarah after Isaac's birth – is, traditionally, father to Islam. Abraham weeps, therefore, both for Sarah's infertility "ánd" (Hill stresses the conjunction) the injustice done to Hagar.

14.4 make mourning instrumental The 'instrumental' case (as compared with the accusative) denotes the means with which or by which an action is done; here, Abraham's weeping ('he mourns') is revised into a statement of instrumentality: by means of Abraham's mourning God's purpose will be done.

14.5 Spare us As in the beggar's demotic 'give a little'; but also 'allow us to live a little longer, vouchsafe us salvation'.

14.6 grafted to the condemned stock Redemption is "grafted", as the cross of Jesus onto the tree of Paradise.
14.7 original justice The 1910 *New Catholic Dictionary* defines 'original justice' as the "aggregate of all those organically correlated prerogatives which constituted the state of our first parents in Paradise. This primitive state before the Fall included the gift of sanctifying grace, exemption from concupiscence, bodily immortality, habitual infused science, and the non-necessity of suffering. The first named gift is purely supernatural; the others, less strictly supernatural, and more commonly called preternatural gifts, were allied with this to form the rich endowment which Adam was to transmit to all his descendants" ('Original Justice', *New Catholic Dictionary*).
14.8 contestant juries A contestant is one (here not individuals but theological sects) who enters a formal challenge to a will or verdict or decision. Here, the sense is that of jurors (theologians) adjudicating between divergent faiths.

15. Powerful in its strong grammatical coherence and strong in its Biblical phrasing, this stanza presses home the ideas of stanza 14. Predestination entails that the calendar of the Christian church is always "fulfilled"; Pentecost is anticipated by the Nativity as the New Testament is by the Old. The Church or "bride of tongues" remains "*Intacta*", despite her many trials ("roads despoiled"). This unsullied "bride" has an "untimely" (eternal) perfection; she is perfect irrespective of the many imperfections which litter history, the unfolding of God's will in time. That perfection is part of an eternal plan; it will not be manifested in "our day". However, the hidden "revelation" of the moments in the Christian calendar when the spirit ignites on earth ("flint arrow- / head touched to a vapour") – when the Word is made flesh – anticipates the day when all shall be revealed. The spiritual instruction ("Believe it") sets the tone for the rest of this stanza: a prophetic Hill provides a vision for which Augustine "saved himself", an ever-vigilant ("watch and ward") "City of God" (towering above its storm-sewers), eternally prepared for the Day of Judgement.
15.1 About time Meaning 'finally!' in common parlance; also 'concerning time'. Cf. Eliot's *Four Quartets*, 'Burnt Norton' I: "Time present and time past / Are both perhaps present in time future, / And time future contained in time past. / If all time is eternally present / All time is unredeemable". Eliot's central

mystery is the incarnation of God to Man in time, and so the Christian mystery as revealed *at this time*, i.e., at Pentecost.

15.2 when all / her days are fulfilled Cf. Exodus 23:26: "the number of thy days I will fulfil". Prophetically, the New Testament as the fulfilment of the Old, and God's promise as manifest at Pentecost.

15.3 Pentecost / or at the Nativity Two points in the church calendar when eternity touches the present: the Nativity, or Incarnation, when the Word becomes flesh; and Pentecost, the 7th Sunday after Easter, commemorating the descent of the Holy Spirit on the apostles, after Christ's ascension.

15.4 flint arrow-/head In ancient weaponry, a shard of hard grey flint stone used as an arrowhead, but also with the sense of flint as striking a spark.

15.5 *Intacta* In Latin: untouched, intact, pure, as the Virgin Mary (as in the phrase '*virgo intacta*'). Here, *intacta* refers to Ecclesia, the Church itself (feminine in its Latin form), to which the many roads (sects) lead. Jean Ward discusses this stanza in terms of Hill's "apprehension of Catholic doctrine concerning the role of Mary in redemption" ('Geoffrey Hill, *Little Gidding* and the "Christian Poetics" of Michael Edwards', p. 11).

15.6 bride of tongues As the Bride of Christ, Jesus is betrothed to the Church (see John 3:29 and Matt. 9:15). Here, this metaphor entails glossolalia, the practice of speaking in tongues, a miraculous gift of the Spirit made at Pentecost. See Acts 2:4: "And they were all filled with the Holy Ghost, and began to speak with other tongues, as the Spirit gave them utterance".

15.7 saved himself Literally, 'attained salvation', but in popular usage, 'remained chaste'.

15.8 City of God The title of Augustine's mammoth defense of Christianity against its pagan critics, with its uniquely Christian view of history. Augustine regarded all history as God's providential preparation of two mystical cities, one of God and one of the devil, to one or the other of which all humankind will eventually belong. Cf. *The Triumph of Love*: "The whole-keeping of Augustine's City of God / is our witness" (CXVVI). See also stanzas 112, 115 and 117.

15.9 watch and ward In the Christian sense of one who witnesses and watches. The Boston 'Watch and Ward Society' (late 19th to middle 20th century), was responsible for raising obscenity charges against such works as Voltaire's *Candide*,

Whitman's *Leaves of Grass*, and Huxley's *Point Counter Point*; the phrase reflects militias charged with the duties of keeping *watch* at night and *guard* by day.

15.10 hidden in revelation The stanza is filled with paradoxes: the Virgin is at once intact and despoiled, the City of God both "exposed to obscurity" and "hidden in revelation".

16.
In this impressionistic stanza, Hill paints a picture of primitive creation, an elemental landscape that, for all its bleakness, is eternal: ground cover is "perennial" and its glaze "stubborn"; hawthorn persists, against the odds, amongst "rough soggy drystone". Hill's picture – "patched" in a palette of "dark ochre" and "oil of verdure" – is of the survival of life tenaciously clinging to the rocks beneath it. This is an "indigenous" landscape, in existence since Genesis ("First day of the first week"), that yet sustains humanity "beyond and below life" (a prelapsarian still life). The remembrance of the real and tangible – the natural world or "that which ís" – offers the possibility of "self's restitution"; like the Tetragrammaton, which appears in stanza 62, it is "Finally / untranscribable". The signature of the stanza is that of the paradox of Matthew: through the difficult ("hard-come-by") abandonment of the mortal self the "self's restitution" is won. This is the companion piece to stanza 15, but offers instead of the vision of the City of God that of the elemental landscape, virtually bare of prophecy and revelation save for the first line of the stanza – which somehow sets up the challenge of the final line, that of "self-restitution" in such a bleak setting.

16.1 perennial Lasting or existing for a long or apparently infinite time, like plants, such as mosses, that live for several years (as opposed to annual, or biennial).

16.2 oil of verdure The greenness of growing vegetation, but phrased in the language of painting in oils (compare "ochre" and "glaze"). Rocks in many arid, desolate surroundings are coated with a dark highly-reflective sheen, known as 'rock varnish' or 'desert varnish', a coating made up of clay particles that bind iron and manganese oxide. There is still debate as to whether this sheen is chemical (black strips of manganese oxide alternating with orange layers of clay and iron) or microbial (manganese oxide to protect microbes from harsh UV rays). Details from Barry E. Gregorio, 'Life on the Rocks', pp. 40-43.

ANNOTATIONS

16.3 drystone Walls built without mortar.
16.4 fell Chiefly Northern and Scots: a stretch of high moorland, a ridge, a cliff, or a mountain face. But cf. Hopkins, 'I wake and feel the fell of dark, not day', where the sense is both that of the Fall and an animal's pelt; here, the thin cover of vegetation clinging to the rock beneath.
16.5 hawthorns The hawthorn is a thorny shrub or tree of the rose family native to northern temperate regions, with white, pink or red blossoms and small dark red fruits.
16.6 indigenous Originating in and typical of a region or country; here, related to the landscape, the primal impulse.
16.7 inuring In discourse of law, something coming into operation or taking effect. Hill discusses Whitman's use of 'inure' in *Collected Critical Writings*, pp. 516-517.
16.8 hard-come-by loss of self / self's restitution Cf. the words of Jesus in Matthew 10:39: "He who finds his life will lose it, and he who loses his life for my sake will find it". For Jean Ward, this apparent paradox has a broader provenance: "it is by inward discipline that mortifies the self – the only form of 'violence' that *is* truly Christian – that the Christian, in Pauline terms, is delivered from 'this body of death' (Rom. 7.24) and participates in Christ's redemption of the world. The last line of poem 16 in *Speech! Speech!* presents a kind of paraphrase of this Christian paradox, maintaining that resurrection comes only by way of the Cross" (*Christian Poetry in the Post-Christian Day*, p. 192).

17. Images of philosophy and elemental landscape now give way, perhaps unexpectedly, to the more or less contemporary: an English familial wartime setting – radio on, tuned to the BBC. Hill briefly and gently parodies Hughes, Joyce, Powell and Sitwell: twentieth-century literary luminaries. The controlling image is that of a highbrow cast playing working class roles – the literary travestied as the demotic. "Trust" is repeated nine times in the stanza; iterated in this context, it is stripped of its potential to issue the instruction 'Have faith', and instead denotes – idiomatically, repeatedly – the idiosyncrasies of a variety of characters. These characters, and the stanza as a whole, are expressed in a deliberately British colloquial style: "tart", "Old Man", "have to go" and "queen it" suggest a particularly English tableau, while Joyce's "grand wake" is unmistakably Irish. Lying between the ecclesiastical charge of stanzas sixteen and eighteen, the casual domesticity and the hint of social satire constitutes a significant tonal shift, both contemporary and temporary.

17.1 WORKERS' PLAYTIME *Workers' Playtime*: comedy and music programme from the BBC (1941-1964), broadcast live each week from a factory canteen "somewhere in Britain"; conceived as a Home Front morale-booster for industrial workers during World War II (*Radio, Television and Modern Life*, p. 45).

17.2 Aunty Beeb British Broadcasting Corporation, or BBC, fondly known as 'The Beeb' or 'Aunty'.

17.3 Trust the Old Man / to pawn his dentures Presumably, to buy drink.

17.4 have a go Colloquially, to 'have to go' is to require the bathroom; here, the sense is of "Grandma" being mildly incontinent.

17.5 Ted-next-door Ted Hughes (1930-1988), author of *Crow* (1970), a bleak collection of poems based around the (talking) bird character 'Crow'.

17.6 Irish Jim James Joyce (1882-1941), author of *Finnegans Wake* (1939).

17.7 Uncle Tony Anthony Powell (1905-2000), whose twelve-volume omnibus *A Dance to the Music of Time* concerns the changing nature of the English upper-middle class from the early 1920s until the 1970s. To drink from the saucer is to reveal (here, intentionally) lower-class origins.

17.8 Mad Bess Although 'Bess' typically represents Queen Elizabeth I, 'Mad Bess' denotes Poor Tom's companion in *King Lear* and features in Henry Purcell's [Mad] Bess Ballad. Edith Sitwell (1887-1964), the English poet and critic, wrote two books about Queen Elizabeth I (with whom she shared a birthday), had similarly angular features, and regularly sported elaborate regal gowns of velvet and brocade.

17.9 Sandy / MacPherson Sandy MacPherson was a prolific radio broadcaster and organist during the dark days of World War II. The *Radio Times* of 4-10 September 1939 in a special issue declared: "Broadcasting Carries On!" (*A Concise History of British Radio, 1922-2002*, p. 71). The Regional Service and the National Programme were replaced by a single show, which for the first few weeks consisted almost entirely of news, records and Sandy MacPherson at the BBC Theatre Organ.

ANNOTATIONS

18. The rhetorical question which opens this stanza responds to the previous three: the gravitas of 15 and 16, and the worldly chatter of 17. Hill asks how, in this age ("nów") of confusion and "without distinction" (stanza 10), the Pentecostal spirit can survive, how language can be intensified to the point where words can approach 'the Word' ("grammar / to the power x"). Hill (perhaps still seated in front of the mirror) debates with himself and his audience (or editor, as in stanza 3) about how and what to write; the problem is how to bear poetic witness without being either a self-righteous pharisee or a philistine. The Christian image is the vehicle for the poetic scrutiny and Hill is or must be (regardless of the difficulty) a "Steadfast" witness to that poetic truth or mystery. The intent is to persist with language which attempts representation of the spirit touching earth, to strive to express the divine. The last third of the stanza is imagined as a more mundane dialogue with Hill's disgruntled editor, who, communicating in a kind of telegraphese, rates as worthless ("zero") his use of "RECENT PAST / AS DISTRESSED SUBTEXT" (disjointed, fragmented contemporary material artfully disarranged implicitly to question its value). Hill is "BEHOLDEN" to his editor; there are "Penalties" for lateness – inexcusable in a world of "fax" and "e-mail", and he must be more serious ("Cut out the funny speech"). Alternatively (he reflects), he might just as well discard the draft ("Commit to landfill") or "recycle" it as waste. The last lines are self-mocking: the poet as pharisee, unable to critique his own methods without self-righteousness; the voice of the editor is mingled with his own, with a self-awareness that is its own defence against (while still an admission of) pomposity.

18.1 Who nów 'Now' implies 'then': Hill contrasts our age with a past age of scholasticism, when the transcendental might have been embodied (as now it cannot be) in grammar, which is here compared with the mysteries of mathematics (the 'Word' as the 'word' raised to the power x).

18.2 Write whát | I ask Double meaning: 'write what I demand' (both imperative and interrogative), or 'write what?, I ask.' Compare the syntax of Eliot's 'Journey of the Magi': "All this was a long time ago, I remember, / And I would do it again, but set down / This"; and Isaiah 40:6: "The voice said, Cry. And he said, What shall I cry? All flesh is grass, and all the goodliness of the thereof is the flower of the field".

18.3 Steadfast / witnesses Although not precisely Biblical, "Steadfast / witnesses" (those ever-vigilant who testify on behalf of the Gospel and bear witness to God) is very much a Christian cliché.

18.4 pharisees / not philistines 'Pharisee': one who is self-righteous or hypocritical, especially with regard to rules and formalities; 'philistine': a materialist indifferent to artistic values. Here, the New Testament distinction between the self-righteous Pharisees and the infidel Philistines, the former making a public show of their devoutness, as in Luke 18:11: "The Pharisee stood and prayed thus with himself, God I thank thee, that I am not as other men are".

18.5 DISTRESSED SUBTEXT Both 'distressed' and 'subtext' refer to trends and fashions, the former being the deliberate ageing of paint or furnishings and the latter (literally an underlying theme) an overused term in the discourse of literary criticism.

18.6 Penalties [...] Or recycle waste The telegraphese of the final three lines suggests an impersonal dialogue between Hill and his editor who, in frustration, implores (with the typo "Plead" for 'please') Hill to send a new (perhaps a more serious) version of the poem.

19. The etymological link between the pomegranate and the grenade is here the central conceit, expressed through the image of Lord Morley as a still life of 'Lord with Pomegranate' with the motto "FIDUCIA", though the seriousness of this is, perhaps, somewhat compromised by the sense of 'tagging' a stately picture "with" a pomegranate. The dark, mysterious mythology of this fruit – one that can send the eater to Hades – is contrasted with the explosive violence of the grenade; the fruit is filled with seeds and life, while the grenade is filled with deadly shrapnel. The sense is of how Colonel Fajuyi's *faithfulness* (the transition is from "FIDUCIA" to "Fajuyi") was betrayed ("wrong-footed"), and the inadequacy of Hill's words ("praise-songs") to paint the portrait of that tragedy. Fajuyi's simple individual commitment to his values would be more difficult than ever to re-enact; against it, emergent cohorts "mass for mutation", deviate *en masse* from his right action. Hill is aware of the weakness of the 'word' against the 'sword', and thus expresses his sense of the futility of his "praise-songs"; given the reality of "mutation" as 'mutilation' and

"Semiotics" as "semiautomatics", such surreality is a pathetic defence. As Wainwright notes, a sad rhetoric is being uttered: "Where does the defeat of reason and ethical responsibility take us?... Does an assertion that the 'surreal' is the natural state of affairs relieve us of bothering with 'ethics and suchlike'?" (*Acceptable Words*, p. 100). Words or poetry may make amends, as a military 'tribunal' might restore justice, but "not right now".

19.1 Dürer's Albrecht Dürer (1471-1528), German painter, thinker and printmaker, now deemed to be one of the Old Masters.

19.2 LORD MORLEY Henry Parker, Lord Morley (1476-1556), translator of Italian and Latin masters into English. His version of Petrarch's *Trionfi* features a frontispiece portrait of Morley by Dürer (1523); this frontispiece was adapted for the cover of the hardcover Houghton Mifflin edition of *The Triumph of Love*. The pomegranate is from another Dürer, a portrait of Emperor Maximilian I (c 1519), holding a pomegranate (his personal emblem) in his left hand. There is a touch of parody in the phrase, as a still life with a standard title, '*x* with *y*'. See Appendix, fig.2.

19.3 POMEGRANATE Fruit ('the Food of the Dead') laden with mythological significance. For eating pomegranate seeds Persephone is confined to Hades (see stanza 61). The fruit is mentioned frequently in the Bible (see Exodus 28:33-34); in some accounts Eve eats a pomegranate. Hill refers to the "Henrician scholar-diplomat Henry Parker, Lord Morley" as translator of Tasso in 'The Eloquence of Sober Truth' (*Collected Critical Writings*, p. 345).

19.4 FIDUCIA Literally 'he inspires trust'; an emblem of Faith or Trust; here, a *motto* for the portrait.

19.5 GRENADE The pomegranate named the grenade from its shape, size, and the resemblance of its seeds to a grenade's fragments. In many languages the nouns are identical.

19.6 in re Literary instruction meaning 'with regard to'.

19.7 Colonel F. Fajuyi Lt. Colonel Francis Adekunle Fajuyi (1926-1966) assassinated by counter-coupists during the Nigerian civil war along with General Johnson Aguiyi-Ironsi, Head of State and Supreme Commander of the Armed Forces, who had appointed Fajuyi as first military governor of the Western Region and was at the time Fajuyi's house guest. Wale Adebanwi notes: "when the northern soldiers came to Government House, they only demanded to take Ironsi away.

The dominant narrative has it that Fajuyi was asked to abandon Ironsi to his fate, but he refused to do so and chose rather to die with his guest and Supreme Commander" ('Death, National Memory', p. 425). Fajuyi "should remind us of Lot defending the two angels, his guests in Sodom" (Logan, 'Author! Author!', p. 65). Hill's interest in Fajuyi reflects his association with Christopher Okigbo (see stanza 87).

19.8 praise-songs See stanza 99 for Hill's awareness, after arriving in Nigeria in 1967, of the "praise-songs" broadcast for Fajuyi, a month or two after his death.

19.9 Cancer to Capricorn The two tropics, marking latitudes 23°26' north (Cancer) and south (Capricorn) on the equator. Here, the time of year (summer) of the Nigerian conflicts.

19.10 emergent Wainwright hears the newspeak phrase 'emergent nations' (*Acceptable Words*, p. 99).

19.11 but not right now Cf. Augustine of Hippo's *Confessions* (as in Pusey's 1853 translation), "Give me chastity and continency, only not yet" (p. 98).

20. "THEY" are the snake oil merchants of the New Age, peddling their dubious wares ("Spiritual osmosis / mystique of argot"). A cant Spirituality – syllabised to ensure mocking comprehension – is saluted with the same honourable futility as dying gladiators might greet Caesar and accept their fate. Hill acknowledges this; like Luther, he cannot do otherwise, despite his distrust of the mindless acceptance ("cultic pathology") that invites instead ethical satire, so difficult in such a protean age. However, accepting his complicity, Hill resolves to say more. Reverting to the role of radio showhost, he must ask his audience to don the "earphones" so that they may listen more keenly to his secret offering: not music, but poetry, poetry that aspires to the dark mysteries, to the "condition of Hebrew"; and can utter the mildly pretentious phrase – "a wind in the mulberry trees", with its quasi-Biblical resonance – nobody will "know" enough to contradict him. That is, he assumes the role of the broadcaster, aspires to the condition of Hebrew by using fancy biblical quotations, and poses as an expert. Hill, too, may be a snake-oil merchant, peddling inauthentic wares: who would know?

20.1 Spiritual osmosis In biology and chemistry, the process by which certain molecules pass through a semi-permeable

ANNOTATIONS

membrane; here the sense of language acting as a membrane or screen between the Word and the ineffable.

20.2 argot The jargon, slang, or peculiar phraseology of a social class or group; originally the cant of rogues and thieves.

20.3 I salute you As gladiators to Caesar in the Colosseum: "Cesare morituri te salute" [Those about to die salute Caesar]. The semi-correspondence of syllables implies a deliberate echo of the phrase.

20.4 *Ich kann nicht anders* In full, "Hier stehe ich. Ich kanne nicht anders. Gott helfe mir. Amen" [Here I stand. I can do no other. God help me. Amen], traditionally the final phrases of Martin Luther's reply to Counsellor Eck's question, at the Diet of Worms (1521), "Would Luther reject his books and the errors they contain?" See also stanza 6.

20.5 shape-shifter An image of the age (or the attempt to capture it in poetry) in terms of Proteus, god of the sea, who had the power of prophecy but would avoid questions by assuming different shapes, until, in Homer's *Odyssey*, he was finally pinned down by Menelaus.

20.6 Poetry aspires / to the condition of Hebrew By tradition, Hebrew is the language of Eden, the unified language spoken before the destruction of the Tower of Babel. Cf. Walter Pater (1839-1894), in *The Renaissance* (1873): "All art constantly aspires towards the condition of music. For while in all other kinds of art it is possible to distinguish the matter from the form, and the understanding can always make this distinction, yet it is the constant effort of art to obliterate it" (p. 140).

20.7 a wind in the mulberry trees Blending Samuel 5:24: "the sound of a gong in the tops of the mulberry trees", with Isaiah 7:2: "And his heart was moved, and the heart of his people, as the trees of the wood are moved with the wind", as emblems of the mystery of God. Hill is not alluding to these biblical quotations so much as deliberately making a non-allusion: the desired effect is to *sound* biblical rather than to quote the Bible (the title of Yeats's *The Wind Among the Reeds* [1899] has a similar, though not sardonic, effect).

21. Hill's sense is that the apparently surreal is the natural order of things, so that by definition no ethical considerations can be valid (see stanza 20); and that the limits ("how far") of the surreal cannot be established artificially ("*in vitro*") by the "inflicted" self (the "self | inflicted"). Let the "CHORUS" (otherwise, the "PEOPLE") reply to that, even if they don't like it. Stoicism offers an alternative, but not for the poet, who rejects both its austere moral doctrine and its rational basis. To "Think surreal" (like Robert Desnos with his automatic writing) entails the elimination of the distinction between the central and the peripheral vision and, with reference to moral vision, the discounting of the ethical, of what others might think. Thus casual clichés, such as "See if Í care" (eye-care), "sight unseen" and "Body / language my eye", invoke the irrational image of the mantis shrimp and its extraordinary vision, this in turn introducing its role as predator ("EYE TO EYE") and its reputation for ferocity. This final image of the shrimp *is* surreal, with irrational, peripheral associations conjuring up disjunctive effects, but it affirms the *truth* of the opening gambit: "SURREAL is natural" ... "IT IS TRUE".

21.1 SURREAL A 20th century avant-garde movement in art and literature that sought to release the potential of the unconscious mind, as by the irrational juxtaposition of images. The etymology of the word is 'sur' *real*, i.e., on top of or beyond the real, or natural.

21.2 perpetuity A restriction marking an estate inalienable perpetually or for a period beyond certain limits fixed by law; a bond or other security with no fixed maturity date.

21.3 *in vitro* Referring to processes taking place in an artificial environment such as a test tube rather than inside a living organism. It is now used most frequently in 'in vitro fertilization', the artificial conception of babies outside the womb.

21.4 how far is HOW FAR Cf. the publisher's note appearing on the first hardcover edition of *Speech! Speech!*: "With a poem for each of the 120 days of Sodom, it may go too far – but then, as T.S. Eliot said, it is only by going too far that you find out how far you can go."

21.5 self | inflicted The verticule allows two readings: a) 'the 'self, inflicted' (the wounded self); and b) 'self-inflicted' (wounded by the self).

21.6 CHORUS Cf. the "acclaimed chorus" of stanza 13.

21.7 Stoics Members of the ancient Greek school of philosophy founded by Zeno (fl. 300 BC) and characterized by austere ethical doctrines; hence, those who practise repression of emotion, indifference to pleasure and pain, and patient endurance in adversity.

ANNOTATIONS

21.8 vis-à-vis French, literally 'face to face'. Here, the loss of peripheral vision implies the discounting of the ethical and/or the values of others (the "peripheral"). See 21.11.

21.9 Desnos Robert Desnos (1900-1945), French surrealist poet and proponent of automatic writing, by which rational links between the critical and the peripheral are purportedly erased. Hill's 'Domaine Public', the second of 'Four Poems Regarding the Endurance of Poets' in *King Log*, is written in memory of Desnos.

21.10 my eye A clichéd exclamation of disbelief which here leads into the remarkable "Body / language" of the shrimp. The term 'body language' was popularized during the 1970s via the work of Julius Fast (*Body Language*, 1971) and Desmond Morris (*Manwatching*, 1977).

21.11 Regarding the shrimp / as predator The eyes of the mantis shrimp sit atop mobile stalks which move independently of each other, giving the shrimp very advanced – almost 360° – vision (cf. "peripheral / vision" in lines 7-8). This exceptional power has contributed to the reputation of the mantis shrimp as a fearsome opponent: the truism is that – size for size – it is the most voracious predator of the ocean.

21.12 EYE TO EYE A phrase usually expressed in the negative, to describe two individuals who do *not* agree ('see eye to eye'). Cf. "vis-à-vis" in line 8.

22. At this point, the poem introduces for the first time the figure of Diana, Princess of Wales, who had at the time of publication only recently been killed in a car crash in Paris, her death marked by an astonishing outpouring of mass emotion. The controlling image of this stanza is that in this age of mass communication Hill may use Diana ("go global") for his own ends – he could, like Herod, be violent and moody, forget nothing, reprieve no one, excusing only the titled aristocracy (her children). Thus, he could dismiss as immoderate the outraged (if excessive) grief of the public ("the PEOPLE"), conjured by the media. Instead, in a change of focus, Hill is now Prospero calling the spirit of Diana (his Ariel) on "this island", which is both England and the lake island at Althorp on which she is buried. Even as her memory settles into obscurity, her spirit is sensed as restless. Hill presents the image of Diana, once Princess of Wales, her youth at engagement reflecting the "age of mass consent". That Diana was 'crucified' by a relentless and brutal media is a commonly held belief of "the PEOPLE", and Hill here details it in a series of relentless imperatives: the often vicious actions of the press before her death becomes Herod's slaughter of the innocents, while the questions and rumours surrounding the circumstances of her death – at the time of Hill's writing, not yet resolved by a formal inquiry – are suggested by her "nowhere / coming to rest". Diana is here an embodiment of spirituality: the people's princess, while the clinical approach of the Windsors and the vicious heart of the fourth estate 'gone global' are emblematic of a modern loss of faith.

22.1 age of mass consent The age of consent (cf. "compliance" in line 8) is the age at which a person is considered to be legally competent to consent to sexual acts, which here suggests Diana's youth at her engagement (she was 19). However, given the media focus, the phrase here suggests 'mass communication' – the approval of Diana by the international masses having become a global phenomenon, a "mass consent".

22.2 go global with her The reference is to Diana, Princess of Wales (1961-1997), former wife of Charles, Prince of Wales (1948-), heir to the British throne. The daughter of the 8th Earl Spencer, Lady Diana Frances Spencer was a kindergarten teacher in London before her 1981 marriage to Charles. They had two sons, the princes William (b.1982) and Henry (b.1984), but separated in 1992 and were divorced in 1996. Diana and Charles were rivals for acceptance by the British public after their marriage unravelled spectacularly; her death in a Paris car crash in August 1997 brought a huge outpouring of sentiment.

22.3 day-star The day-star is a (chiefly poetic) expression of the morning star, a bright planet (usually Venus, or Lucifer) visible in the east before sunrise. Hill is also invoking the dog-star, the binary star in the constellation Canis Major that appears as the brightest star in the sky, to suggest a sense of moodiness, irritability, of the doldrums ('dog-days') as experienced by Herod.

22.4 moody as Herod Herod's slaughter of the innocents. Matthew 2:16: "Then Herod, when he saw that he was mocked of the wise men, was exceeding wroth, and sent forth, and slew all the children that were in Bethlehem, and in all the coasts thereof, from two years old and under, according to the time which he has diligently acquired of the wise men".

22.5 *jus natalium* In Cambridge, the privilege whereby sons of noblemen were excused from taking examinations, abolished

ANNOTATIONS

only in 1884; here, exempting Diana's young children from the slaughter of the innocents, or the ferocity of the media.
22.6 PEOPLE Here 'the masses', rather than the magazine.
22.7 Inscrutable Í call Both a) I, inscrutable, call [up] her spirit; and b) I call [describe as] her spirit inscrutable.
22.8 on this island Both a) England, and b) the island on the lake at Althorp, the Spencer family estate, on which Diana is buried. Hill also implies Prospero's island in *The Tempest*, with its Ariel, the spirit nowhere coming to rest.

23. This stanza turns back to the radio, with particular reference to its role in the Low Countries in the time of war. The signal from beyond, the mystery of the voice that must be attuned, is introduced using the indefinite, indeterminate "It". The Dutch (like the Brits and the Poles later in the poem) are heroes, "living as they have to" (anticipating the "Stoicism" that might serve to counter the "vacancy" of the troubled or, in his case, empty age). Hill avoids Radio Luxembourg, the first pirate radio station, though he recalls "the atmospherics" (the static and poor reception, but also the controversy) of the 1960s, when pirate radio stations were an issue. Despite the poor reception, Hill is called to speak, asked to "Step forward" in the radio studio, where a red light indicates that he is 'on air'. But what is he to say (how is he to affirm his being)? He would welcome suggestions, preferably antagonistic ones, but everything (on this talk show) sounds "THE CRY OF THE AFFLICTED", that is, precludes other matters, just as the case of "Gallant Little Belgium" (a voice still heard) invokes only the Great War even though the pathos of that case is no reason not to discuss others. The spiel returns, first with the language of officialdom ("delete other options"), though, ironically, he is the one who needs to be 'talked' through the crisis.
23.1 Hilversum A province in the north central Netherlands, the centre of Dutch radio and television broadcasting, of especial significance during World War II.
23.2 The Dutch [...] as they have to The phrase 'The *x* (Poles, Brits, or Dutch) are heroes living as they have to' is a motif used repeatedly; cf. stanzas 38, 40, 84, 94 and 103. The stanza reflects a 'Benelux' structure, an association of Belgium, the Netherlands and Luxembourg. As Jeffrey Wainwright notes, the "phrase 'living as they have to' is a running joke in *Speech! Speech!* But it has deep implications because it invites

judgement between the contingent and the freely chosen" (*Acceptable Words*, p. 105).

23.3 Give Luxembourg a miss A pioneer of pirate radio, Radio Luxembourg, one of the earliest commercial radio stations, began broadcasting in 1933 to an international audience including Britain. The BBC (which held a monopoly on UK airwaves until 1973) vehemently opposed the station and made repeated attempts to cease its operations (*Television and Radio in the United Kingdom*, pp. 20-22). To 'give x a miss' is a British colloquialism meaning to avoid or not do something.

23.4 atmospherics a) Electrical disturbances that interfere with telecommunications; and b) effects to create mood in music.

23.5 Stoicism Stoicism fills its own "vacancy" by its self-affirmation of authentic choice in an otherwise meaningless universe. See 'Stoics' in stanza 21.

23.6 Speak at the red light During a radio broadcast, a red light indicates to the presenter that the microphone has been switched on (a green light gives ten seconds warning of this).

23.7 What else proclaims us? Compare Eliot, *The Waste Land*, line 405: "By this, and this only, we have existed".

23.8 THE CRY OF THE AFFLICTED Job 24:28: "So that they cause the cry of the poor to come unto him, and he heareth the cry of the afflicted".

23.9 delete other options As on bureaucratic forms, e.g., 'Please tick the boxes as appropriate or delete other options'; here phrased as a question: 'Is thát any reason (to do so)?'

23.10 Gallant Little Belgium Germany's violation of the neutrality of Belgium stirred British public sympathy at the outset of WWI and WWII; the courageous but futile resistance led to the popular sentiment: 'gallant [or brave] little Belgium'. The metaphor is that of a resistance cell, communicating (faintly) by clandestine radio.

24. With the radio of stanza 23 now fading out, this stanza reveals a reluctant paradox: diminishment is the lead-up to death, but it is also a necessary part of being (whether "animal" or something more). The ageing mind can be easily distracted, and so must eliminate, or give up, even the most beautiful, the most arresting (the "dark / roses" in their "rain-bleached tubs"), to allow the "threatened attention", to "LEAD" itself "BACK" into the "right way", to fundamental questions of what really matters. This is "mortal self-recognition": the positive realisation that the inevitability of death and the diminishment which constitutes old age equally 'leads back' to essential questions ("hard, reductive"), and finally to that primal scene in the Garden of Eden. But it takes patience to accept the reduction to nothingness. With a voice like that of Eliot's Gerontion, Hill reflects that we must be "animal / to some purpose"; the search is to comprehend our diminishment, among other things, of the soul (*anima*) to the level of brutes, and the purpose of such 'reduction'. The Serpent in the Garden of Eden (perhaps overheard by God, as part of His plan) ordered Eve to eat the fruit that cursed mankind with death, but Eve, as here presented, ate all too willingly: the stress on "and dı́d she?" implying the demotic emphatic affirmation, 'and did she ever'.

24.1 dark / roses in rain-bleached tubs These roses may intimate the rose-garden in Eliot's 'Burnt Norton' II or Gerontion's contemplation of disintegration as a part of the human process of dying (see line 11), but they are also a powerful image in and of themselves, like William Carlos Williams' red wheelbarrow, with a sense of immediacy and 'thereness'.

24.2 let me confess Both a) I must admit; and b) let me undergo confession (as a condition of salvation). Compare "taken / further" and "how far is HOW FAR" in stanza 21.

24.3 REDUCE means LEAD BACK From O.Fr. *reducer*, from L. *reducere*, from *re-* "back" + *ducere* 'bring, lead'. The etymological sense is preserved in the military 'reduce to ranks'. *Reduction* is attested from 1483; *reductionism* in philosophy is recorded from 1948. Hill writes specifically about the word in 'Common Weal, Common Woe' (a review of the second edition of *The Oxford English Dictionary*): "The entry for the word *reduce* (in the July 1904 fascicule, edited by W. A. Craigie and his assistants) is an exemplary 'reducing' (as in: 'reduce. 14*a-c*') of its own 'series of significations' running to just under seven columns of print" (*Collected Critical Writings*, pp. 273-4); and in 'Unhappy Circumstances' (an essay from *The Enemy's Country*): "'reducing' it, that is, 'bringing it into proper order', 'making it conformable or agreeable to a standard'" (*Collected Critical Writings*, p. 187). Here, the sense is of the "Diminishment", of old age 'leading back' to fundamental questions ("mortal self-recognition"). Cf. *Scenes from Comus*: "To reduce is to lead back, / to rectify" (1.15). See also "reductive" (line 9).

24.4 Patience / is hard 'Hard' here means both 'difficult' and 'dealing with precise and verifiable facts' (as in 'hard science'). There may be an echo of Pound's "beauty is difficult", a motif that runs through *The Cantos*. Cf. Gerard Manley Hopkins's 'Patience, Hard Thing': "Patience, hard thing! the hard thing but to pray, / But bid for, Patience is!".
24.5 we múst be animal As in both a) brute; and b) the Latin *anima*, the soul, the paradox of *animated* brutality.
24.6 to some purpose Cf. Eliot's *Gerontion*: "Think at last / I have not made this show purposelessly."
24.7 UN- / HINGE YOUR JAW, DO IT LIKE A PYTHON A distinctive feature of *Homo sapiens* (one that makes language possible) is the flexible jaw. But snakes can also unhinge their jaws, to consume things bigger than their girth.
24.8 and díd she? She: Eve, in the Garden of Eden, tempted by the serpent. Hill's choice of "python" may also intimate the oracular mysteries of Delphos, and the question of 'What comes next?'.

25. After an ambiguous opening phrase (Hill has faith and hears; Hill recalls that he has heard), the stanza uses the relationship between the deaf and their music to assert that, although "Luck / is against the many", being blessed with exceptional talents ("to be gifted") "cannot be bad". The astounding (because stone deaf) percussionist is Dame Evelyn Glennie, here described in the language of her art (a "striking" and "instrumental" beauty). Glennie's practice of playing barefoot in order to 'feel' the music reminds Hill that his friend David Wright (to whom *Speech! Speech!* is dedicated, and who had died of cancer six years earlier), could "draw music up through heel of hand"; he could transmit the music to his soul via the physicality of his body, an extraordinary and rare ability. Glennie's and Wright's mode of 'listening' – active, visible, "material", unifying – is, in a sense, more active and involved than the usual empathy (passive hearing with the ears). Regardless, both sympathy and empathy – all modes of hearing music, and music itself – are unwritable and untranscribable ("*unbeschreiblich*"); but the gift of beauty (both physical and musical, and by implication poetical) "cannot be bad".
25.1 the astounding / percussionist is deaf Dame Evelyn Glennie (1965-), Scottish virtuoso percussionist, profoundly

deaf, who writes in her 'Hearing Essay' that "Deafness is poorly understood in general" and that "Hearing is basically a specialized form of touch" as it requires 'feeling' the movement of vibrating air (evelyn.co.uk/live/hearing_essay.htm). Glennie achieves this, in part, by playing barefoot, stating in an interview transcribed on the Public Broadcasting Service website: "When a particular sound is made, you can truly, truly feel that in certain parts of your body, and you just have to be so unbelievably sensitive to begin to translate certain sounds" ('Beat of a Different Drummer').

25.2 not Saul's David Saul, the first king of Israel, who, jealous and suspicious of David's popularity, was charmed and soothed by his playing of the lyre. David was a poet-king and writer of the Psalms; one of his most beautiful poems is a tribute to Saul and his son Jonathan after their deaths in battle.

25.3 David of Deafness David Wright, author of the prose autobiography *Deafness* (1969) and to whose memory *Speech! Speech!* is dedicated. Hill's connection with Glennie and Wright, and his interest in a soundless experience of the world, is strengthened by his own experience: due to a severe case of mastoiditis, he has been deaf in his right ear from the age of eleven. See also *The Triumph of Love*, in which Hill plays on his own condition: "For definitely the right era, read: deaf in the right ear" (XV).

25.4 harp Recalls both "harp of nerves" (stanza 3) and "Harps / in Beulah" (stanza 7), although there may be some private association as well.

25.5 material Meaning a) concerning physical objects rather than the mind or spirit; b) important, essential, relevant; c) law (of fact) significant, influential, relevant, especially to the extent of determining a cause or affecting a judgement.

25.6 *unbeschreiblich* German, meaning 'indescribable' (literally, 'unwritable').

25.7 instrumental beauty Another play on the lexicon of grammar: an "instrumental beauty", recalling the instruction in stanza 14 to "make mourning instrumental". Hill uses the same terms to describe the impact of the deaf poet David Wright (see line 4): "It is a creative paradox that we owe to a deaf man some of the most striking images of sound in contemporary English poetry" (as stated in Wright's obituary in the *New York Times*, 5 September 1994).

26. The central sentiment of this stanza is the fleeting sense of eternity ("a thousand years" but also "No time") and – by implication – the challenge to what Hill wants to do, in this, the age of the 'quick fix', when "peerless" computers call up dystopia on the Internet, and sordid "folk / festivals" reflect the profile of the times. Great gifts (art and talent) are "unprized", not valued; tabloid papers, feigning boldness, offer cowardly 'shocking' headlines; the PEOPLE favour disgusting large-spun plastic wigs to draw attention ("*cat-calls, cheers*") to themselves. The text, like the safety cap of a medicine to be applied "FOR FAST RELIEF", cannot always be manipulated to effect: Hill tries, but cannot open the bottle, cannot apply the quick fix. As the second millennium ticks over (a thousand years, "No time at all"), Hill recalls that, in sharp contrast to the present, the seers and thinkers of the past wrote of "LOVE". As a poet, he should "perform", but rather than write of "LOVE" he is required to address subjects of less solemnity. Here performance, our answer to doubt, is both "these orations" and sexual performance requiring prophylactics (obtainable on the Web), the mention of which is still hypocritically taboo ("*cries of 'shame'*"), with the cheap, stand-up comedy innuendo of "Stick to" and "much-used", as well as the more obvious "CHECKMATE".

26.1 No time [...] a thousand years Cf. 2 Peter 3:8: "But, beloved, be not ignorant of this one thing, that one day is with the Lord as a thousand years, and a thousand years as one day".

26.2 peerless Unlike a client-server network, a peer-to-peer network has no central server, but computers connected to the network can share files, printers and other resources. There is a suggestion of the millennium bug (also known as Y2K), the mass computer malfunction expected to occur (but not eventuating) as clocks ticked over to the year 2000, to usher in a further "thousand years".

26.3 APPLY FOR FAST RELIEF As in the discourse of medicinal instructions.

26.4 Dystopia A dysfunctional community seeking "FAST RELIEF" on the internet, which offers quack medications, condoms and grotesque images of a sick society.

26.5 gifts unprized Cf. Paul in Romans 6:23: "For the wages of sin is death; but the gift of God is eternal life through Jesus Christ our Lord." Paul uses the word 'prize' in much this sense in 1 Corinthians 9:24 and Philippians 3:14.

ANNOTATIONS

26.6 Starved [...] mystics write of LOVE As did Julian of Norwich (d. after 1416), English religious writer, an anchoress, or hermit, of Norwich called Mother (or Dame) Juliana or Julian. Her work, *Revelations of Divine Love* (c.1393), is an expression of mystical fervour in the form of visions of Jesus. Eliot quotes Julian throughout 'Little Gidding'. *The Fire of Love* by Richard Rolle (1290-1349), is another, in which the English hermit describes his various mystical experiences.

26.7 CHECKMATE In chess, placing an opponent's king into inextricable check, by which the game is won. Here, an actual brand of condom, Ansell's 'Checkmate', somewhat ambiguously described as "much-used".

27. The theatre of war is here the theatrical district of London, as Whitechapel is "swept away" and shaken apart by the V1/V2 'flying bombs' of the German attack during World War II. Yiddish theatre was a casualty of the Blitz, and with its demise "Something of London" was lost, even if not regretted by all ("not / music to all ears"). Rosenberg, son of a Jewish Russian immigrant to the city, for instance, had ignored the theatre in his day, a generation earlier. Then, the farce of the stage gave way to the farce of life in the trenches, a tragedy so great and brutal as to be unbelievable, absurd. That farce was 'redeemed' by Rosenberg through the realist brutality of his early poetry and through the shift away from anger to a sardonic humour in his later poetry (in which rats and lice are not the "sole victors" of conflict). Cruelly, he was killed; he did not survive, but his work did. This redemption constitutes an atonement for Rosenberg as he remade and remastered his history and his poetry, and his history into his poetry; but also for Hill, as he looks back on both World Wars I and II. Though he avoided his Jewish (Hebrew) roots and did not survive the war, Rosenberg in his last poems atones both for the war and the culture he rejected. But acts of positive atonement coming out of a gruesome death: is Hill serious? Well, he's not "joking exactly"; he is unwilling to say 'yes', though that is his serious, and honest answer.

27.1 Whitechapel Yiddish theatre in London was created by and for the Jewish immigrants from Eastern Europe who settled in the East End in the late nineteenth-century. During the Victorian era, Whitechapel was a centre of Jewish and Irish immigrants. The area suffered great damage in V2 German rocket attacks and the Blitz of WWII, especially on 7 September 1944, when much of East London was destroyed. A passage in Hill's essay 'Isaac Rosenberg, 1890-1918' is significant here: "Whitechapel High Street and Whitechapel Road, together with the adjacent Library and Art Gallery, were the meeting places for Isaac and a circle of friends and acquaintances, a group at once closely- and loosely-knit, which included David Bomberg ... a magnificently unmute throng" (Collected Critical Writings, p. 453).

27.2 Rosenberg Isaac Rosenberg (1890-1918) was born into a working-class Jewish family that had emigrated from Russia and eventually settled in the East End of London. Although his working-class origins and economic circumstances prevented his attending Oxford or Cambridge, he was a talented artist and enrolled in evening classes in the Art School of Birkbeck College, London University. He hoped to make his living as a portrait artist and had moved to South Africa to pursue his career when the war broke out. He returned to England in 1915, enlisted in 1916, and was killed on 3 April 1918. Before going to the front Rosenberg published a small volume of poems, *Youth*; T.S. Eliot and Ezra Pound knew and admired his poetry. One of Hill's first published poems was 'For Isaac Rosenberg', in which he admires Rosenberg's realist verse as opposed to that of the commemorialist war poets.

27.3 LOUSE / HUNTING Rosenberg's 'Louse Hunting' (1917) begins: "Nudes – stark and glistening, / Yelling in lurid glee. Grinning faces / And raging limbs / Whirl over the floor one fire. / For a shirt venomously busy / Yon soldier tore from his throat, with oaths / Godhead might shrink at, but not the lice. / And soon the shirt was aflare / Over the candle he'd lit while we lay."

27.4 THROUGH THESE PALE COLD DAYS Rosenberg's 'Through These Pale Cold Days': "Through these pale cold days / What dark faces burn / Out of three thousand years, / And their wild eyes yearn, // While underneath their brows / Like waifs their spirits grope / For the pools of Hebron again – / For Lebanon's summer slope. // They leave these blond still days / in dust behind their tread / They see with living eyes / How long they have been dead."

27.5 atonement Yom Kippur, the Jewish day of atonement and the most important and sacred Jewish holy day, falls in September or October. It is a day of fasting, worship and repentance (see also stanza 7).

ANNOTATIONS

28. In stanza 26 "a thousand years" may have been "No time at all", but here, in Rosenberg's trenches, thirty days counts as long term survival. The trivialities of trench life ("Hoarding", "looting", each the consequence of the other) may seem insignificant in comparison to the horrors of death and the brevity of life, but are a microcosmic description of all life: some steal, some hoard, all lose in the end. Hill – like Rosenberg – must attest to these trivialities, "Haruspicate / over the unmentionable" (specifically, the obvious manifestations of diarrhoea). Hill's position when speaking of these soldiers (*almost* his contemporaries) is difficult; born between the wars he knows of the trenches and their occupants only "IN IGNORANCE". He invokes "mental / hygiene" to free himself of such horrible images, but (lest he forget), pays tribute in capitals to those whom he has known (in ignorance) called up ("CHARMED"), however vain ("BARREN") their sacrifice (or his words) might be. Narrow focus and attention to detail ("Scrupulosity") can draw attention away from what is most significant, and yet the horrors must be discussed; the past must be resurrected in order to lay it to rest. Unlike Rosenberg's louse hunters, Hill enjoys a perspective that only time allows. Distance permits a better view of how what was once called the "irresistible / beauty" of the advance reveals (in hindsight) the desolate spectacle of the dead and dying.

28.1 thirty days Compare "files pillaged and erased / in one generation" (stanza 1) and "No time at all really | a thousand years" (stanza 26).

28.2 Haruspicate From the Latin 'haruspex', one who inspected the entrails of sacrificial victims to foretell the future. Compare Eliot, 'The Dry Salvages' III: "To communicate with Mars, converse with spirits, / To report the behaviour of the sea monster, / Describe the horoscope, haruspicate or scry, / Observe disease in signatures, evoke / Biography from the wrinkles of the palm / And tragedy from fingers". See also stanza 29.

28.3 mental | hygiene The social or mental hygiene movement of the late nineteenth and early twentieth centuries was an attempt to control venereal disease, regulate prostitution and vice, and disseminate sexual education through the use of scientific research methods and modern media techniques. In 1908, the mental hygiene movement took root as a public reaction to Clifford Beers's autobiography, *A Mind That Found*

Itself, which described his experiences in institutions for the insane; Beers adopted the term 'mental hygiene' (suggested by Adolf Meyer) to describe his ideas.
28.4 CHARMED BARREN 'Charmed' here suggests Pound's sardonic use of 'charm' in 'Hugh Selwyn Mauberley' V (in which the waste of WWI is laid bare): "Charm, smiling at the good mouth / Quick eyes gone under earth's lid".
28.5 Scrupulosity See stanza 11.
28.6 gifted with hindsight Cf. the ironic phrase, 'the gift of hindsight', used to refer to the underwhelming feat of being knowledgeable about something only after it has happened.
28.7 irresistible / beauty The irresistible (yet appalling) spectacle is reminiscent of the refrain in Yeats's 'Easter 1916': "A terrible beauty is born".
28.8 advance Ironically, a) of civilization; and b) on the front.

29. The setting is primitive, primal, but even after the sacrifice (the sanctuary "hung with entrails"; "Blood / on the sackcloth" suggesting a return to the previous stanza and the trenches of World War I) we have not learned our lesson, we are not "word-perfect". Ironically, Hill scrutinizes "HARUSPICATE", a word which sounds like clearing one's throat, and can come up with nothing better than a series of facetious rhetorical questions ("is the Pope to be trusted?") that lead to an answer of despair: "No-hope to redeem / all covenants". Through (primal) visions one can determine that all is unaltered ("NOTHING has changed") or that the nature of nothing itself has altered (the nothingness has changed). The sense is that of time passing from the age of sanctuaries and sackcloths to the present with no change, but with a change in what no change means. Hill is clearing his throat: yet again he is called to speech, however fraught and futile an activity that might prove to be. The language of sacramental ritual is preferred, as the stanza ends prophetically with apocalyptic, mystical phrases: "the moon burns, fire / quenches water". The image is that of the poet, as a would-be acolyte before the bloody shrine, unable fully to participate in the ritual; he does not know his lines, there are too many facetious (yet BIG) questions to be answered, and so, despite all the intimations of the apocalypse, nothing has finally changed.
29.1 sanctuary The inmost recess or holiest part of a temple, or the part of the chancel of a church containing the high altar.

ANNOTATIONS

29.2 sackcloth A coarse fabric used to make sacks or wrap bales; formerly worn as a sign of penitence or mourning; a penitential garment made of this.
29.3 we are not / word-perfect That is, we lack both the words, and the Word. There is perhaps an echo of Jeremiah 8:20: "The harvest is past, the summer is ended, and we are not saved".
29.4 HARUSPICATE To divine by entrails (see stanza 28).
29.5 is the Pope to be trusted? A variation of the more usual statement of the obvious: 'Is the Pope a Catholic?'
29.6 divide / night from day Genesis 1, God's first act, beyond the power of even an infallible Pope.
29.7 sphere of desire Pope Alexander VI in 1493 sanctioned the Spanish and Portuguese empires by dividing the non-Christian world into two spheres of influence assigned to either Spain (the West) or Portugal (the East).
29.8 one-octave / chant of candles An eight-branched candelabrum, lit – one candle at a time – during the eight days of Hanukkah, using a special candle called a 'Shamash'.
29.9 No-hope Cf. "WANHOPE" in stanza 37.
29.10 redeem / all covenants As in God's promise to Noah that He would never send another flood to destroy the earth. He made a rainbow as the sign or covenant of that promise.
29.11 the sun roárs Cf. Dylan Thomas's 'Vision and Prayer': "Now I am lost in the blinding One. The sun roars at the prayer's end".
29.12 water Revelation 6:12: "And I beheld when he had opened the sixth seal, and, lo, there was a great earthquake; and the sun became black as sackcloth of hair, and the moon became as blood". Here, the sense is of the world enduring a permanent ("Now as ever") apocalypse, with ongoing sacrifices that change nothing.

30. What do poets do? Does the writing of poetry qualify as work? For Hill, it is a "Symbolic labour" akin to alchemy: its product is either priceless or worthless. The poet, like Rumplestiltskin, makes something out of nothing. The true difficulty, then, is not in the production itself, as there is copious low-quality material available, but in the battle against "procrastination", delivered with a jibe at the writer's 'sentence' to "hard labour" and the hope of some miraculous intervention that will turn clichéd words into gold. The great shame, according to Hill, is that this battle is often won by lacklustre poets of questionable merit, merchants of a smug contemporary dialect. The language of the people has, through time, been the poet's choice; now, a "coarse" hybrid Australian phrasing is "triumphalist", just as Dante's use of the vernacular Tuscan (instead of a bookish Latin) was in its day itself an affront; there is an irony, too: Dante's vernacular became the vehicle of real poetry, not just demotic rubbish. This kind of "Culture-shock" is easily generated, simply by using (as Dante did) the language of the people – using little effort ("NO SWEAT") to say "NO SWEAT". And yet not all poets are created equal, and for most the use of the vernacular is merely a mechanism by which they can "make real" their fantasy of being current, pertinent, feted (the phrasing is deliberately clichéd). These poets achieve renown and "Courtesy / titles"; their protest ("Rage") becomes a popular aesthetic. But they stand (or think that they stand) somehow beyond reproach, as the "Culture shock" that their product elicits is regularly mistaken for mystery: they (we) remain (or fancy that we remain) untouchable.

30.1 Symbolic labour According to Sean Sayers, Hardt and Negri identify two main forms of immaterial labour: "'symbolic' or intellectual labour and 'affective' labour, dealing with feelings or attitudes." Neither has material products nor is designed to meet material needs. Symbolic labour is primarily intellectual or artistic. "It includes computer programming, graphic design, various sorts of media work, work in advertising and public relations" ('The Concept of Labour', p. 444-445).

30.2 spinning straw to gold In the Brothers Grimm fairy tale, the gnome Rumpelstiltskin appears to a girl enslaved by the King, who has been given the impossible task of spinning straw to gold. This task is completed by the manikin on condition that her first-born child be given to him as payment. The King marries the girl, and after the birth of the child Rumpelstiltskin appears to claim his payment, but offers her a riddle – 'Guess my name' – unaware that he has been overheard singing his own name. His plan thwarted, Rumpelstiltskin stamps his foot deep into the earth and tears himself apart in rage.

30.3 hard labour Labour as an additional form of punishment beyond imprisonment alone.

30.4 Courtesy / titles A form of address in the British peerage used for wives, children, former wives, and other close relatives of a peer. These may mislead those unacquainted with the system into thinking that they are substantive titles.

ANNOTATIONS

30.5 licence plates That is, *personalized* licence plates, re-sold by auction. See also stanza 9.

30.6 NO SWEAT No sweat: Australian slang for very easily, without worry. After the Fall, Adam and his descendants were condemned to hard toil (see "Symbolic labour" in line 1); see Genesis 3:19: "In the sweat of thy face shalt thou eat bread, till thou return unto the ground; for out of it wast thou taken: for dust thou art, and unto dust shalt thou return."

30.7 the tongues Ironically, as in 'the gift of tongues', the power of speaking in unknown languages, regarded as one of the gifts of the Holy Spirit (Acts 2). See stanza 15.

30.8 Australian-Tuscan A reputedly uncouth vernacular (Australian) likened to that of Dante's age (Tuscan) with an ironic appreciation of the way that this uncouth Italian dialect became the vehicle of some of the world's greatest poetry. There may be a suggestion of the Australian feminist writer Germaine Greer, who was arrested for using obscenities during a 1972 tour of New Zealand.

30.9 Culture shock The disorientation experienced by someone who is suddenly subjected to an unfamiliar culture, way of life, or set of attitudes; here, the disjunction (in language) between the entitled and the demotic. The phrase originates from Alvin Toffler's *Future Shock* (1970), which addresses the disorientation of those living in a highly technologized society.

30.10 nothing to it Both a) very easy, and b) of no substance.

30.12 they can't touch us That is to say, they cannot make a legal case against us.

31. The alchemic transformation of the poet's work is now replaced with the enactment of "This WORD", a deliberate scatological 'play' upon the reverse process – not spinning straw to gold, as in the previous stanza, but the WORD as "CHIE" or *merde*, output that is excremental. The metaphor is that of a game of charades; a word-association game in which he promises to outbet ("overreach") even Daumier in terms of social satire – the list of contemporaneous detritus which closes the stanza is a testament to this. In this game of charades the poet is lost for an answer ("I pass"), but cannot resist a litany of anal puns: "strenuously", "let drop", "pass", "end", "SENNA", "AUGEAN" stables. The stanza is itself a game of word associations: from the "WORD" to "CHARADE", to "CHIE", to "*Merde*"; then, "let drop" to the roulette wheel ("stake"), from "overreach" to "viziers", thence "Soccer versus Islam". Hill then issues the directive to "Ríp through thís lot"; "thís lot" being topics for a game of charades, examples of verbal diarrhoea (*merde*, again) apposite for the stanza. Amidst this muck ("SENNA", "AEGEAN") Simone Weil – that most patient philosopher – is instructed (as in a basketball game, or as a naughty child) to "TAKE / TIME OUT", hardly an instruction she needed to hear, but a requirement (for sanity) given the babel of confusion in the preceding lines.

31.1 WORD Here the "WORD" stands for the Logos, the poet's word, and the answer in a game of charades. Cf. 'To the Lord Protector Cromwell' in *A Treatise of Civil Power*: "If the WORD be not with us, what is our / present legal position?" (Penguin edition, p. 16).

31.2 CHIE [...] *Merde* "CHIE" is a French vulgar intensifier with the same root as the English 'shit'; "*Merde*" (French slang, also meaning 'shit') here expresses dismay for not having the right words.

31.3 Daumier / was his latest Muse Honoré Daumier (1808-1879), French caricaturist, painter, sculptor and social satirist. The covers of all editions of *Speech! Speech!* feature his 1864 work, 'On dit que les Parisiens sont difficiles à satisfaire' [It is said that Parisians are hard to please]; a cartoon lithograph which – with bitter irony – ridicules the bourgeois society of his day (see Appendix fig.3). See also stanza 100.

31.4 viziers A high-ranking government officer, especially in the Ottoman Empire. Here, "overreach" suggests Marlowe's *Tamburlaine* (the 'Overreacher'), the Persian setting of which suggests vizier, then Iran (see note 7), with a hint of a gambling official, or croupier.

31.5 Soccer versus Islam A possible reference to Iran's 2-1 victory over the USA in the 1998 soccer World Cup.

31.6 END OF THE WORLD CUP A conflation of the apocalyptic 'end of the world' and the soccer World Cup held every four years. Brazil's 1970 third World Cup victory entitled them to keep the Jules Rimet trophy permanently; 1970, therefore, marked the 'end' of that World Cup.

31.7 SENNA A laxative prepared from dried pods of the cassia tree; and a form of Eddic poetry in which participants exchange insults. Also Ayrton Senna (1960-1994), Brazilian Formula 1 driver and three-time world champion killed in an horrific accident at the San Marino Grand Prix (cf. "BELT UP" in line 11). Cf. the demotic 'Go easy with the sauce'.

ANNOTATIONS

31.8 PECCAVI RESCINDED 'Peccavi' was the one-word (Latin, 'I have sinned') telegram reportedly sent to London by British General Charles Napier from Sind, the Indian province he had captured despite orders not to do so. His message, already a perfect pun, is augmented by 're-sinned'.

31.9 THE AMUSEMENT / PARK TWISTER AND OTHER STORIES Cf. John Barth's *Lost in the Funhouse and Other Stories* (1968).

31.10 MORE FAUNA OF THE AUGEAN One of the Herculean tasks was to clean the stables of King Augeas, a task that took thirty years. Here, as a topical coffee-table bestseller, a scatological variation of an imagined volume, *Flora of the Aegean*.

31.11 BELT UP Both a) 'be quiet'; and b) 'fasten seatbelts'.

31.12 PHAZZ Sounding trendy and short-lived, a conflation of fantasy, phantasmagoric, fizz and jazz. Cf. De-Phazz, a contemporary German jazz ensemble.

31.13 SIMONE WEIL Simone Weil (1909-1943), French mystic philosopher and political activist who converted from Judaism to Christianity and promoted the faculty of patience above all else (see her *Waiting for God*). She demonstrated supreme self-sacrifice, dying in Kent after trying to live on the same rations as those enduring German occupation.

32. The rant of the previous stanza has come to a close, and the short sentences which begin this stanza ("Take issue. About time") force the poet to contemplate making an objection ("Take issue"); it is "About time" (at about a quarter of the way into the poem) that he did so. But how to do so is the issue: whether to rant ("shout down / darkness"); or try to communicate ("Invent the telegraph"); whether to face death with frivolity ("dancing"); or go out in a blaze ("set fire" to one's bed). More seriously the poet must "MAKE ANSWER" to his age, must attempt to "make / reparation" – but this is "not / easy". There is a paradox implicit in "MAKE ANSWER": to submit a "bulk recognizance" – to speak on behalf of others – one must be in tune with one's own body. The elemental words of the final lines defy conventional syntax, are an attempt to reach the deepest recesses of the individual consciousness ("lost sensation", "heart's blood"), ultimate truths against which there is no appeal. Hill's poetry may have public, social, historical functions – may "make / reparation" and be submitted as a public document ("bulk recognizance") – but it must equally and at the same time be read as deeply ("unselfknowing") and ultimately ("to the bone") confessional.

32.1 About time Invoking both the temporal patience of Simone Weil (see stanza 31) and Eliot's 'Burnt Norton' I. See also stanza 15.

32.2 shout down / darkness above all Cf. "And universal Darkness buries All", the final line of Pope's four-book *Dunciad* (1743). Also Russell Hoban's *Riddley Walker* (1980), in which, as part of Lissener's story 'The Other Voyce Owl of the Worl', Owl tries to maintain darkness and prevent light by repeating the word 'dark' (p. 85).

32.3 Invent the telegraph As did Samuel Morse, who first used the device in 1835 to transmit the words, 'What God hath wrought'. See also stanza 33.

32.4 you would be wise to Colloquially, 'to be wise to' something is to have experienced it previously, to be aware of its pitfalls.

32.5 Some go / dancing, some set fire to their beds The words "go / dancing" are ambiguous: one can go dancing for fun, but also to death; likewise, setting fire to one's bed can be an attention-seeking act, or one of suicide. Here, the likely reference is to a fire which devastated Hampton Court in 1986 having originated in the apartment of pensioned aristocrat Lady Gale; according to forensic scientists "between the bed and the window ... the result of the ignition of furnishing fabric or paper by a naked flame or a lit cigarette" (*The Great Fire at Hampton Court*, p. 31). Cf. "we may not need / to burn the furniture" in *The Triumph of Love* (LVII).

32.6 mock-up The preliminary layout of a publication, showing the size and arrangement of material to be included. The phrase echoes the familiar upper-class frivolity, 'Anyone for tennis?'

32.7 make do To 'make do' is to cope with a given situation, to get by.

32.8 reparation To put right wrongs, as a convicted offender might be instructed to do.

32.9 MAKE ANSWER As the defendant must make answer (in Latin, *ad respondendum*) in a legal action or suit. Also, as an examinee in an exam (see stanzas 41 and 44).

32.10 recognizance A formal agreement made before a judge, or the sum of money to be forfeited if such an agreement is not honoured; "bulk" because many parties are involved; and the poet must speak for all.

ANNOTATIONS

32.11 heart's blood Cf. *The Triumph of Love*: "When I examine / my soul's heart's blood I find it the blood / of bulls and goats" (LXIII).
32.12 slammers Slang for gaol, from the 'slamming' of the prison door. The word also conveys a sense of urgency, as in to 'slam a proposal or idea' (to discount it) or to forcefully 'slam dunk' a goal in basketball. There is a hint of 'tequila slammer', a potent cocktail mixed by slamming the glass on the hard surface of the bar.
32.13 instress A neologism of Gerard Manley Hopkins (1844-1889): 'instress' is "the *sensation* of inscape – a quasi-mystical illumination, a sudden perception of that deeper pattern, order, and unity which gives meaning to external forms" (*Hopkins: Poems and Prose*, xxi).

33.
Framed by the quiz show answers, "YES", "NO" and "PASS", this stanza offers a general recognition that "fantasies" could give "us" (poets, *et al.*) a hollow sense of approbation ("YES"), and that accordingly, however guilty we feel, we might find common cause with our age – talk fashionable nonsense, acknowledge (but not deeply) our complicity with the violent past. This is the voice of reason, of the *homme moyen sensuel*, prepared to "give" or concede, to come to terms with his age. So, Hill invites himself to respond in a fashionably cryptic manner ("talk telegraphese") and make frivolous puns ("FORTITUDE / NEVER MY FORTE"). An alternative, however, is to say NO to such things as fiddly accounts, popular recognition and dubious honours — and PASS to all societal obligations, the final phrase "of despair" sounding the one authentic note in a stanza which tries to reconcile one's sense of deeper complicity within a shallow society prepared to forgive this for the sake of superficial values. The thrust is theological (though the language is legal), the sense of admitting common complicity, yet needing to make "common cause" between this recognition and the deeper sense of personal and individual complicity.
33.1 YES […] see us out Compare Yeats's rueful admission in 'Meditations in Time of Civil War': "We have fed the heart on fantasies." See also "sex / fantasies" in stanza 10.
33.2 amnesty A political pardon, but here (following the "confessional" of stanza 32) the sense of a whitewash remission of sins.

33.3 *son / et lumière* Literally 'sound and light' in French; the term usually implies shabby aesthetics, specifically outdoor multimedia shows telling the history of notable structures.

33.4 Something múst give Cf. the demotic 'something's got to give', meaning something must surrender, give way, be flexible.

33.5 make common cause In legal language, parties make common cause when working together to achieve a satisfactory outcome for all (cf. "MAKE ANSWER" in stanza 32).

33.6 frank exchange An abbreviation of 'full and frank exchange (of views)', a euphemism used by journalists and in public relations for anything from the unrestrained trading of opinions to a stand-up argument.

33.7 defamation Legally, maligning the reputation of another without justification.

33.8 telegraphese A terse, inelegant form of language used in telegrams (see stanza 32) and featuring (since charged by the word) as few words as possible.

33.9 FORTITUDE / NEVER MY FORTE As Algernon says in Oscar Wilde's *The Importance of Being Earnest*: "As far as the piano is concerned, sentiment is my forte" (I.i).

33.10 BLOOD-IN-URINE The sense is of prisoners being beaten until they pass blood in their urine (haematuria); an indictment of "EURO-CULTURE".

33.11 RUIN EURO-CULTURE Suggesting a cryptic crossword (see stanzas 1 and 85), which matches 'urine' with 'ruin' and 'Euro', to hint at the legacy of violence.

33.12 makeshift honour Cf. "Courtesy / titles" in stanza 30.

33.13 by royal appointment 'By appointment' are the words entitled to be displayed by holders of the royal warrants granted to suppliers of goods and services to the Crown. Here, perhaps, a conjectured offer of the Poet Laureateship.

33.14 all / duties [...] of despair From the discourse of legal statutes, the list properly ending not with "despair" but with 'responsibilities', 'immunities' or 'obligations'.

34. In this stanza, unusually coherent for the first eight lines, Hill contrasts the inherent (and often inadvertently slapstick) humour of the films of the silent era with the horror of the reality of war. The implied setting is a cinema, depicting, first, a newsreel of the front in World War I, with soldiers going 'over the wire' into battle; Hill wonders if the audiences of those days could "adjust" their minds to compensate for the primitive technology, and to see the tragedy beyond the visual "farce"; for the deaths were not farcical, but tragic. First is shown the newsreel (documentary, and "nót farce"), in which the soldiers are depicted marching and walking with "stiff gallantry" and a "jig-jog" gait; then, the men break out of the trenches to attack across No Man's Land (over "the wire"); they are (silently) "howling" with pain, but (perhaps when the attack is over) persist with the "formalities" of soldier life ("dress ranks"), to see who is still alive, so thin is the line between living anonymity and heroic death ("fame and luck"). The other feature, perhaps preceding this ("after"), is a "rare / projection of WINGS", in which the genuine tragedy of a crash on a final sortie is represented unflinchingly: not Hollywood glory or valour or fine slogans ("PER / ARDUA"), but pilots dying in agony, choking on their own blood.

34.1 caught-short The jolty effect of early motion pictures (see "jig-jog" in line 3, and Charlie Chaplin's jerky on-film movements in line 7), whereby those walking or marching (soldiers, for instance) looked as if they were "caught-short", i.e., in desperate need of the latrine. Hill has spoken of the "curious twitchy movement" of early film ('The Art of Poetry', p. 286).

34.2 half-over the wire That is, shot as they come out of the trenches, and so draped across the barbed wire.

34.3 whatever else [...] howling Note the implied contrast between silent movies and things of that kind ("in thát line") that make an audience howl with laughter, and the agonies to be suffered by the soldiers, "in thát line".

34.4 dress ranks In its military stance, 'dress ranks' means to line up shoulder to shoulder, specifically after a sortie, to determine who was still alive; here, also, the neatly seated ranks of movie-goers watching the soldiers do so, in a jerky Chaplinesque manner, that might seem funny but is not.

34.5 Chaplin's Sir Charles Spender ('Charlie') Chaplin, Jr., KBE (1889-1977), English comedy actor and one of the stars of Hollywood cinema, whose principal character was 'the Tramp', a vagrant with the refined manners and dignity of a gentleman, and a dyspraxic walk.

34.6 forwards-backwards fame and luck That is, one jerky step backwards or forwards could make all the difference between fame and anonymity, life or death (see "fame and luck").

34.7 WINGS A 1927 Paramount Pictures silent film about WWI American fighter pilots and their love-lives, directed by William A. Welman and starring, among others, Clara Bow and a young Gary Cooper; the first winner (for best picture) of an Academy Award.

34.8 heroic lip-readers Both pilots reading directions from the ground before take-off, and watchers of silent films decoding the images through a mixture of lip-reading and subtitles (see "mouthings" in line 11).

34.9 sortie An attack made by a small military force into enemy territory, or by a single aircraft, here shot down.

34.10 bingo A 1920s expression (deriving from the game of Bingo, or Housie) of satisfaction or surprise at an outcome or event.

34.11 ventriloquists The etymology of "ventriloquists" ('belly-speakers') anticipates the "eloquent belly-blood" of the final line.

34.12 PER / ARDUA Latin words which form the first half of the epithet of the Royal Air Force Regiment '*per ardua ad astra*' [through adversity to the stars]. The final images ("choked mouthings", "belly-blood") invoke Wilfred Owen's 'Dulce et Decorum Est' (see also stanza 35): "guttering, choking, drowning ... If you could hear, at every jolt, the blood come gargling from the froth-corrupted lungs".

35. The focus shifts from the First World War to England and, more specifically, to the end of the British Empire. The social order ("hierarchies") of pre-1914 England now seems bizarre ("Fantastic"), but also as leading inevitably to the destruction of war ("fatalistic"). A remade society is readjusting, but without the "demotic splendour" of the past: the 1920s and 30s were gloomy years. Edwardian England, with its quaint ways (its polite "modicum of the outrageous") may have been destroyed, but a certain type of wilful patriotic joviality survived throughout the war, here represented by the soldierly ("martial") charwomen who danced (and marched) at the rehearsal of Holst's *Jupiter* (1918), carrying the everywoman's armour of "bristles and pails". A melody from this piece was used for the hymn 'I vow to thee my country', the first to be sung at the funeral of Princess Diana, an occasion of vast and (in Britain) unprecedented public outpouring of grief and mass unity. And so, however much one disputes the

ANNOTATIONS

"audit" of the casualties and the true cost of the war, and however ridiculous one finds the relentless patriotism of Land-of-Hope-and-Glory-England (or disputes the worth of Diana as the recipient of endless bouquets), one cannot deny the solidarity and sincerity of the dancing of the charwomen, nor the rank and file singing of Blake's *Jerusalem*, nor the outpouring of public grief in 1997.

35.1 to her intended (or to her intended) The words before and inside the parentheses can be read as either a) intended to her; or b) her fiancé. The "her" is Britannia, emblem of the Empire, as well as Diana, Princess of Wales (see stanza 36).

35.2 near fatalistic / love of one's country A sentiment almost identical to Owen's identification of "the old lie" in 'Dulce et decorum est', which exposes the fallacy behind "Dulce et decorum est pro patria mori" [Sweet and fitting it is to die for one's country].

35.3 love of one's country [...] over-subscribed Christopher Ricks notes that these lines "bear witness to at least some attachment to 'Little Gidding' III: 'love of a country / Begins as attachment to our own field of action'" (*True Friendship*, p. 43).

35.4 modicum of the outrageous The paradox of decorous provocation, as, for example, outfits worn to the Last Night of the Proms.

35.5 dancing – marching – in and out of time The words hint at the title of Anthony Powell's *A Dance to the Music of Time*, a 12-volume series of novels documenting the changes in English upper class social mores between 1920 and 1970. Eliot in 'Little Gidding' talks of moments "in and out of time". See stanza 17.

35.6 Holst's JUPITER The melody of the slow middle section of Gustav Holst's (1874-1934) 'Jupiter, the Bringer of Jollity' (from *The Planets*) became popular as the hymn tune 'Thaxted' (named after the village where Holst lived for many years) with words (written as a response to the cost of WWI) beginning "I vow to thee, my country" added by Cecil Spring-Rice. Although Holst had no patriotic intentions for his music, the Jupiter melody inspired fellow-feeling among listeners: at the first (private) performance of the work in 1918, "The whole performance had been perfect – even charwomen scrubbing the floors outside the auditorium had danced to Jupiter" (Paul Holmes, *Holst*, p. 68). At the 1997 funeral of Diana, Princess of Wales, 'I Vow to thee, my country' was the first hymn to be sung (it was, allegedly, her personal favourite). The dancing, marching "bristles and pails" also suggest the 1940 Disney animated film *Fantasia*, in which (in the sequence 'The Sorcerer's Apprentice') small squads of brooms come to life and – all the while marching in formation – carry buckets in each 'hand'.

35.7 JERUSALEM The short poem, 'Jerusalem', by William Blake (1757-1827), beginning with the words 'And did those feet in ancient time', put to the music of Sir Charles Hubert Hastings Parry in 1916, and subsequently championed as a nationalistic anthem. The stress upon "ás" invites the comparison with Holst, but equally implies a 'step' towards Jerusalem (a promised land), as in 'Onward Christian soldiers, marching as to war'.

36. Diana, like her namesake, the goddess of the hunt, is now also fantastic and apocryphal, a "creature of fable" lionized extensively after her death, although she was "hunted" by the press and her public (to whom she was "inescapably / beholden") during life. The words from the *Book of Common Prayer* ("funeral sentences") uttered at Westminster Abbey, "Half forgotten" by the public during Hill's own lifetime, regained currency (were "resurrected") after the occasion of the television event that was her funeral (with its estimated 2.5 billion viewers worldwide), a feat which elicits wonder from the poet. The tone of the final five lines of the stanza is elegiac, with a contrast between the "bio-degradation" of the physical body after death and the eternising capabilities of memory: Diana's body may lie and rot at the island in the lake at Althorp, but there remains a worthy mystery to the love felt for her by her public, who remember her even "in sleep". The 'little death' of sleep implies a unity with those from whom we lie "apart", a sentiment which may be "tired" but which is nevertheless grounded in a truth, however much it "lies apart" from the biological finality of the "half-rotted black willow leaves / at the lake's edge".

36.1 Huntress [...] creature of fable The "Huntress" is Diana, Princess of Wales (see stanza 22), whose life and death are the stuff of modern-day "fable". Here she is contrasted with Diana, Roman goddess of chastity, the moon and the hunt.

36.2 for her | / like being hunted Hill's description of Diana as hunted echoes the words of her brother Charles Spencer during her 1997 funeral: "a girl given the name of the ancient goddess

ANNOTATIONS

of hunting was, in the end, the most hunted person of the modern age" (*The Oxford Dictionary of Quotations*, p. 732).

36.3 beholden Cf. "beholden" in lines 4 and 6 of stanza 18.

36.4 tired but not / emotional A variation on 'tired and emotional', the euphemistic phrase coined by British satirical magazine *Private Eye* in 1967 to describe the recurrent drunkenness of Labour Cabinet Minister George Brown, now a journalistic cliché (*From the Horse's Mouth: Oxford Dictionary of English Idioms*, p. 357).

36.5 funeral sentences The seven texts in the Anglican *Book of Common Prayer* which constitute the burial service, and which have been put to music by a number of composers; at Diana's funeral, Henry Purcell's interpretation was preferred.

36.6 Whatever of our loves Sophie Ratcliffe identifies this phrase as "both an echo of Prince Charles's awkwardness on the day of his engagement about whether or not he was in love ('whatever "love" means'), and an attempt at reconciliation" (*On Sympathy*, p. 235).

36.7 whatever it is | you look for in sleep Both a) whatever it is that you look for in sleep; and b) whatever it is – that is what you look for in sleep.

36.8 willow leaves / at the lake's edge Although Ophelia's drowning takes place not in a lake (which recalls Diana's resting place) but in a brook, the willow and its leaves recall Gertrude's report of her death: "There is a willow grown aslant the brook, / That shows his hoar leaves in the glassy stream" (*Hamlet*, IV.vii).

37. Hill now imagines not a landscape of decay but the "humble homes" occupied by readers of *The Sun*, the daily newspaper of Hill's demotic mass: the voice of the PEOPLE. This, at least, is how it should be, but Hill fails to hear the voice of democracy, whether Churchill's or that of some other, for instance, Joseph Wanhope, whose name ('faint hope') is the "clue" to what is missing – the authentic voice of society, as opposed to the frivolity of celebrity. But wait! – says Hill, the clue is not lost, since Hill is its inheritor. Hill has now himself become a social critic, a Daumier-like "WANHOPE" with, verily, *wan hope*; the Langland, Chaucer, or Skelton of his age. The tongue-twisting "sashaying your shadow self" is to be said at "normal walking speed", but even then is difficult, a task of vocal agility, just as walking a straight line (when inebriated and at the behest of a policeman) can pose a challenge. Words, as in stanza 31, are playthings: the partly palindromic, almost anagrammatical twin phrases of "SURE SUCCESS OF RAP" and "PAR FOR THE COURSE" and the auditory possibility of 'rapper' out of "RAP PAR" are sensationalist *Sun*-like snippets, proof of the "game / celebrity plays us for". Somehow, somewhere between these forces, Hill has to find his authentic (not his "shadow") self and voice.

37.1 SUN This UK tabloid has the highest circulation of any English-language newspaper. It focusses heavily on gossip relating to the entertainment industry and, in particular, the British royal family. Hill uses "condescends" to suggest the efforts of the daily newspaper to curry favour with its target audience, with a smugness as inevitable as the daily rising and setting of the sun.

37.2 Churchill's Sir Winston Leonard Spencer Churchill (1874-1965), heroic UK Prime Minister during World War II, renowned for his stirring radio addresses.

37.3 WANHOPE "Wanhope" is used twice by William Langland in the allegorical *Piers the Plowman*: "Syre Wanhope was sibbe to hym as som men me tolde" (12.198); "And wedded on Wanhope a wenche of the stewes" (23.160). William Logan identifies Wanhope as from Chaucer's 'The Knight's Tale': "Well oughte I sterve in wanhop and distresse. / Farwel my lif, my lust, and my gladnesse" ('Author! Author!', p. 65). Here, the word offers a "clue" to its own etymology ('faint hope'); there may also be a reference to Joseph Wanhope, a London journalist and prominent socialist at the beginning of the last century.

37.4 Jack! John Skelton (c.1460-1529), an English poet whose 'Skeltonical' verse resembles *Speech! Speech!* in its comic admixture of languages, its breathless volubility, and its frequent turn to invective.

37.5 sashaying The sashay (a corruption of the French *chassé*, meaning 'driven out') is a dance movement in which gliding steps are performed ostentatiously, with dancers strutting and parading sideways; here, 'sashaying' refers to the jagged movement of Skelton's verse.

37.6 shadow self In the writing of Carl Jung (1875-1961), the shadow or shadow self is an archetype of that part of human, psychic possibility that we deny in ourselves, as in R. L. Stevenson's 1886 novella, *The Strange Case of Dr Jekyll and Mr Hyde*. Here, the alliterative "sashaying your shadow" suggests

ANNOTATIONS

Skelton's alliterative style (see Hill's reference to him as a "right rapper" in stanza 95).

37.8 normal walking speed, toes on the line As in a police test of sobriety, in which one is asked to walk a line without deviation, and to say a tongue-twister at normal speaking (not "walking") speed. Also, to 'toe the line', to behave with propriety.

37.9 SURE SUCCESS OF RAP Here rap is summoned as an example of contemporary demotic entertainment, guaranteed "SURE SUCCESS" due to its up-to-the-minute 'rapport' with its audience.

37.10 PAR FOR THE COURSE In golf, the score used as a standard for the course, or a given hole. The phrase is almost palindromic, pivoting upon "RAP PAR" (see also stanza 120), and the partial anagram of "SURE" and "COURSE".

38.

In this stanza, which follows from stanza 37 in its sense of decaying democracy, Hill begins to hypothesize. If, he wonders, he senses something of the demotic within himself, then one option (other than the "despair" of stanza 33) is to conform to the expectations of his age ("assume the PEOPLE'S voice"). And if Hill were to conform, to assume this antithetical voice, what would ensue? What follows in the stanza is a kind of conditional in which he explores this idea, the resulting "circus act", the "short-cuts", the many "thwartings", the spouting of hackneyed phrases ("heroes / living as they have to"). There is, for Hill, "no darkness" more "difficult" than this self-willed plunge into the worse-than-ordinary, where in speaking he produces nothing more than "dumb insolence", insolence expressed despite saying nothing. Assuming the democratic voice, Hill might even become a working-class hero, perform one circus act after another, might even able to "Show the folks" (note the homespun idiom of U.S. television game shows) Caravaggio, that is, translate highbrow art into something for the masses. The last two lines are self-mocking: in this demotic voice (that of a *Sun* reporter, for instance, as in the previous stanza), Hill asks himself, his other self being that of a pretentious poet, what the hell is this old wreck up to? And suddenly to be the voice of his age and speak "well" of it – what sort of unlikely story would that be?

38.1 Do nothing but assume the PEOPLE'S VOICE Cf. Walt Whitman in stanza 26 of his *Song of Myself*: "Now I will do nothing but listen". Here, the sense is that of 'assuming' a demotic voice, one propounded by *People* magazine (see stanza 1).

38.2 Xenophobic Having an intense and irrational dislike of foreigners and their cultures.

38.3 the Brits are heroes / living as they have to Marcus Waithe notes that "At first, the speaker assumes the superior tone of the internationalist. But the reprimand of xenophobia collapses with the line break. It mutates to become an affectionate characterization of compatriots expressed in a sort of mid-Atlantic journalese" ("'The slow haul to forgive them'", p. 79). See also stanzas 23, 40, 84 and 94 for reiterations of and variations on this phrase.

38.4 Powers Cf. stanza 13: "power among powers". One common affliction of the Brits, in both the interbellum and post-war periods, was the frequency of power cuts.

38.5 Caravaggio's FLAGELLATION A c.1607 oil painting by Caravaggio (1571-1610), with a permanent home in the Museo Nazionale de Capodimonte, Naples, depicting a near-naked Christ at the mercy of three torturers; the palette is restricted, and the dismal colour and unflinchingly horrific scene combine to give the composition a grim force. See Appendix, fig.4.

38.6 what's it worth Were Caravaggio's 'Flagellation' to be shown to the PEOPLE ("the folks"), then their first (perhaps only) response would be a cynical inquiry about the monetary value of the painting.

38.7 damages Those monies awarded to a claimant after success in a civil suit; Hill is imagining himself as having assumed the role of public arbiter.

38.8 wreck still singing Cf. Hopkins's 'The Wreck of the Deutschland', in which five Franciscan nuns sang their threnody as the ship sank. Hill described the poem as a "magisterially eccentric work of genius" in a 2008 interview-by-post ('Civil Polity and the Confessing State', p. 7).

38.9 A FINE STORY! In the demotic sense, a story which cannot be entirely believed, often far-fetched, a 'likely story'. See stanza 9: "*welch ein Gruss*".

ANNOTATIONS

39. The central metaphor of this stanza is that of an early surveillance flight over the bleak landscape, itself a further metaphor of the human mind. Launching his stanza, Hill imagines a pilot pushing off (probably for "one last sortie" as in stanza 34) from a runway; still alive to do so, he has already "outlived" statistical expectations of the World War I airman. The pilot has a bird's eye view of the landscape beneath; the body ("husk") of the aeroplane (possessing that unique "light-heavy" quality), its wings and fuselage, leave a shadow on the industrial landscape (likely, because of the "coal-staithes", to be Northern English). This shadow (see the "shadow self" in stanza 37) is explicitly associated with the dark portions of the mind, the parts of ourselves which, repressed as they are, appear to be a "stagnant / puddle" but may instead conceal a "maelstrom". The personality is "sick", the landscape is sullied, the pilot does not return from his patrol; from his elevated perspective, the difference between still "stagnant" puddles and the dark vitality of the "maelstrom" cannot be discerned. What looks like quiet grimness from a distance may in fact be, up close, swirling whirlpools, and to come too close might mean not to return.

39.1 push off As in a) the demotic 'go away'; b) aircraft leaving the ground or a boat leaving shore; and c) the act of dying.

39.2 without coverage That is, from the press, or public notice.

39.3 coal-staithes Waterside depots for coals brought from collieries for shipment, furnished with staging and chutes for loading vessels.

39.4 blistered hardtop Literally, a parched, unyielding landscape, a hard surface; here the word implies (psychologically) a tough carapace concealing a vulnerable inner being.

39.5 *nerdlich* A faux-German coinage, presumably Hill's own, based on the faux-English 'nerd'.

39.6 maelstrom A great whirlpool in the Arctic Ocean off the west coast of Norway formerly supposed to suck in and destroy all vessels within a long radius. The word (Norwegian) was introduced into English by Edgar Allan Poe ('A Descent into the Maelström', 1841), and was made famous by Jules Verne in his *20,000 Leagues Under the Sea* (1870).

39.7 Í'll sáy Meaning both a) indeed; and b) I shall report.

39.8 failed / to return from patrol The reference is to surveillance by air, and particularly to those flights with spying as their aim, a practice common in WWI and persisting to this day. Here, a metaphor for the "sick personality" that has failed to return to the "routine" world.

40. This is what World War II has done: the Poles (in Hill's by now hackneyed phrasing) are "heroes living as they have to", but it is not a gift given to them exclusively (the phrase is used elsewhere for the Brits and Dutch); hardship is not discriminate, but instead is a blank cheque, upon which many names might be entered ("PAYABLE TO BEARER"). What was unmade can be made again: Bernardo Bellotto (known to the Poles as Canaletto) is invoked as the individual responsible for making the city of Warsaw "fly | together again"; his architectural detail standing as a memorial to the order of the old world, and as a starting point for its rebuilding. The "Gouvernement Géneral" in occupied Poland destroyed this order, worked as a bellows-fuelled fire (a "drawn furnace") in which everything (from books to people) burned. It is not a happy story to tell (hence the sardonic reference to "mirth"), but – like *"Galgenfreude"* – it is tattooed into our bones. And what has changed in our world? The stanza ends with a blasé, sardonic sense of self-advising ("Brush-up mnemonics. Unearth / survival kit") that finds expression only in mottos and clichés, and in the sense of the inevitability of such recurrent destruction and death ("Change date of expiry").

40.1 The Poles [...] See stanzas 23, 38, 84 and 94 for other iterations of this phrase, the impersonality and irony of which is here indicated by the instruction "PAYABLE TO BEARER", words used on personal cheques to indicate that it can be redeemed by anyone who has possession of it (see also "Change date of expiry" in the final line).

40.2 exploded / city they made fly | together again Warsaw, the Polish capital left in ruins after WWII, and subsequently rebuilt painstakingly; the process of restoration here envisioned as a film running backwards. The phrase "fly | together" suggests its opposite, the more usual 'fly apart', and gives an image of Warsaw being put back together by a force equal to that which destroyed it.

40.3 Canaletto The reference is not to the Venetian landscape painter Canaletto (1697-1768), but to his nephew and fellow Venetian Bernardo Bellotto (1720-1780), who in 1764 became court painter in Warsaw and is known in Poland as 'Canaletto'.

Annotations

Like his uncle (whose name he sometimes exploited for the purposes of self-promotion), Bellotto produced meticulous landscape and architectural views; his paintings of Warsaw were used as historical records during the restoration of the city after WWII.

40.4 Gouvernement Géneral Polish territories under German military occupation between September 1939 and 1945, which endured extreme repression and deprivation (those "things unmentionable", such as the furnaces of the Holocaust) during WWII.

40.5 your lot One's "lot" is one's allotment in life, position and death.

40.6 *Galgenfreude* A word not in general currency, but which exists in the Grimms' *Deutsches Wörterbuch* (with a single example in literature) as meaning 'joy in another's execution'. It derives from *Schadenfreude* [joy in another's misery]. Here, it brings to mind the "hideous" names of the concentration camps (see also stanza 83), as well as the cruelty of those who took satisfaction from the deaths of millions. Cf. "This is late scaffold-humour, turn me off" in *Without Title* (p. 11).

40.7 tattooed / into our bones As identification numbers were tattooed onto the flesh of concentration camp victims, so the names of Auschwitz and Buchenwald etc. are indelibly now a part of our past.

40.8 Activate motto As if to set up and mobilize a military unit, or to treat a substance such as charcoal to increase its capacity for adsorption. The specific motto 'activated' could be anything: 'Arbeit Macht Frei', or 'Per Ardua ad Astra' (see stanza 34), or "The Poles are heroes". Like a blank cheque, the sentiment can be cashed at need.

40.9 Change date of expiry As of a cheque, a culture, or an individual life (including his own).

41. Hill begins with what may be simply a rhetorical (empty) speculation: anything of the human past could assume Lusitanian (read: *titanic*) proportions of "sorrow" were it 'raised' from unknown depths. Still a defendant, Hill 'makes answer' with only "NO or NO COMMENT". Just as he is not certain of the nature of his question, so he is not certain of his response. Perhaps it is a question of lack of knowledge and context: *hoch* plus *zeit* does not equal *Hochzeit*, though to the ignorant eye it is a clear deduction. The translations (between times, places) can be "Dreadful". The problem, as ever, is how to speak, given the inherent difficulties of speaking and the futility of history and conflict. Generations have been too easily duped by stories and deductions, willing to accept inferior translations, to imagine easy redemption of promissory notes to the past ("IOUs"), to believe in the World War I Christmas truce (temporary, amidst mass bloodshed) as a symbol of peace. Mankind continues, through time, to tolerate the institutions ("Devil's Island"), the organizations ("Fenian Men"), the mouthpieces ("Stahlhelm") and instruments ("Lambeg") of torture, warmongering and "sententious" bloodshed. How, given all of this, can any individual speak – "raise" the past – without causing immense "sorrow". Here, like a child in school, Hill is sure of neither the questions nor the answers.

41.1 Lusitanian The sinking of the unarmed British-registered liner *Lusitania* by a German submarine off the Irish Coast on 7 May 1915 was a turning point in WWI. Of the 1,198 casualties, 128 were United States citizens, and although there was, at this time, still considerable sympathy for Germany in the United States, the deaths led to demands from many for an immediate declaration of war.

41.2 raise it Both a) 'raise the question'; and b) 'raise the sunken wreck'.

41.3 NO or NO COMMENT See also "YES", "NO", and "PASS" in stanza 33 for other responses to the instruction to "MAKE ANSWER" (stanza 32).

41.4 *Hochzeit* German "*hoch*" implies 'hands up', in surrender (as by those "won over", convinced or defeated by the Germans), though the metaphor is equally that of a test in high school, where the translation of German compounds can have "Dreadful" results: literally, *hoch* and *zeit* mean 'high' and 'time' respectively, but when compounded translate not to 'high time' but to 'wedding'.

41.5 Christmas of the truce During the Christmas Truce of 1914, thousands of soldiers on the Western Front acting from not a single initiative but rather independently and spontaneously, temporarily ceased combat. Their actions – now considered an expression of peace and brotherhood – were at the time criticized by those "spoilsports" in higher command.

41.6 Sarn't A contraction of 'Sergeant', the military rank; sometimes used as a general address.

41.7 *dévots* French for the devout, but with the connotation of 'excessively pious', and perhaps also the suggestion of the

ANNOTATIONS

'conchies', or conscientious objectors. Cf. *The Orchards of Syon*: "Both you and I / who pray with the *dévots* yet practise / every trick in the book" (XLV).

41.8 Devil's Island The Île du Diable, off the coast of French Guyana, infamous as a prison island and site of atrocities (as depicted in Henri Charrière's *Papillon*). Alfred Dreyfus, a French artillery officer wrongly accused of spying for Germany, was imprisoned there, until "spoilsports" like Zola agitated for his release. The prison was phased out in the early 1950s.

41.9 Stahlhelm A journal (the 'Steel Helmet') edited by Count Hans-Jürgen von Blumenthal (later hanged for his part in the 20 July 1944 assassination attempt on Hitler), and a mouthpiece for anti-Weimar sentiments. See *"Constellation Kreisau"* in stanza 111.

41.10 Lambeg A large traditional Irish drum made of oak and goat skin, and a provocative nationalist symbol used chiefly by Northern Irish Unionists and the Orange Order during the street parades of 'The Twelfth' of July (to celebrate the Battle of the Boyne).

42. Still in the courtroom ('trying' to decide), Hill is now the defendant, a "Recídivist" or repeat offender who dares to question the process of judgement ("íf / there is leeway?"). He imagines an eighteenth-century courtroom drama, the circuit judge presiding over cases ("righteousness") financed by dubious sources (South African speculation) and forcing the articulate barristers, the various Edward Halls (who are in it for the game, the "forensic oratory") to confess that Hill merits his "nark's wages" – that is to say, that he has done a good job of telling the truth, of detailing what is going on to those arbiters of right and wrong, though at times (like an audacious highwayman) at risk of being "unmasked". At last the exact nature of the case is disclosed: Hill has been caught with the potentially poisonous "eau-de-Luce", or "vitriol", "defiling" those classics of elegy and good taste – and urges his audience to keep his secret ("No, no; not a word"). The "jury is oút", have not yet reached a verdict ("húng"), since they are unable to understand the implications of the "forensic" details cited. And yet the defence was a joke, it "laughed us to tears": in the previous stanza Hill wondered how to speak without inviting sorrow, but here oratory, articulacy and trickery lead to laughter. The reason is simple: in stanza 41, Hill wondered how to take responsibility for the past, how to speak of it in a constructive way; here, in a less honourable cause, he wonders how to evade responsibility, to escape the charges.

42.1 Grace In Christianity, the undeserved infinite love, mercy, favour, and goodwill shown to humankind by God; in legal terms, time to enter or reject a plea.

42.2 withdraw – or enter – an appeal The stanza is littered with legal terminology: here, "withdraw" (a plea), "enter" and "appeal", in the next line "Recídivist" (repeat offender), then "argue" (a case), "Confess" (to a crime), "caught" (in the act), "jury is out, hung" (on their verdict), "forensic oratory" (submitted as evidence), and then finally "defence".

42.3 restore a lost glory to your circuits The judicial proceedings known as assizes and conducted by itinerant judges were abolished in England and Wales in 1972 (hence, "a lost glory").

42.4 the Rand South African currency of strong value until 1982, when political upheaval began to weaken it; with reference, perhaps, to various shady speculations by Western firms in South Africa, despite sanctions.

42.5 Edward (alias Marshall) Hall Hill refers with economy to two great lawyers of England. Edward Hall (c.1498-1547) was both a barrister in the City of London and the author of *Hall's Chronicle*, one of the prime sources for Shakespeare's history plays. Sir Edward Marshall Hall (1858-1927) was a barrister with a formidable reputation as an orator, and known as 'The Great Defender' for his successful defences of defendants accused of notorious murders.

42.6 nark's wages Monies paid by the police to informants ('narks').

42.7 eau-de-Luce An ammonia-based composition used as an antidote for insect and snake bites, and as an agent for 'bringing to' those afflicted with apoplexy or extreme intoxication; to be used with caution, as excessive use (as with any ammonia product) may be disastrous.

42.8 vitriol Sulphuric acid, especially as used as a projectile ('vitriol throwing'), as in Graham Greene's *Brighton Rock* (1938).

42.9 *Pearl* The Middle English alliterative poem, *The Pearl* (c.1400) is an allegorical dream-vision and elegy by the *Gawain*-poet for his young daughter ('the *Pearl*-maiden') who is dead and who he hopes is at peace in heaven; here, she is the victim of the poet's vitriolic attack (see *Middle English Literature: A Cultural History*, pp. 178-179).

ANNOTATIONS

42.10 jury is oút, hung A jury is 'out' when still debating; and 'hung' when unable to reach a verdict.
42.11 laughed us to tears A conflation of the idioms 'reduced (or bored) us to tears' and 'laughed till we cried'.

43. Truth stares unflinchingly (like the blind, or a victim of a vitriol attack) at the poet, and demands he speak for at least a half-minute (that is, a stanza's worth of time, or the time it takes to vote), that he make his pleas ("cast our intercessions") to those who are in charge of the world ("grand / chefs of World Order"), those Bushes and Blairs who will 'make a meal of' the world to come. He wonders how to do so without causing offence or "defilement"; should he "Sieve" his words, filter the passion out of them? He answers 'no', "Not that." He must instead invest the (polite, passionless, inherently "inauthentic") vocabulary of bureaucracy with sincerity; this may be fundamentally 'fraudulent' but it can still express a necessary "empathy". Hill argues that his vitriol is not unprecedented; those desperate to inaugurate the United States Constitution" wrote with similarly passionate invective ("PUBLIUS" in the "FEDERALIST PAPERS"). In order to achieve justice, in order to secure the victory of democracy and of righteousness, one ought to do what is necessary, with precise foresight. But what kind of monster (Cerberus, a hell-hound) will this beget?
43.1 VERITAS The Roman goddess of truth, whose name is used as all or part of many university mottoes, notably those of Harvard ('Veritas') and Yale ('Lux et Veritas'). See also "CARITAS" and "AMOR" in stanza 57. Here, Truth stares blindly, while Justice is blind to bias and prejudice.
43.2 intercessions Pleas and prayers made to gods or saints on behalf of another; here, the vote.
43.3 World Order Globalization systems, controlled and facilitated by such organizations as the World Bank, the United Nations, the World Trade Organization and the International Monetary Fund; "chefs" in the sense of 'chefs de mission', leaders of such enterprises. There is perhaps a hint of the 1978 comedy film, *Who is Killing the Great Chefs of Europe?*
43.4 Roman / love elegists Catullus and Ovid, for instance, but particularly the latter for his political persecution and exile (his verse interpreted as "slanders").
43.5 three-headed / PUBLIUS [...] FEDERALIST PAPERS Publius was A Roman consul (d.503 BC) and one of the first

statesmen of the Republic. His name was used as an allonym – to honour his role in establishing the Roman Republic – by the three authors of *The Federalist Papers* (1787-1788) in a series of articles written under the pen name 'Publius' by Alexander Hamilton, James Madison and John Jay (hence 'three-headed'). Madison, widely recognized as the Father of the Constitution, was later President of the Unites States; Jay became Chief Justice of the US Supreme Court; Hamilton would serve in the Cabinet and become a major force in setting US economic policy. *The Federalist Papers* articles were written to gain popular support for the proposed Constitution, and the three authors succeeded magnificently in achieving this end, which they foresaw precisely. But Hill's monster is also Cerberus, the three-headed guard dog of Hades.
43.6 exact foresight Cf. "gifted with hindsight" in stanza 28.

44. In this stanza, Hill leaves the courtroom and enjoys a moment of crystalline reflection. He considers it likely that he has had a "vision or seizure", a "stroke of luck" which has somehow cured him of that maelstrom of the mind which dominated stanza 39 (*"supra"*). The dark yet playful humour which emanates from "stroke of luck" and "HE'S GOT A NERVE" lightens the mood; the "monster / of exact foresight" from stanza 43 (now a "basilisk") which affected his ability to speak is now "behind bars", and can be pencilled in or written out, 'cross-hatched', as it were. Hill, *sui generis* like the dandelion (or, perhaps, 'in solitary'), can survive even when enemy sources have eradicated all sustenance, or destroyed the environment. Here is the explanation of Hill's recent prolificacy: relieved of his mental burdens, he writes so freely that he must be told – like a child by a teacher ("STOP WRITING. HANDS ON HEADS") – to stop. Vitriol (the adult weapon of the "difficult child") is no longer required. Hill has begun to "understand / history", and in so doing he endures a loss of ignorance, the fall from innocence into experience, an inevitable transition both desired and feared, as we desire both change and constancy simultaneously. The harsh, unforgiving nature of revealed, half-welcome knowledge is softened by the fresh, clean, purifying fall of snow, covering the "scorched earth", in an elegiac final line which draws on the perennial – and conventional – wisdom of the poets.

Annotations

44.1 stroke of luck Both a) unexpected good fortune; and b) a severe (and unlucky) disabling attack caused by an interruption of blood flow to the brain, a seizure that has somehow led to insight. If the narrator has suffered a stroke, it stands to reason that he is at this point writing as opposed to speaking, as the stroke would have affected his speech. This supposition is strengthened by the composed tone of the stanza, and the instruction in line 7 to "STOP WRITING".

44.2 *supra* A formal literary instruction to refer back to an earlier point in the text; here, to the "shock" of stanza 39.

44.3 HE'S GOT A NERVE! Cf. "harp of nerves" in stanza 3. Also, the imagined response (of the "PEOPLE") to one making such a claim (hence, put him behind bars, give him the third degree).

44.4 Cross-hatch the basilisk The basilisk is a mythological reptile, whose gaze or breath is fatal, hatched by a serpent from a cock's egg, and sometimes used to describe a person with destructive and malicious influence. Here, the basilisk is 'cross-hatched', which suggests both the hatching of the cock's egg and the stripes of the prison bars ("behind bars"). The sense is the colouring of a picture (in pencil, black and white), this being a metaphor, perhaps, for the 'hatching' of a poem. INCLUDE CROSS HATCH IN BOLD?

44.5 Cryptic third-degree Intensive interrogation, here "Cryptic" because the questions are not only difficult to answer, but difficult to understand. "Cross-hatch" (line 4) may also suggest 'cross-examine'.

44.6 parthenogenic The dandelion reproduces asexually from a gamete without fertilisation – that is, it is *parthenogenetic*.

44.7 scorched earth The military strategy in which anything which might sustain the enemy is destroyed, such as food, shelter, communications and vegetation.

44.8 STOP WRITING. HANDS ON HEADS. As a primary school teacher would say to mark the end of a test. See stanza 41.

45. After the stroke and seizure of the previous stanza, Hill requires – like an ancient automobile – regular maintenance. The necessary checks and adjustments are made, both to the body ("alignments"; "brake-fluids"; "Shocks") and the mind ("slackened / memory"). The tone is no longer "MORTIFIED" (that was "last season's" theme, the tenor of Hill's pre-*Canaan* work), but rather "Thánksgiving", with a new appreciation of common life, the economy of home. Instead of sounding Hill's personal note (that of the child breaking into experience of stanza 44), it represents a "fable of common / life", a collective rather than an individual voice, yet one that is "neither / at one with the wórld" nor with itself. If this is a voice without atonement, it does at least profess humility. Œconomy is used as a metaphor: the word (like the poet) is public, official, even global, but at its "heart" is the domestic, the private, literally the 'home', with the blind prophetic venture reliant upon "forgiveness" and "MERCY".

45.1 Shocks, alignments, brake-fluids The first three words of the stanza invoke an automotive warrant of fitness: shock absorbers (part of the suspension system) to ensure a smooth ride; alignments, or the adjustment of the wheels for straighter driving; and brake fluid for hydraulic braking systems. Along with the poet's "slackened / memory", these are "checked and adjusted" as part of servicing. Cf. the poet's mind being "tuned" and "untuned" (there, not as a car, but as a musical instrument) in stanza 3.

45.2 MORTIFIED Here used in the religious sense, in which self-imposed discipline and even pain is used in an attempt to control desires; also, punning on being dead.

45.3 Thánksgiving An annual holiday of the United States, held on the fourth Thursday in November to commemorate the 1621 harvest of the Pilgrims, as an example of the "common / life".

45.4 GO HOME Cf. 'Go home Yankee', graffiti directed at American occupying forces.

45.5 ŒCONOMY From the Latin *eco nomos* (itself from the Greek *oikonomia*) 'the law of the home'. Here, the emphasis is on the household as the centre of the economy.

45.6 importunate Both a) an importunate ghost; and b) slightly importunate. See "a shade too painful" in stanza 6.

45.7 Least said; this said; / to be said at least The proverbial 'least said, soonest mended'.

45.8 MERCY Here "MERCY" is that dispensation delivered by a judge to mitigate the severity of 'blind' justice; the paradox is that, were Hill blind, he could "see his way" to forgiveness. The (perhaps mixed) metaphor here is that of Oedipus, after his blinding and anagorisis, led from Thebes by his daughter, Antigone; or, the blind prophet, Tiresias, led by his daughter,

ANNOTATIONS

Manto. The image of the daughter as giver of mercy also recalls *The Pearl* (see stanza 42).

46. The historical conflicts between France and Germany are here represented linguistically: the French battleground versus the German battleground, with Germany (the now defunct "Prussia") named as the "clear victor" (as in 1871, 1914 and 1939). Victor invites "VECTOR", a word now more "widely used", specifically ("hów exactly") because of 'advances' in technology that have increased the range and firepower of conflict. Moving from the nineteenth century to the twentieth century, and using Saki's *When William Came* as his template, Hill imagines a 'what if?' world in which Germany won the First World War: instead of tea with the Queen, he imagines tea with the Hohenzollerns, his newly-learned German producing distortions of etiquette ("*Die Zuckerzange, bitte!*"). By this time, the best of that generation would have died, and his own "ticket" would be long overdue, had he been in the trenches ("in No Man's Land"). At some point ("Somewhere"), like many others, Hill has confused the pseudonyms of two popular writers, "SAKI" and "SAPPER", yet another clanger ("*Tray no bong*"). In the closing image, Saki is described as "lambasting" the Jews of England ("luxury underclass"); according to those turncoats who now take tea with the Hohenzollern victors, he was "right on target".

46.1 *Champ d'honneur* versus *Schlachtfeld* French battleground (literally 'field of honour') versus German battleground, here specifically representative of various Franco-German conflicts.

46.2 Prussia emerges the clear victor The Franco-Prussian War (1870-1871) established the German Empire and anticipated WWI. The catalyst was the offering the Spanish crown to Prince Leopold of Hohenzollern-Sigmaringer, a Catholic relative of the Prussian king, which the French felt would give too much power to the Hohenzollerns.

46.3 VECTOR In gunnery (see "fállen" in line 7 and "target" in line 11), the trajectory of a shell.

46.4 *Die Zuckerzange, bitte!* German, 'Pass the sugar tongs, please!'; but a perverse translation might be, 'Please pass the forceps'. See stanza 41 for another "Dreadful" German translation.

46.5 Hohenzollerns The German princely family that ruled Brandenburg (1415-1918), Russia (1525-1918) and Germany (1871-1918) until its abdication following the formal dismantling of the German Empire as dictated by the Treaty of Versailles in 1919 (see 46.2).

46.6 my own ticket / long overdue Colloquially, one's ticket is up (here, "overdue") when one is due to die.

46.7 No Man's Land The stretch of disputed land between one's trenches and the enemy front lines.

46.8 SAKI Pseudonym of Hector Hugh Munro (1870-1916), satirical short story-writer. His *When William Came: A Story of London Under the Hohenzollerns* (1913) describes, after an imagined (and portentous) war, a London under German rule. Munro was a virulent anti-Semite, and *When William Came* characterised the London Jews as having weakened England and of having surrendered too easily to the German invaders. "'They grew soft,' he resumed; 'great world-commerce brings great luxury, and luxury brings softness'" (*The Complete Saki*, p. 766).

46.9 SAPPER Pseudonym of Herman Cyril McNeile (1888-1937), popular novelist between the wars and creator of *Bulldog Drummond*, the leading character (a WWI officer *cum* private detective) of ten of his novels. A 'sapper' in warfare is one who digs trenches or tunnels.

46.10 *Tray no bong* In dog French (of English soldiers), 'very no good'. Hill may know the phrase via Ivor Gurney (see stanza 111); see Hill's 'Gurney's "Hobby"': "'No bon', like 'Tray bong' and 'Na pooh fini' is a bit of the pidgin French that Gurney enjoyed'" (*Collected Critical Writings*, p. 446). See "*Napoo Finee*" in stanza 5.

46.11 SAKI 'as is' 'Saki' may be rendered as 'ça qui' in French.

46.12 Lance-Sergeant A corporal acting in the rank of sergeant, used from the 19th century until abolished in 1945. Saki, who enlisted in his forties as a private, attained the rank of Lance-Sergeant.

46.13 BEF The British Expeditionary Force, formed after the Boer War (1908) to provide overseas troops in the event of another international war. The force was sent to France and Belgium during WWI and to various parts of Europe from 1939-1940 during WWII.

ANNOTATIONS

47. Hill begins this reflective stanza with an image of the "moon in its stained ice-clouds", but ice-clouds are "themselves memorable", and as such "sharply" recall for the poet the image of his recent ("late") driving (a return to the automobile imagery of stanza 45), the pleasure in and value of the journey itself. His philosophical musing is brusquely interrupted: his poetry may be reflective, insightful, confessional, but – Hill asks himself – is it "CANONICAL" and "EPOCH-MAKING?"; or is it mechanical, the stops and starts ("Slow down here; / stop at the volta") timed to tug at the emotions of the readers, turned out on demand by one with an enviable facility (compare stanza 44), an "Unstoppable" work schedule? The poet spits out "blanks" for the critics and reviewers ("quote research / unquote", "junk-maestro") to sort through. Hill has "BEÉN THERE / DÓNE THAT"; filled in the blanks with what was wanted (including blank verse); whichever titles he has been awarded and whatever titles he has published, these may disappear, worn out (*"épuisés"*) by the changing fashion of interest and appreciation ("instantly wiped applause").

47.1 ice-clouds Ice (or hypocumulothermic) clouds are a rare phenomenon, occurring when clouds become so frozen (and therefore heavy) that they are unable to continue floating, and so plummet to earth.

47.2 my late driving The dominant sense is of his driving being recent, but there is also a suggestion of the poet being past the age at which he can (or wants to) drive, or of his driving at night.

47.3 hoping / not to arrive Cf. Robert Louis Stevenson's now proverbial, "to travel hopefully is a better thing than to arrive" (from *Virginibus Puerisque*, 1881). Here, there may be a suggestion of the driver entertaining suicidal thoughts. By the time of writing *The Orchards of Syon*, Hill could definitely refer to his "late driving" as in the past (rather than late at night): "I'm not driving / fortunately" (XXX).

47.4 CANONICAL Part of a biblical canon, or a set of artistic works believed to represent the peaks of human or cultural achievement.

47.5 volta The 'turn' that is (in a sonnet) usually after the eighth line, at the end of the posing of the problem but before the statement of the resolution. Hill's instructions to "Slow down" and "turn" may be the utterances of the 'back-seat driver', telling the driver what to do.

47.6 blanks A cartridge which, when fired, produces the sound of explosion, but which is harmless as it contains no bullet. Here, blanks are also the swear words, terms of abuse (replaced by blank spaces) for the "research" of the "junk-maestro" (cf. "Don't bleep shop" in stanza 48). See line 10 for the sense of 'blank verse'.

47.7 world-surfing As in, 'surfing the world wide web'.

47.8 quote research / unquote That is, "research", the authenticity and merits of which are undermined by the quotation marks; specifically, material that derives from the Internet, often full of obscenities (hence the need for blanks).

47.9 junk-maestro There is an echo here of 'junk bonds', the high-risk financial product sold, most often, to finance takeovers.

47.10 BLÁNK BLANK BLÁNK BLANK Blank verse: verse without rhyme, especially iambic pentameter. Although dismissed with the tourist's cliché "BEÉN THERE / DÓNE THAT", Hill was soon to 'go there and do it' again with the blank verse poem, *The Triumph of Love*, published in 2002.

47.11 My own titles Book titles (now including Hill's 2006 untitled-titled volume *Without Title*), but also honours awarded. Cf. "Courtesy / titles" in stanza 30.

47.12 *épuisés* French, meaning 'exhausted', 'worn out', or, in the discourse of publication, 'out-of-print'.

47.13 instantly wiped applause Pre-recorded 'canned' laughter used extensively in non-studio recorded sitcoms. See "spools of applause" in stanza 8.

48. This stanza considers the natural world as a testimony to faith. As lichwort ("pellitory... of the wall") stands to "old faith", so stands the "fieldstone" as a testament to the natural world. The rock (the "fieldstone", *petros* of Matthew 16:18) though dobbed with the "white crut" of ages, still stands. What stands unshaken, unshakeable through the fashions, fads and upheavals is "old faith" – the church – which is depicted as a kind of Hadrian's Wall, its coating of "moss", "lichen" and "crut" serving not to defile it but instead surviving as a testament to its age and durability. What remains is the affirmation of faith, the "*Credo*". And after this *credo*, the natural world – however debased ("car radio"), whatever the aggravations and frustrations of the profession ("wound-up / laughter"), whatever compromises must be made ("Accept

ANNOTATIONS

contingencies"), whatever dark forces ("the *duende*") must be admitted – is "ALL RÍGHT"; and because of that faith in the natural order of things the retreat from the world (Hill's "late / vocation to silence") may be revoked.

48.1 pellitory *Parietaria officinalis* (lichwort or hammerwort, pellitory of the wall), a plant of the nettle family which routinely takes root on stone walls.

48.2 common / signatories Cf. "common / life" in stanza 45 and "commonweal" in stanza 74, and the title of Hill's essay 'Common Weal, Common Woe', first published in *Style and Faith*. Here, "signatories" implies the sense of reading the book of the world, the doctrine of signatures.

48.3 fieldstone Stones in their natural, found forms, often used for walls.

48.4 *Credo* In Latin, 'I believe'; a statement of religious belief, immediately mocked by its crass echo, "*car radio*", a "mishearing" that Jeffrey Wainwright describes as "incongruously funny" (*Acceptable Words*, p. 97).

48.5 passive aggressions Passive aggression (Hill's nominal use is unusual) is a personality trait/disorder, which entered the public consciousness during the 1990s, but about which professionals are divided. The term is used to describe such behaviours as procrastination and pouting when they are intended as a form of indirect resistance to the demands of others and an avoidance of direct confrontation.

48.6 the claques People hired to applaud (or heckle) a performer or public speaker, or a group of sycophantic followers originating at the Paris Opera and popular throughout the early to mid-19th century. See the cover of *Speech! Speech!* for Daumier presenting the bourgeoisie as *claqueurs* (literally: clappers), and his 1842 lithograph 'The Claqueur'.

48.7 HAS BEEN / EDITED The sense of the self as an old 'has been', one who has been 'edited' and not given the go-ahead (for publication, or for affirmation). Cf. the voice of the editor in stanza 18.

48.8 Don't bleep shop 'Don't talk shop' is the expected phrase; "bleep" is often substituted for an expletive in radio and television broadcasts. Here, Hill compares the claques to their modern-day equivalent, the laugh track, in which the laughter is "wound-up" at the appropriate moment in the broadcast. See also "spools of applause" in stanza 8; and "Hurdy-gurdy" in stanza 53.

48.9 duende A Spanish concept of a demon or goblin, or more broadly of a dark power, described by Federico Garçia Lorca in his lecture, 'La Teoria y Juego del Duende' as "the mystery, the roots thrusting into the fertile loam known to all of us, but from which we get what is real in art" (*Toward the Open Field: Poets on the Art of Poetry, 1800-1950*, p. 198).
48.10 Revoke a late /vocation to silence Hill's revoked silence (cf. *Speech! Speech!*) is "late" both because it is passed, and because it occurred late in his life and career.
48.11 THÁT'S ALL RÍGHT THEN Here, this demotic phrase carries a measure of irony, as if in response to a weak and insufficient explanation (such as 'I didn't mean it!') for some irredeemable disaster.

49. In stanza 49, the focus is again the modern martyr, hence the opening "Not to forget". The central conceit is that of the poet travelling through Nigerian Customs – a memory of Hill's 1967 trip (shortly after Fajuyi's death) and of being "robbed" (by Customs officials) of a small "cache" of Nigerian banknotes. But that is a triviality, compared with the courageous "slow" and "foul" death of Colonel Fajuyi. Like Bunyan's Faithful, he was martyred for his decency – in Fajuyi's case for protecting a house guest. The difference between the pilgrim and Fajuyi is that the former achieved a death in fiction worthy of a martyr ("went like Elijah"), while the latter suffered an all-too-real, demeaning, "hide and seek" and "bushed kill". In this ignoble environment, even the insignia of peace – left-over or unused United Nations uniforms and armoury – are recycled, in a primitive ("neo tribal") manner. But worse was to come: the tableau of Nzeogwu's death in the night, separated from his support troops ("Where did you / ditch the platoon?"), his corpse horribly defiled and his eyes gouged out.
49.1 Colonel Fajuyi Lt. Colonel Fajuyi, Nigerian military leader and martyr. See stanza 19.
49.2 dead / before I arrived Hill visited Nigeria in 1967 (two months after the death of Fajuyi); see stanza 19.
49.3 cache A hidden store of things, especially weapons or valuables.
49.4 ten-shilling notes Cf. Hill's poem 'On Reading *Milton and the English Revolution*': "my Commonwealth shilling from an

ANNOTATIONS

oddments box" (*A Treatise of Civil Power*, Clutag edition; Hill replaces "my" with "a" for the later Penguin edition).

49.5 Faithful's / death In Part II of Bunyan's *Pilgrim's Progress*, Faithful is tried and executed as a martyr by Judge Hate-good for the crime of his disdain of Vanity Fair. See stanza 60 for further references to Bunyan.

49.6 went like Elijah That is to say, in a glorious finale. See 2 Kings 2:11: "And it came to pass, as they still went on, and talked, that, behold, there appeared a chariot of fire, and horses of fire, and parted them both asunder; and Elijah went up by a whirlwind into heaven".

49.7 Remaindered UN helmets The United Nations, which had had a presence in Nigeria since the 1960s, to such an extent that it could be considered "neo-tribal" (see 49.8). Here, "Remaindered" suggests not only 'left-over' but also 'unused' – as if Nigeria had no use for peace.

49.8 neo tribal The phrase 'Neo tribal' picks up the potential pun on "Customs" (line 2): Colonel Fajuyi died as a victim of "neo tribal" traditions, something that renders Hill's encounters with small-scale bureaucratic corruption entirely trivial.

49.9 platoon A subdivision of a company of soldiers, usually led by a lieutenant and consisting of two or three squads of ten to twelve people.

49.10 Major / Nzeogwu's eyes Chukwuma Kaduna Nzeogwu (1937-1967), leader of the failed 1966 military coup against the Nigerian First Republic, who achieved – after a period of imprisonment and after the Biafran secession – the rank of Biafran Lieutenant Colonel. Nzeogwu was killed on 29 July 1967 by federal troops while conducting a night reconnaissance (without appropriate support); sometime between the discovery and identification of his body and burial, his corpse was mutilated (by whom it is not known) and his eyes gouged out. A photograph of Nzeogwu's corpse is displayed at the National Archives at Kaduna.

50. The imaginative site of this stanza remains the airport (see stanza 49), though this is only made explicit in the final lines. Although this stanza begins with the *vieillard*'s resignation to being out of touch with the times, of living in the past, it quickly becomes a call to "ACTION", of the need to "restart" old "battles", even if it "kills" him. The link between this and stanza 49 is the sense of going through Customs (or airport security); but now (like Her Majesty on his coins) he is much older, and treated with scant respect. As Hill 're-jigs' the coins in his pocket to the 'heads up' ("ageing right profile") position, he wonders if having called attention to HM's ageing will earn him "censure". Meanwhile, the *vieillard* is herded around the terminal to the air gate ("go to the door"), where (once aboard the plane) the hostesses ("threshold / angels") will bring food and drink ("gifts"). But Hill imagines himself as missing his meal: like the 'waiter' or 'vigilant' who falls asleep at the crucial moment (as in W. B. Yeats's 'At the Hawk's Well'), the moment of the miracle for which he has been waiting, Hill the *vieillard* is slumbering when the hostess passes.

50.1 Old men to their own battles Cf. Eliot in 'East Coker': "Old men ought to be explorers".

50.2 advisement For "self-advisement", see stanza 6.

50.3 ACTION THIS DAY The phrase 'Action this day' has become emblematic of Churchill's strong wartime leadership and can-do attitude: when Bletchley Park codebreakers (see stanza 7) wrote to him complaining of insufficient staff due to budget constraints, Churchill minuted his Chief of Staff: "ACTION THIS DAY Make sure they have all they want on extreme priority and report to me that this has been done" (*The Essential Turing*, p. 336).

50.4 about time Here, the phrase is used in the demotic sense of 'overdue'. But see also stanza 15.

50.5 armatured The armature is the moving part in an electro-magnetic device, wound with coils that carry a current; here, the airport metal detector.

50.6 Even if it kills me A demotic phrase meaning 'irrespective of the consequences to myself'. Hill must "Carry this through" (i.e., complete the poem) at all costs. But he is also entering the killing fields (see stanza 49).

50.7 Empty your pockets for the cage The image is that of a traveller passing through customs and required to empty his pockets before being screened by metal detectors. The sense of the prison cell is also implied, with prisoners being stripped of all personal effects before being confined.

50.8 Re-jig / HM's ageing right profile on sterling / zinc of the realm Since 1998, the Royal Mint has issued coins to the United Kingdom and Commonwealth bearing the Ian Rank-Broadley effigy of Elizabeth II; on it, the sovereign is notably aged as compared with the previous issue (1984). Here, the

ANNOTATIONS

sense is of the silver coinage debased to nickel and zinc; 'sterling silver', however, is still the cliché.

50.9 Vieillard French, 'old man'; specifically, as a figure from the poetry of Baudelaire (cf. 'Les Sept Vieillards'); here, the old man is rudely told to pass through the check-point.

50.10 threshold-angels Literally, those who will soon conduct his soul to the next world; more prosaically, the flight attendants (bearing gifts); even more despondently, the sense of having slept through life and of not having made use of his gifts.

51. In a ghastly *tour de force* of imaginative extravagance, Hill in this stanza expatiates upon the experience of undergoing a rectal examination. The patient experiences grief, agony, pain – some of the "wording" of the *Book of Common Prayer*, but made "INORDINATE" and (like the patient's rectum) "dilated". The procedure is inflicted upon the body (is an "Outrage" to it), and invites "SORROW"; the "hulks moving in convoy" are both the various incarnations of human suffering in procession, and the proctologist's endoscope. The use of "hulks" leads Hill to develop a conceit: the surgical steel tools of the proctologist are as naval missiles; the doctor is now a destroyer heading into battle, sending out an endoscope as a torpedo (the vernacular 'steel eel', now a "tin fish"). Without an enema (*"de rigueur"*), there might be "mud" in the proctologist's eye (no "glycol" on his goggles, nor on the endoscope camera). The doctor announces the beginning of the procedure ("Nów he expatiates"); Hill takes a moment to reflect (with an appalling pun on "POSTERITY") on the "daring" of this stanza. Although some readers may dismiss it as a "Waste of effort" (and "write this off"), Hill does not believe it to be such, and nor will those who read it sympathetically ("it shall not be read so").

51.1 Common Prayer The *Book of Common Prayer* contains the order (and so is an *ordinal*) to be followed in Church of England services. What follows is inordinate; the ordinal is out of order.

51.2 dilated In the literary sense, discoursed on or written about at large; but of an eye (and hence an anus), the sense of the pupil as enlarged.

51.3 SORROW Here used as if the name of a ship. Cf. "Lusitanian / sorrow" in stanza 41.

51.4 hulks A ship that is afloat but unseaworthy; an abandoned wreck, often used as a prison ship.
51.5 Destroyers Fast and manoeuvrable warships that escort larger vessels in a convoy.
51.6 boomerangs Curved flat wooden missiles of native Australians, which can return to the thrower; actions or statements that recoil on the originator, that backfire. Here, the image is of destroyers destroying themselves as their torpedoes 'boomerang' back, a fate famously endured by the USS *Tang* in 1944 off the coast of Taiwan when it failed to clear the turning circle of its own torpedo.
51.7 tin fish Navy slang for torpedo; hence the transition from "tin fish" to 'steel eel'.
51.8 Enemas Used loosely to suggest suppositories, torpedo-shaped preparations inserted into the rectum; the "third eye" (see 51.10) is thus that of the camera at the end of the endoscope.
51.9 *de rigueur* Required by current fashion or etiquette; here, before a rectal examination.
51.10 third eye In both Eastern and Western spiritual traditions (and especially New Age), the third eye is the gate that leads to inner realms and places of higher consciousness. However, a proctologist is a medical practitioner concerned with the anus and rectum.
51.11 glycol The common name for ethylene glycol, the clear syrupy liquid which, due to its low freezing point, is used as a de-icing fluid for windshields. Cf. the toast, popular during WWII, 'Here's mud in your eye'.
51.12 windshield 'Windshield' is the North American term for the British 'windscreen'; here, the windshield is the doctor's protective eyewear, and the "steel eel" of the proctologist, which serves (in an absurd conceit) to protect him from the patient's wind.
51.13 Nów he expatiates The stress on "Nów" suggests the idiomatic '*Now* he tells us', but in this context suggests the moment of rectal insertion.
51.14 POSTERITY | how daring! What is "daring" is the etymological pun on 'posterity' and that area of concern to the proctologist, the 'posterior'.
51.15 I do not / so understand it Jeremy Noel-Tod identifies the "terse imperative suggested by the enjambment" ('Curious and Furious', p. R.16).

ANNOTATIONS

51.16 Yoú may / write this off Meaning a) dismiss from consideration as a hopeless failure; b) write of it as being in poor taste, unacceptable; or c) include as an expense account or insurance claim.
51.17 it shall not be read so That is to say, this stanza (and perhaps the entire poem) shall not be a) read as trivial; nor b) considered by the discerning to be in bad taste.

52. At the centre of this stanza – typographically and thematically – is Psalm 90, specifically as put to music by Charles Ives. In it, God is eternal, unchanging, beyond the physical; here in the poem, the body (with its 'strange workings') has its own temporality, and is attuned to its own age ("knows / its ówn tíme"). It also knows its time to cease: "after all", Hill was himself sixty-eight when writing: "near enough" to the Biblical lifespan of 'threescore years and ten'. The image is that of an ancient damson tree, at the gable's end, which can be seen by anyone leaving (the house or yard). Then, but only then, it becomes an image of the old man, one more or less ready to 'depart' (as in the *Nunc dimittus*, or Eliot's 'Song for Simeon'). At the centre – physically and thematically – of this stanza is an attestation to the constancy of God and the Church: "FROM ÓNE / GENERÁTION TO ANÓTHER". The source of these words (Ives's *Psalm 90*) leads Hill to move from the landscape of the damson to images of dance and rhythm: the musical instruction, "*lento*", dignifies the sense of slow deliberation, and the acceptance of one's place in the pattern ("bow and return"). The Ives piece, "grief's thánksgiving", functions as a catalyst for reconciliation: "found late" by the poet and by its composer, it balances the temporal and the eternal, and renews time as time: the poet, in old age, experiences a "renewed" and heightened appreciation of the rhythms of his time.
52.1 seventy years near enough Born in 1932, Hill was sixty-eight years old when this poem was published, so "near enough" to the Biblical lifespan: "The days of our years are threescore years and ten; and if by reason of strength they be fourscore years, yet is their strength labour and sorrow; for it is soon cut off, and we fly away" (Psalm 90:10).
52.2 damson tree Originally the 'plum of Damascus' or 'damascene plum', later contracted to 'damson'.

131

52.3 stands in the sight of him departing In this image, the tree and the poet (approximately the same age) share characteristics: weathered and damaged ("resin-knurled") and bent with age ("crookt"). Resin-knurled suggests a particular image: the lumps of resin which form over a tree's broken or severed branches, and are a sign of age. There are echoes here of the *Nunc dimittus* (The Song of Simeon) in Luke 2:29-32 and of Eliot's 'A Song for Simeon': "Let thy servant depart / Having seen thy salvation".

52.4 LŎRD | / THOÚ HAST BEEN OUR DWELLING PLÁCE From Psalm 90:1-2: "Lord, thou hast been our dwelling place in all generations. Before the mountains were brought forth, or ever thou hadst found the earth and the world, even from everlasting to everlasting, thou art God"; the words are presented as in the score of Charles Ives's *Psalm 90* (see line 9).

52.5 *lento* A musical direction, indicating that the previous sentence is to be 'played' slowly, as is the music which accompanies the words in Ives's *Psalm 90*.

52.6 out of step As in a dance, recalling the "daunsinge" in Eliot's 'East Coker' for its sense of "Keeping time ... The time of the seasons and the constellations / The time of the milking and the time of harvest / The time of the coupling of man and woman / And that of beasts. / Feet rising and falling. Eating and drinking. Dung and death".

52.7 boy and return As a dancer (to his partner) at the start and end of a dance, or a stage performer for an encore.

52.8 Charles Ives's /*Ninetieth Psalm* Charles Edward Ives (1874-1954), American composer and organist, was an insurance agent until the "late" age of 56, his music fully appreciated only after his death, and perhaps by Hill only "late" in his own life. "*Ninetieth Psalm*" is Ives's *Psalm 90 for Chorus, Organ and Bells* (1924), completed only three years before Ives abandoned composing.

52.9 bell arpeggios The notes of a chord played in succession, either ascending of descending, in Ives's *Ninetieth Psalm* by bells. Cf. Eliot's 'Burnt Norton' IV: "Time and the bell have buried the day". These lines testify to both Ives's and Eliot's sense of life renewed in time.

52.10 páces Both a) measures; and b) sets the speed, as a metronome.

ANNOTATIONS

53. The key image of this stanza is that of Bill Clinton's affair with Monica Lewinsky; from the first line ("Fine figure of a man") to the last (with Clinton starring as a greasy John Travolta) *Herr Präsident* is present. The imperative "say it" punctuates (no less than five times) successive clichés ("Fine figure of a man", "Try thís for size", "why are we waiting"); as Clinton prepares for his next sexual climax ("Get stuck in", "Hurdy-gurdy the starter / handle"), Lewinsky's menstrual cycle is also considered ("monthlies"). The President narrowly escaped impeachment because of the Lewinsky scandal, a crisis "Too close / for comfort"; and Hill critiques the "show" of repentance made ("lubricant and brimstone") as a rather smug Clinton avoids being called to account. The phrase "wipe yo' smile", with a suitably Arkansas twang, has connotations of the oral sexual encounters at the centre of the affair. The President, who should have been concerned with "COMPETITIVE DEVALUATION", has devalued the presidency itself – the "great find" of democratic Union (as well as the promise of Clinton's regime) was "wasted", as the scandal assumed the role of public entertainment. Clinton became little more than a playboy bad-boy heartthrob to the public: Hill imagines him first as James Bond ("licence to silence"), then Tarzan, and finally (and with the least dignity) as John Travolta riding on the carousel in the closing scene of the film *Grease*. The presidency has been devalued to the status of sleazy schmaltz.

53.1 why are we waiting? As sung to the tune of 'O Come All Ye Faithful' by frustrated British audiences or queues, or passengers on a bus.

53.2 Hurdy-gurdy To turn an engine with a "starter / handle", as a barrel organ, or a vintage car.

53.3 backfire An explosion within an engine.

53.4 Call monthlies / double-strength stale *fleurs du mal* The "monthlies" (journals, newspapers), like a heavy menstrual cycle, are "stale"; here, the sense of *ennui* suggests Baudelaire's *Les Fleurs du mal* [Flowers of Evil], first published in 1857, and revised in 1861, a volume of verse focusing on decadence, boredom and eroticism.

53.5 Too close / for comfort So dangerously close as to be unsettling; here with reference to Bill Clinton ("*Herr Präsident*") and the Lewinsky affair, specifically his narrow escape from prosecution for perjury (see 53.7).

53.6 lubricant and brimstone A corruption of the familiar 'fire and brimstone' found throughout the Bible, notably in Psalms 11:6: "Upon the wicked he shall rain snared, fire and brimstone, and an horrible tempest: this shall be the portion of their cup". Here, the substitution of "lubricant" for 'fire' provides the link to President Clinton. Cf. "Watch my lips" in stanza 55.

53.7 wipe yo' smile A reference to the scandal (1998) in which then President Bill Clinton was almost impeached for lying under oath about the nature of his relationship with White House intern, Monica Lewinsky; the phrase "wipe yo' smile" mocks Clinton's Arkansas accent.

53.8 COMPETITIVE DEVALUATION The devaluation of a currency to make a country's goods more competitive on the international market.

53.9 a great find An excellent discovery; cf. *"Ben trovato"* in stanza 76.

53.10 pleasantries of intermission The image is that of the bourgeois crowd socializing during a break in performance, but given the weeping of line 6, there is an echo of Lamentations 3:9: "Mine eye trickleth down, and ceaseth not, without any intermission".

53.11 licence to silence The echo (almost anagrammatical) is of Ian Fleming's Bond title *Licence to Kill*; here, it completes the oxymoronic imperative: 'voice your right to silence'.

53.12 me / Tarzan, you | diva of multiple choice A corruption of, 'Me Tarzan, you Jane', an off-set quip from Johnny Weissmuller, star of the 1932 MGM film *Tarzan of the Apes*; Weissmuller claimed that his original utterance was simply "Tarzan. Jane." (Johnny Weissmuller, Jr., W. Craig Reed, *Tarzan, My Father*, p. 58). The phrase is emblematic of masculine strength coming to the aid of helpless femininity; here there is no defenceless Jane, but a "diva of multiple choice", a woman who has become a public spectacle.

53.13 arousal-cárrousel In the final scene of the 1978 film *Grease*, John Travolta (who later starred as the Clinton-figure 'Stanton' in the 1998 film *Primary Colors*) and Olivia Newton John sit astride carousel horses while singing 'You're the One That I Want'. Hill's preference for the French spelling (*carrousel*, rather than *carousel*) is unclear.

ANNOTATIONS

54. The reiterated "say it" of the previous stanza becomes the rhetorical "Take it". This stanza begins with the imperative "Take", used to introduce examples which support an argument, but also with the milder sense of 'accept'. The pervasive nature of God (His "plenary immanence") is not transcendent but "eternal"; though, like summer, it may seem to pass, its season always returns. One must 'take' the temporal to be eternal, despite its presentation as temporal. Likewise, "you" – the reader, humanity at large – are evidence of our mysterious beginnings ("obscure / origin"), of the "clairvoyance" of God, of his "giving". The words of Prospero thus affirm our curious equivocation as both material and spiritual beings. And "by / these words", Hill (like Dante) can sense and affirm the ebb and flow of time (see stanza 52), the "cycles of the unstable"; the gifts intermittently spurned and recovered. The sins – inherent in our obscure and sinful origin – are too numerous to be "counted"; and counting is futile. And yet for all the theological argument it is the natural world – the daisy that opens for the sun and closes without it, the ancient aster, the exotic sumac – which "swáys / argument across the line" of the poem. "Contemplation" of these things – these natural things – is where 'love' lives (its "estate", its flower garden). So convincing is the natural world as evidence of the "immanence" of God that it may serve as proof rather than evidence, leaving no space or need for "argument". Even so, Hill's final credo ("OH I BELIEVE YOU") is not unequivocal; rather, it is both sceptical and fervently longed for.

54.1 plenary immanence "immanence" is used in its theological sense of the permanent and sustaining presence of God, here "plenary" because entire and unqualified. Cf. 'plenary indulgence', in Roman Catholicism, the complete remission of temporal punishment.

54.2 passing hence of summer Cf. the song 'Thou'rt Passing Hence, My Brother', by Arthur Sullivan with words by Felicia Hemans: "Thou'rt passing hence, my brother! / Oh! My earliest friend, farewell! / Thou'rt leaving me, without thy voice, / In a lonely home to dwell." See also Edgar in *King Lear*: "Men must endure / their going hence, even as their coming hither; / Ripeness is all"; and Joyce's *Finnegans Wake*: "thou art passing hence, mine bruder, able Shaun" (p. 427).

54.3 clairvoyance The supposed ability to see things beyond the range of human vision. God too, then, must have clairvoyant capabilities.
54.4 *Mein / Ariel, hast du, der Luft, nur ist...* Hill's German [Hast thou, which art but air, a feeling...] is identical to the title of an aria from the third act of the Frank Martin (1890-1974) three-act opera, *Der Sturm*, with libretto from Wilhelm Schlegel's German translation of Shakespeare's *The Tempest*; Hill's choice of the Martin aria title identifies the reference as being to *Der Sturm* the opera as opposed to Schlegel's translation. In 1996 the London Philharmonic recorded a suite from *Der Sturm* (including this piece) along with two other Martin works: the *Maria-Triptychon* and *Sechs Monologe aus Jedermann* (see stanza 83). See also stanzas 65, 79, 91 and 115.
54.5 And by / these words From the 'Paradiso' of Dante's *Divine Comedy*: "And by these words, if thou hast gathered them / As thou shouldst do, the argument is refuted / That would have still annoyed thee many times" (from Canto IV, here in the Longfellow translation [pp. 24-25], though others include the same words).
54.6 cycles of the unstable Cf. "Manic / depressive" in stanza 58; the sense of psychological disorder is emphasised by "recovered" in line 6.
54.7 Contemplation Devout meditation, here identified as the home and property of love, its garden filled with the plants of the following note.
54.8 wild aster [...] goldrenrod [...] sumac The plants are of a European landscape: *aster*, the showy plant whose daisy's eyes open with the day's eyes; *goldenrod* with its petite yellow flowers; and the *sumac* shrub, known for its use as a dye and as a poison.
54.9 OH I BELIEVE YOU Cf. "I sáid I believe you" in stanza 55.

55. The controlling metaphor of this stanza is that of Sade's *120 Days of Sodom*, which serves as an analogue to *Speech! Speech!* Hill's conceit is that of readers reading his poem for titillation ("You turn me on"; "THE LENGTH OF THE THING"), and the sense of authorial condescension, with Hill self-styling as a kind of Marie Antoinette (see "You can eat cake" in stanza 56), crying "Let them imagine...". What follows are a few well-wrought, clichéd sentiments from one on a trip ("Í am in the pink. Wish you were here. / In Abraham's tent and bosom. DID

ANNOTATIONS

YOU EVER...?"), and then a return to seriousness: "I saíd I believe you ÁND here I háve you"; the poet asserts his authority "Among the ellipses" on the page. Hill's suggestion is that the touch of eroticism may have attracted the attention of his audience, but he, like a president threatened with impeachment for sexual impropriety (Clinton's *120 Days*) or dishonesty (Bush's "Watch my lips") must now deliver. The stanza closes with an uncertainty which seems a manifestation of the untrustworthiness of its subjects: this very stanza, attests Hill, lacks fluency ("more end-stopped than usual"); the question "WHY?" remains unanswered.

55.1 As many as the days that were | of SODOM The Marquis de Sade's 1785 novel, *Les 120 journées du Sodome ou l'école du libertinage* [The 120 Days of Sodom, or the School of Licentiousness]. Hill may refer to Sade to suggest our own world is similarly depraved, or, as Johnson suggests, merely to determine "THE LENGTH OF THE THING" (note the sexual innuendo): "to help himself establish an (invented) end point for his own work" (*Why Write Poetry?*, p. 265).

55.2 You turn me on Meaning a) as a radio or television; b) make me sexually aroused; and c) to use recreational drugs (1960s). Cf. "did I turn / myself on?" in *The Orchards of Syon* (XXXI).

55.3 Hoick To spit phlegm, or lift out with a sudden yank; David Yezzi mistakenly identifies "Hoick" ('yoicks!' is correct) as "a call to incite hunting dogs" ('Geoffrey Hill's Civil Tongue', p. 22).

55.4 signal blessing Here, "signal" functions both as a broadcast signal "sent but not received", and as an indication of the seriousness of the "blessing" broadcast.

55.5 Í am in the pink 'In the pink', now meaning 'in rude good health', has its origins in eighteenth-century fox-hunting culture, when Thomas Pink was the aristocracy's preferred maker of red hunting jackets – to be stylishly turned out in one of these was to be 'in the pink' (*Frommer's London 2010*, p. 342).

55.6 Wish you were here The stereotypical postcard sent home by one on holiday.

55.7 In Abraham's tent and bosom Luke 16:22-23: "And it came to pass, that the beggar died, and was carried by the angels into Abraham's bosom: the rich man also died, and was buried; / And in hell he lift up his eyes, being in torments, and seeth Abraham afar off, and Lazarus in his bosom." In the Old

Testament, Abraham is the first of the patriarchs, the father of Isaac and founder of the Hebrew people (Genesis 11-25); thus, to be in his 'tent' is to be one of the chosen on earth; likewise, in death, the just repose in Abraham's 'bosom' in heaven (see Luke 16:22). See also stanza 14 for Abraham weeping for the mothers of his children.

55.8 DID YOU EVER...? Cf. "Were you ever!" in stanza 59.

55.9 ellipses The set of dots (...), indicating an ellipsis, here likened to salt grains on the page. Note the alliterative connection of "ellipses" to *"Tristis lupus"* and "lips".

55.10 *Tristis lupus* 'Sad wolf', from C.S. Calverley's translation of Milton's 'Lycidas' into Latin, as published in his *Translations into English and Latin* (1866). Milton's "Besides what the grim Woolf with privy paw / Daily devours apace, and nothing sed" becomes Calverley's "Expleat ingluviem tristis lupus, indice nullo?" (*Translations into English and Latin*, p.199).

55.11 impeachment The 'impeachment' of Charles I, Milton being of the Parliamentary persuasion. See stanza 53 for the proposed impeachment of US President Bill Clinton.

55.12 Watch my lips 'Read my lips. No new taxes' was the promise made by US presidential candidate George Bush, Sr., to America; in 1991, as President, he introduced a raft of new taxes.

55.13 end-stopped In verse, without enjambment, with a distinct pause at the end of each line; as in all but two (lines 4 and 10) lines of this stanza.

56.
This stanza returns to the Western Front of World War I: the (unique) "Flanders poppy" (using the scientific phrase "no trial variant" to mean 'the real thing'), gas attacks and decaying bodies ("bad breath"); an anonymous Belgian known as "YPRES MASTER"; the gendered male and female "MARK IV tanks"; old songs of war now sung again (*"Marlbrough s'en va-t-en"*), the soldiers freezing in trenches ("frozen mud wrestlers"). Following these images, Hill offers bad jokes (gendered tanks, "superflux", "LIGHT RELIEF") as a way of coping with "grief of no known cause", and asks that we "excuse" him for them. In Hill's 'great battle', the poem (like the phoney war of 1914-1915) might seem superfluous, but just as the war, supposed to be over by Christmas, ultimately cost the "best part" of a generation, so does this effort (Hill is aware of the incongruity of the comparison) reflect "unnatural / wear and tear". The war

ANNOTATIONS

itself was no joke: the 'Beef of Old England' in every sense went off; the rabble-rousing myth of England could no longer sustain the very real deaths of very real men for whom eating cake was no more a solution than it was in Marie Antoinette's France. A pitiful joke closes the stanza: the Yeomanry are Beefeaters, and Hill's deliberately pathetic, "HORSEPLAY FAILS AS LIGHT RELIEF" (uttered in the style of a telegram, or a snippet or war correspondence from the Front) acknowledges the danger of the poem being seen not as the work of a Ypres Master but rather as a "superflux", no more than the jesting of a 'bit player'.

56.1 Flanders poppy Cf. "In Flanders field the poppies grow", the opening line of the elegiac 'In Flanders Fields' (1915) by Canadian poet John McCrae.

56.2 unknown YPRES MASTER Ypres is a town in Flanders near the border with France: the scene of many sieges and battles in WWI, when it was completely destroyed. The phrase combines 'unknown soldier' with the trope (in painting) of 'the *x* master' (an anonymous artist).

56.3 MARK IV tanks, rostered by sex Mark IV tanks were armoured vehicles (produced in 1917 and 1918) categorized by gender, the 'males' having four Lewis machine guns and two Sponson guns, while the 'females' had six machine guns and no Sponsons.

56.4 *Marlbrough s'en va-t-en* 'Marlb[o]rough s'en va-t-en Guerre', French folk song (to tune of 'For He's a Jolly Good Fellow') written in satirical honour of John Churchill, First Duke of Marlborough (1650-1722), and sung to Louis XVII, son of Marie Antoinette and Louis XVI (see 56.12). Longfellow's English adaptation is here imagined: "Marlbrook the Prince of Commanders / Is gone to war in Flanders, / His fame is like Alexander's, / But when will he ever come home? / Mironton, mironton, mirontaine" (*Stories of Famous Songs*, pp. 15-16.)

56.5 Jocks Scots troops who, with their ANZAC and Canadian counterparts, fought at Passchendaele. The mud wrestlers are the soldiers, frozen by the extreme cold, an object of amusement to the newly arrived Scots.

56.6 Arrest yourself A literal translation of the French '*arrêtez-vous*' (meaning 'stop'; here an instruction to himself, as poet, to stop making bad jests); the image is of rustic Flanders recruits struggling to make sense of the French officers' orders.

56.7 grief of no known cause Many WWI soldiers suffered from pyrexia of unknown origin ('PUO', or 'trench fever').

56.8 superflux "superflux": a) superfluity, too many; b) irrelevant, as his jests and poetry might be; c) a rush of diarrhoea or bodily fluxions; and d) an unexpected hint of tears.
56.9 best part "best part": as in the sense of the 'best part' of a generation destroyed.
56.10 finished by Christmas Refers to the promise, and generally held belief, that WWI troops would be home in time for Christmas 1914; in reality, many troops were not demobilized until the 1920s.
56.11 Beef of Old England's off *Roast Beef of Old England*, melody Richard Leveridge (1735): "When mighty Roast Beef / Was the Englishman's food, / It ennobled our brains / and enriched our blood. / Our soldiers were brave / and our courtiers were good / Oh the Roast Beef of old England / and old English Roast Beef" (*England's Elizabeth*, p. 119). Here, Old England's beef is "off", withdrawn from a menu or gone bad.
56.12 You can eat cake Cf. Marie Antoinette's famous – and perhaps apocryphal – reply upon hearing that the poor people of France had no bread: "Let them eat cake."
56.13 YEOMANRY English commoners who cultivated their own land, and a British cavalry force that formed a home guard from 1761 until 1907, when it became part of the Territorial Army.

57. The logic of this stanza is the progression from obscurity to abundance, and to redemption; it begins with a confidential, almost conspiratorial phrase: "Shów you something" (as in, *let me* show you something). What Hill 'shows' is the way in which the sparseness of Shakespeare's late plays – his "elliptical" syntax – serves not to inhibit understanding, but rather to give clarity ("clear the occlusions") and to invite a sense of close attention to language ("cálls us to account"). The ellipsis may suggest sparseness, austerity; on the contrary, it is "abundance", and from this abundance – the plenitude of clarity – we can "understand redemption" (the first-person pronoun – notably absent in lines one and six – is here complicit). We are then invited to imagine *The Winter's Tale* – romance but also tragicomedy, in which both Leontes and the Clown have a place. But today, when an admixture of comedy and tragedy is no longer viable, "our / clowns" are nowhere to be found. Will, asks Hill, the absurdity of our age be discernable from photographs? Will they "reveal all" aspects of the age? The photograph may not be the accurate static description history demands; we may be caught "mid- / gesture" – the image is one of humourless pomp, a mock-senatorial tone introducing the highfaluting "noble CARITAS" and "proud AMOR". But "all" is miraculous – common and uncommon, Leontes and the Clown – all occupy the same festive (winter, and *The Winter's Tale*) landscape of "mistletoe" and nested "boughs". We must revise our understanding from a bleak to a beautiful landscape (see stanza 63). And we can "hope" for even more than this, something even more abundant and redemptive than this abundant and redemptive landscape, for which *The Winter's Tale* acts as emblem (see stanza 61).

57.1 occlusions Obscurities and unknowns, with particular reference to the misunderstandings within the plot of *The Winter's Tale*, as well as the sixteen-year gap between Acts III and IV.

57.2 abundance Shakespeare's plays are themselves examples of "abundance", in their superfluity of number, of character, of ages, of language, of settings and scenery. Brian Gibbons notes that "abundance is a great strength in Shakespeare's plays ... they are designed deliberately to expand the mind – to generate a sense of concentrated vigorous life in emotions and ideas" (*Shakespeare and Multiplicity*, p. 1). Cf. *The Triumph of Love*, in which Hill uses the rhetorical term *copia* to refer to the 'abundance' of the Renaissance humanists: "Wealth – *copia* – was required / to buy moderation" (CXVI).

57.3 Whó – where – are our / clowns Cf. 'Send in the Clowns' from the Stephen Sondheim musical *A Little Night Music* (1973): "But where are the clowns / Send in the clowns".

57.4 WET 'N' DRY [...] photographs The image is of photographs produced in a darkroom, removed from the developing tank ("WET") and pinned up to dry. There is a suggestion of the off-colour joke about Shakespeare plays, which designates them as either 'wet' (*Midsummer Night's Dream*, for instance) or 'dry' (*Twelfth Night*). The "clowns" here are those agents of "redemption", in particular the shepherd's son Antolycus (also called 'Clown') of *The Winter's Tale*, whose act of charity (see line 7) saves Leontes's abandoned baby and so allows for the King's recension (see line 11) and redemption (see line 4).

57.5 CARITAS Charity, here addressed – like "AMOR" (love, and a reverse Eternal City) in the next line – as if a character in a Shakespeare play, and in a mock-senatorial style. The words have resonance for *The Winter's Tale*: "proud AMOR" made Leontes suspect his wife, and "noble CARITAS" led to the rescue of his daughter. See Hill's 'Funeral Music' (from *King Log*): "We are dying / to satisfy fat caritas" (II). Cf. the similarly capitalized, nominal "VERITAS" in stanza 43.

57.6 uncommon thoughts 'Common thoughts' would mean 'shared advice'; "uncommon thoughts" therefore suggests personal, individual opinion.

57.7 mistletoe An evergreen shrub with Christmas associations; here, Spanish Moss, a parasitical variety which is 'grafted' to its host tree, and is particularly conspicuous during the winter.

57.8 recensions The revisions of a text, especially those completed with great attention to detail; here, with specific reference to *The Winter's Tale*, in which charity – charitable recensions – allow reconciliation.

58. The final line of the previous stanza is here repeated as the first of this, but with a different intonation. Hill can read without tears ("dry-eyed") Cowper's famous tale of 'The Castaway'. Matter of factly and uncompassionately summed up, Cowper was a "Manic / depressive" who "wrote about hares". "PERFORCE" *was* Cowper's word in 'The Castaway'; he uses it to intensify the word 'pitiless'. The opening refrain is repeated, but now, after a colon, comes the assertion that Hill's word is his bond, his assurance as good as his action ("surety, my entail"). His word is exhibited, proffered, by the twelve lines of each stanza of the poem, twelve distinct pushes, efforts ("Twelve press-ups"), the "heaviness / increased" as the effort required intensifies. The poem is a show of strength, the self-made man's display of both *tour de force* and invincibility. The voice of the self-made man takes prominence as an aside is made: "the mad are predators" (a self-conscious allusion to the *Mercian Hymns*, VIII), feeding as they do on the mental health of those around them, and all the while threatening to kill; for this man – perhaps Hill, perhaps an aspect of Hill, perhaps a modern maker of self – ignoring any cry of pity ("CHILD / OVERBOARD"), the "self-righting hull shears on"; the course is not altered for the sake of human loss and suffering.

58.1 Better | than that I should hópe Reiterated in line 7, meaning a) I should hope for something better than this; b) it is better to have something besides hope; and c) rather than

ANNOTATIONS

simply hoping, assign me to work with some kind of destiny, which I can yet perceive as free will. Cf. Eliot's 'Ash-Wednesday': "Because I do not hope to turn again / Because I do not hope / Because I do not hope to turn".

58.2 assign me / to bond Both "assign" and "bond" (see line 8) have legal meanings: the former is the transfer of rights and liabilities, the latter the deed by which one commits to pay another.

58.3 C. Brontë cleared it with a word – / Olney's own castaway *en famille*. Charlotte Brontë (1816-1855), the eldest of the three Brontë sister novelists, best known for *Jane Eyre* (1847) and for *Shirley* (1849). 'The Castaway' is a poem by William Cowper (1731-1800), author (with John Newton) of the *Olney Hymns* (1779). Cowper lived (first at Huntingdon and later at Olney, Milton Keynes) with clergyman Morley Unwin and his wife Mary; after Unwin's death, Cowper remained living "*en famille*" with the widow. Cf. Charlotte Brontë's *Shirley:* "Cowper's hand did not tremble in writing the lines; why should my voice falter in repeating them? Depend on it, Shirley, no tear blistered the manuscript of The Castaway, I hear in it no sob of sorrow, only the cry of despair; but, that cry uttered, I believe the deadly spasm passed from his heart; that he wept abundantly and was comforted" (p. 191).

58.4 Manic / depressive Also known as 'bipolar disorder', manic depression is typified by alternate episodes of mania and depression. Cowper oscillated between bouts of zealous evangelism and believing himself rejected by God, damned. Cf. "cycles of the unstable" in stanza 54.

58.5 wrote about hares Cowper cared for hares and wrote about them in prose, in his letters, and in two poems: the Latin 'Epitaphium Alterum' and 'Epitaph on a Hare'.

58.6 PERFORCE Cf. 'The Castaway', stanza 4: "He shouted: nor his friends had fail'd / To check the vessel's course, / But so the furious blast prevail'd, / That, pitiless perforce, / They left their outcast mate behind, / And scudded still before the wind."

58.7 my / word is my bond In his essay, 'Our Word is Our Bond', Hill cites the origins of this motto: "According to its official webpage, in 1923 the London Stock Exchange received 'its own Coat of Arms, with the motto "Dictum Meum Pactum" (My Word is My Bond)' (*Collected Critical Writings*, p. 623).

58.8 press-ups The British term for what North Americans call 'push-ups'); here, like the twelve lines of each stanza, each an arduous task.

58.9 the mad are predators From Hill's *Mercian Hymns*, VIII: "The mad are predators. Too often lately they harbour against us."

58.10 Cry CHILD / OVERBOARD The expected is 'man overboard'; "CHILD / OVERBOARD" adds pathos. Demotically and metaphorically, to 'go overboard' is to overwork, as a cliché (an overworked idiom).

58.11 the self-righting hull shears on The conceit is of Cowper's ship sailing on despite the alarm having sounded that a child is lost overboard. The craft is both merciless and unsinkable ("self-righting"); the poet's craft (hull, 'Hill') self-righteously "shears on".

59.
It is a ruthless world: the ship sails on despite a child overboard, and everyone is "a self-trafficker", dealing in the nasty and illicit parts of themselves, profiting from their own wrong-doing, their own graspingness. We deserve what we get and invite our own punishment; our greedy, avaricious prayers mean that we solicit penitence and then cannot comprehend the penance: "I asked / for stone and so received a toad". Jean Ward notes that the poet is "perhaps suggesting that the point at issue is not the willingness of God to give, but the human inability in the contemporary world to ask for the right things" (*Christian Poetry in the Post-Christian Day*, pp. 89-90). Hill then moves away from avaricious self-traffickers to a remembered/imagined night-time return "trip" to England: the "low-slung", low-lying jets of the hovercraft disturb the surface water of the lit sea-gate. The blackness of the night is not to be mistaken for the blankness of the landscape – indeed it would be dangerous to do so – the true blankness of England is to be found in her Poets Laureate, tedious, "blank-faced", a mere list of names. They make "atrocious static", the sound of "England, My Country", a sound which has ruined Hill's past visits home. England is now theirs, but is claimed by Hill as his: "*Mine*, I say, *mine*": never mind the banality of "Skinflint's last onion", the humours of everyday life which occupy the new poets. Who owns England? Who has owned England? What is England? Was it ever England? And in what sense ("NOW" or "THEN") can he claim it as his (or, as in the next stanza, sign for England)?

ANNOTATIONS

59.1 self-trafficker Literally, one who smuggles himself into a country. The expected words are 'people (or 'drug') trafficker', and so the illicit is implied.

59.2 I asked / for stone and so received a toad Cf. Matthew 7:7-12: "Ask, and it shall be given you; seek, and you shall find; knock, and it shall be opened unto you: / For everyone that asketh receiveth; and he that seeketh findeth; and to him that knocketh it shall be opened. / Or what man is there of you, whom if his son ask bread, will he give him a stone? / Or if he ask a fish, will he give him a serpent? / If ye then, being evil, know how to give good gifts unto your children, how much more shall your Father which is in heaven give good things to them that ask him?"

59.3 low-slung jets blizzard the surface-water The image is of a hovercraft skimming the water, its "low-slung jets" making a blizzard of the water above which they sit.

59.4 jockey To manipulate in a skilful manner, here as a pilot.

59.5 sea-gate The sea-gate is the place of access to the sea; with "gate" and "air-gate", it serves to emphasise the land, air and sea capabilities of the hovercraft.

59.6 The Laureates / process blank-faced for you to name them Poets Laureate, versifiers appointed to the royal household, here as if in procession. The image is of one looking blank when asked to name the Poets Laureate, there being so many poetasters among their number.

59.7 England My Country Cf. Philip James Bailey's *Festus* (1939): "England! My country, great and free! / Heart of the world, I leap to thee!" (*A Complete Dictionary of Poetical Quotations*, p. 152).

59.8 Skinflint's last onion A skinflint is a miser, one who might consume onions for their cheapness. There may be a reference to Dostoyevsky's 'parable of the onion' as told by Grushenka in *The Brothers Karamazov*; the parable tells the tale of a horrible old woman whose only good deed in life was to give an onion to a beggar. Hill may also be making an appalling 'joke' of having eaten one too many French onions, and so belching and jocularly claiming responsibility ("*Mine*" and then "*mine*" again...).

59.10 Were you ever! Cf. "DID YOU EVER" in stanza 55; the phrase is followed by the mock-astonishment of the colloquial "NOW THEN!". Cf. 'Little Gidding' I: "But this is the nearest, in place and time, / Now and in England"; and V: "History is now and England".

60. At stanza 60 – the last stanza of the first half of the poem – Hill believes he "shall get throúgh" to stanza 120, the poem's end. The half-way point is taken as an opportunity for the poet to catch his breath ("a bit of a breather"); being an intermission it will be restful, and not include the weighty material of previous stanzas, not their taxing innuendo ("heavy come-on"). Allying himself first with Bunyan's Pilgrim (and later the dancing Kemp), Hill urges both himself and his reader as "Friend" to keep going, despite the forthcoming difficulty ("Up the Hill"), or humiliation ("APOLLYON"), or the lack of anything intelligent to say or to discuss ("stúck for a treatise"). At the centre of the stanza, and in stark contrast to the professed search for a treatise, is a perverse image: in a porn film, perhaps, or a re-run of the *120 Days of Sodom*, a nun ("Sister Perversity") receives oral sex – or worse ("sinuses choked with shit") – from an anonymous male figure ("ANON on his knees"). That image is in stark contrast to the "simple gifts" that follow; the Pilgrim must continue his journey in this post-Lewinskian climate. And the poet must not be, like Kemp, a newsflash/*Flashdance*/flash in the pan ("nine days' wonder"); he, like a football player (and like Bucer) has now 'signed' for England (see stanza 59).

60.1 breather A short break from exertion, here marking the half-way point in the poem.

60.2 come-on A gesture or remark intended to be sexually attractive, to lure and entice the reader.

60.3 Ón thy way, Friend Cf. Robert Southey's 'To a Friend': "And wouldst thou seek the low abode / Where Peace delights to dwell? / Pause, Traveller, on thy way of life... Pause, Traveller, on thy way, / Nor dare the dangerous path explore / Till old Experience comes to lend his leading ray". "Friend" is also the ordinary Quaker mode of address.

60.4 Up the Hill | Difficulty A pun on the poet's name, and a reference to Bunyan's *Pilgrim's Progress* in which the Hill of Difficulty and its road (also Difficulty) is flanked by two treacherous byways 'Danger' and 'Destruction'. Christian (the "PILGRIM" of line 10) takes Difficulty – the right way – while Formalist and Hypocrisy opt for the other two, which are fatal dead ends. The verticule marks an ambiguity: 'up the Hill *of* Difficulty', and 'up the Hill *with* Difficulty'.

60.5 APOLLYON Revelation 9:11: "And they had a king over them, which is the angel of the bottomless pit, whose name in

ANNOTATIONS

the Hebrew tongue is Abaddon, but in the Greek tongue hath his name Apollyon". In *Pilgrim's Progress* Part I, Apollyon battles Christian in the Valley of Humiliation.

60.6 simple gifts Cf. Elder Joseph Brackett's 1848 Quaker song, 'Simple Gifts': "'Tis the gift to be simple, 'tis the gift to be free / 'Tis the gift to come down where we ought to be".

60.7 nine days' wonder 'Nine Daies Wonder' (now an expression meaning a brief, remarkable event) was the name for Elizabethan and Shakespearean actor William Kemp's 1599 Lent-time dance during his 127 mile journey from London to Norwich. He published a memoir of the journey (*Kemp's Nine Daies Wonder*) the following year.

60.8 Cambridge, full of thy learning Wordsworth's *Prelude, Book Sixth, Cambridge & the Alps*: "I have thought of thee, thy learning, gorgeous eloquence...".

60.9 Flash As in 'newsflash', a piece of news considered so important that it is broadcast outside the times usually allowed for news programming.

60.10 Bucer signs for England – *De Regno Christi* Martin Bucer (1491-1551), German Protestant reformer exiled from Strasbourg after his attempts to preserve the Protestant faith against the Ausburg Interim (a document which imposed Catholicism throughout the Empire and which Bucer was forced to sign to escape imprisonment). Bucer accepted Cranmer's invitation of refuge in England in 1549. He took a position at Oxford University, and tried to diffuse the Reformation throughout England. His treatise *De Regno Christi* [On the Kingdom of Christ] (see stanza 95) urged the King to take control of church reform; and he contributed to Cranmer's 1552 edition of the *Book of Common Prayer*. The phrase "signs for" is commonly used of professional football players; Bucer's acceptance has cancelled his previous signature.

61. Hill is receptive to the cycles of nature, and sees the "good" in both the bountiful (with its obvious benefit of plenty) and the barren (equally "for our good"). The landscape of stanza 61 (like that of 57) is that of a "bare" winter in an industrial landscape, and Hill paints a picture (likely, an *English* picture) which, despite its coldness and its stark "shot-tower", is nevertheless 'vivified'; the sun rising on frost reminds the poet of the potential beauty in the barren, but also of "our violent infirmities" and "our dead", recurrent through history as the changing of the seasons kills and brings to life. The "frosted mantle", or "corolla" over the shot-tower, the sun's "befogged radiance", constitute an emblem of that process. However, Hill does not see Persephone (alive), but rather the body of Diana, killed in a moment (a "soundbite") inside a Parisian tunnel. The horrible image of "Ceres' living child" lying dead "inside the wind-tunnel" emphasizes the brutality of a post-industrial machine age, but also the collapse of England; what looked like winter was in fact death. England is "broken asprawl" instead of spring-ing back – moving from the "limo" of luxurious Empire to the "limbo" of modern-day purgatory in a "soundbite", the contemporary unit of time. Rather than recognizing the inevitable rise and fall that characterizes the history of nations, empires, and civilizations, England (aslumber, not "AWAKE") was taken in by the promises of instant riches ("fell for Aladdin's Uncle") as Diana fell among the Al Fayeds. Here, the Empire, like Diana, is dead, and in this winter the broken nation is cold and seemingly lifeless, needing to be awoken from its sleep of death.

61.1 Open to every season An echo of the shopkeepers' dictum 'Open all hours', anticipating the image of Harrods – a kind of Aladdin's cave – at the end of the stanza (see 61.9).

61.2 shot-tower A tower used for making lead shot during the 19th century. The molten lead is dropped from a height into water, upon contact with which the metal solidifies. Surpassed by other methods, the towers now stand as picturesque landmarks of a defunct industry. The image is of the aurora-like effect of the frost around the top of the shot-tower, with the sense of something like a protective cloak ("mantle") crowning ("corolla", see line 5) the flame of an oil lantern.

61.3 the instant Cf. "*augenblick*" in stanza 80.

61.4 Ceres' living child Ceres, the Roman goddess of grain, harvest and agriculture; counterpart of the Greek goddess Demeter. After her daughter Proserpina (Persephone) was kidnapped by Pluto, Ceres searched the earth for her missing child. In revenge she refused to let crops grow; to restore fertility, Jupiter (Zeus) ordered Pluto (Hades) to return Proserpina, but in the underworld the daughter had eaten pomegranate seeds (see stanza 19), the symbol of marriage; the seeds once eaten, the union could not be broken. Jupiter arranged a compromise: Proserpina could spend two thirds of the year with her mother and one with her husband; during her time in Hades the world became barren, while during her time

ANNOTATIONS

above ground it was fertile. Here, she is emblematic of the promise of spring, which allows winter to be enjoyed as dormancy rather than endured as death.

61.5 wind-tunnel A tunnel-shaped chamber through which air can be passed at a known speed to test the aerodynamic properties of an aircraft or automobile.

61.6 limo to limbo The transformation is from "limo" ('limousine'), the luxurious automobile symbolic of wealth and celebrity, and "limbo", the home of souls not reconciled to God. Only the phoneme [b] separates life and death; the distance between the two no greater than this auditory instant.

61.7 soundbite A bulletin intended for broadcast; here, perhaps, the brief news flash of Diana's death in a Paris tunnel.

61.8 ENGLAND AWAKE William Blake's 'England Awake': "England! awake! awake! awake! awake! / Jerusalem thy sister calls! / Why wilt thou sleep the sleep of death / And close her from the ancient walls?"

61.9 Aladdin's Uncle That is, "one of thóse" charlatans who, like the sorcerer in 'Aladdin's Wonderful Lamp', (a tale with no known Arabic source but included since 1710 in the *Thousand and One Nights*), trick the guileless with the lure of treasure; there is a suggestion of the Egyptian Al Fayed family (the son seducing Diana) and of the takeover of English assets by wealthy Middle Eastern entrepreneurs – the father purchasing Harrods (parts of the store were notoriously bedecked like Aladdin's cave or a Middle Eastern bazaar).

62. There is a literal image at the centre of this stanza: David Bomberg's 1935 portrait of his step-daughter Dinora Mendelson (now Davies-Rees). In it one can "Witness" a naïve yet knowing Dinora ("untutored, unchastened"), bereaved through the experience, the pre-occupation of "time" and "service" devoted to Bomberg, but also experiencing the "reward" of proximity to his talent. "Look at the face!", Hill instructs his readers; the face is burdened, laboured, bereaved. "But daughters do forgive / fathers", we are told – as Cordelia did Lear so Dinora did Bomberg, working to recover his reputation after his death. Bomberg mismanaged his artistic career and suffered for it, never moving beyond an uncertain life of poverty. It is not only the artist but also his family "who gets burnt", aversely affected by the pitfalls of the artistic life, the efforts to approach the "TETRAGRAMMATON", the ultimate abstracted artistic force.

In Hill's "blurred vision" of Bomberg, the artist figures not as the great unnameable, but rather as a kind of dilapidated, "terrible" Jesus, an old man riding his humble donkey. The daughter may grant forgiveness, and God the grace, but the suffering is nevertheless ineradicable.

62.1 occupied The image is of a visitor to an art gallery asserting before a potential usurper his occupancy of the seat facing the portrait.

62.2 PORTRAIT OF DINORA The title of a 1951 oil painting by David Bomberg (see 62.6) of his step-daughter Dinora Davies-Rees (née Mendelson) who, with her mother Lilian Holt, shared Bomberg's obscurity and poverty during and after his lifetime. Bomberg showed no aptitude for self-promotion; after his death his reputation was restored in large part by the efforts of Lilian and Dinora, the latter by then also a practising artist. The name is Hebrew and carries Biblical resonance, being a variation of Dinah, the violated daughter of Jacob (see Genesis 34). See Appendix, fig. 5.

62.3 Grace before arbitration An approximate inversion of the proverbial 'justice before mercy'; both phrases equate the theological and the judicial. There is an echo of 'grace before meat', the saying of short prayers before eating.

62.4 Is it / the artist only who gets burnt That is, by flying too close to the sun (like Icarus); or like the Holocaust, with its etymology of 'mass burning'; or suffering the thunderbolts of an outraged Jehovah.

62.5 TETRAGRAMMATON The Greek term for the Hebrew name of God as revealed to Moses (see Exodus 3:13-15), transliterated into four letters (YHWH or JHVH for Yahweh or Jehovah or, at the risk of thunderbolts, HILL for Hill); in Judaism, the word is considered too sacred to be uttered aloud, the penalty for so doing being death. In the English Old Testament, YHWH is translated 'LORD' (as distinct from the Hebrew *Adonai*, translated 'Lord').

62.6 Bomberg David Bomberg (1890-1957) was born in Birmingham and studied painting at the Westminster School of Art (1908-10) and the Slade School of Art (1911-13). He travelled widely in Europe and the Middle East, and eventually settled in Spain (see 62.7).

62.7 *peon* on donkey In Spanish, a *peon* is an unskilled labourer. The image of Bomberg riding a donkey comes from accounts of the artist's last years, which he spent in Spain; Michael Jacobs writes in his Foreword to the 2004 exhibition of

ANNOTATIONS

Bomberg's Spanish paintings: "Personal reminiscences of Bomberg in Ronda date mainly from these later years. Among the townspeople themselves he is remembered, if at all, as a slightly ridiculous figure riding off on a donkey in search of motifs or to collect his shopping" ('In Celebration of David Bomberg 1890-1957; Daniel Katz Gallery, London, 30 May – 13 July 2007').

62.8 lop- / sided The typography of lines 11-12 is significant: the word "lop- / sided" is itself lop-sided, sprawled over a line break.

63. Hill moves from the familial image of Bomberg and his daughter to the Court of Auditors, which is now not so much a venerable European Union institution as the poet's own audience, his court of listeners. He hears their distant applause, "far back" in place and time: Hill is speaking as much *for* past generations as *to* his own; he was "under constraint" but, paradoxically, could not have spoken more "freely" were this not so. And when addressing his auditors (those who listen, but also those who 'do the books', make the calculations) Hill wonders if he would have "spoken so freely" were he not "under constraint", the constraints of traditional poetic forms (which offer their own freedoms) and of finances ("EITHER WAY THEY GET YOU", the everyman's tax mantra). There is, however, no escape from the conundrums of life: good planning, foresight, preparation (financial and spiritual); but providence would not be credible if there were no final payment. In the rest of the stanza, Hill muses on the poem (which, in unattended moments, sometimes approaches "the sublime"), and on his own late happiness, whatever the odds were against that having come to pass. Although "Not everything" can be as he wants it, Hill has "discovery" and "rehabilitation"; the *Winter's Tale* reference to "Togetherness after sixteen years" with his beloved is met with the strongly affirmative (and resoundingly demotic) "You're on" – providence may be difficult to credit, but despite the note of mild pessimism Hill is happy to bet on this aspect of his personal happiness, whatever the price set on it by any court of auditors.

63.1 Court of Auditors The European Union institution with headquarters in Luxembourg established in 1977 to audit the Union's accounts and to ensure the soundness of its financial management. Here, a listening, judging and even applauding audience.

63.2 EITHER WAY THEY GET YOU A commonplace: payment of tax is unavoidable, either removed from wages before they are paid, or retrieved during the annual auditing process.

63.3 Providence cited [...] without payment The language of financial exchange provides a metaphor for the problem of redemption: Christ redeemed mankind and paid the price of sin; without this redemption, God is neither credible nor creditable.

63.4 cheap entr'acte music moves towards the sublime *Entr'acte music* is played during the break between the acts of a play or opera. Not the focus of attention, it is often inferior ("cheap"). That such music has potential to be "sublime" recalls a line in Noel Coward's *Private Lives* (1930): "Extraordinary how potent cheap music is" (Act I).

63.5 Togetherness after sixteen years? In Shakespeare's *The Winter's Tale* (see stanza 57), sixteen years lapse between the third and fourth acts, as explained in the play by Time: "Impute is not a crime / To me or my swift passage, that I slide / O'er sixteen years and leave the growth untried / Of that wide gap" (IV.i). Sixteen years also approximates Hill's relationship with Alice Goodman, his wife since 1987.

63.6 You're on A clichéd acceptance of a bet or competition; alternatively, 'your turn to act on stage'; here, a final tableau.

63.7 tableau A picturesque presentation in which a group of silent, motionless persons is arranged to represent a scene; specifically, a Victorian parlour game, in which a scene from literature or history is prepared. Here, the "final tableau of discovery" suggests the closing scene of *The Winter's Tale*, in which an apparently lifeless statue of Paulina comes to life – a miraculous "rehabilitation" (see line 11).

64. In this stanza, a long-distance flight is used as a metaphor for the poet. Both pilot and Hill are on a "long haul" journey, arduous and lengthy: Hill is more then half-way through a 120 stanza poem, while the plane is about to "Lift-off". Exhausted, both must push on with their journeys, travelling on autopilot until relieved. The aviation conceit is

ANNOTATIONS

(temporarily) supplanted by the vision of Hill as patient in a clinic, apparently having the area "up to – and beyond – the caecum" investigated, with the all-too common "malignancy" thankfully not present: "No sign there". Hill's autopilot state of mind will be altered when he receives a clean bill of health, when he is relieved by this news. He is, it seems, undergoing a prostate exam. The flickering of the sonograph image reminds him of a hummingbird's wings; the shift from static to movement ("play and replay") is "dizzying". The anal probing reminds him of the body, with (in his terrible jest, for which he apologises) a "full and frank exchange of love-bites" (not soundbites), specifically, on the buttocks (hence the coarseness). And hence the unintentional irony of the Scottish doctor's sympathetic comment, *"Puir / auld sod"*. Life's "adjacent realm" is equally the body (and anal tract), so obviously in contradiction to the life of the mind ("sómething else agaín"); and, returning to the image of the aeroplane ("Lift-off", as one's reaction to being "spitted"), Hill reflects upon the post-Cartesian paradoxes of body and mind and motion in terms of Leibniz's "monad", by curious definition windowless (more prosaically, he does not have a window seat); indeed, it remains a matter of intense speculation as to whether or not "we" are "Óne thing" (unique, isolated), or 'some thing' ("sómething", in the material sense), or "sómething else" again (or should that be, 'a-gaín'?).

64.1 long haul In aviation, a commercial flight with a duration in excess of seven hours; cf. the aviation imagery of "taxiing to take-off" in stanza 1 and here the sense of being on 'automatic pilot' (in marriage, a lasting relationship; in life, longevity) until he is *relieved*, i.e., by the doctor's all-clear.

64.2 spitted up to – and beyond – the caecum 'Spitted' suggests 'spit', the sharp rod on which meat is skewered and roasted. The image is of a surgical probe used to search for cancer, most often of the colon or prostate; the lubricated ("spitted") probe ventures "beyond" the blind gut ("caecum"), the images captured by its camera transmitted to a monitor (see 64.3), then viewed and assessed by the practitioner. See stanza 51.

64.3 sitar's humming-bird-finger-blur An long-necked Indian instrument similar to a guitar, brought to the attention of the West during the 1960s and 1970s through Ravi Shankar, the guru and sitarist favoured by the Beatles; here, the speed of the sitar player's hand movement is likened to the wings of the hummingbird, which is in turn likened to the blurry, shifting

images on the monitor of the sonograph machine (the "free in-house video").
64.4 full and frank exchange A political and journalistic clichéd euphemism for a stand-up argument. Compare "tired and emotional" in stanza 36.
64.5 love-bites Cf. "soundbites" in stanza 61.
64.6 I had forgotten That is, he has "forgotten" both the existence of this "adjacent realm", and his good manners in referring to it thus.
64.7 *Puir / auld sod* 'Poor old sod', as uttered in Scots dialect, presumably by the doctor.
64.8 Lift-off but no window The moment that a rocket or plane leaves the ground; the thrust that sends it upwards, into motion. And motion, in turn, invokes the Leibnizian sense of dynamism, of the motion of monads in the void. The monad (see below) is hermetic – while a 'mirror' of the world, it is 'windowless'.
64.9 Leibniz's / monad In the philosophy of Leibniz, an indivisible unit of being (as a soul, an atom), and an absolutely simple entity. Thus, as well as the demotic meaning of 'one thing' (Greek *monos*, 'unity'), Leibniz's monad really is 'One Thing'. Hill writes in 'What the Devil Has Got into John Ransom?', that "Giordano Bruno, from whom Leibniz may have derived the term, conceived of the 'monad' as being at once a 'material atom' and an irreducible metaphysical element of being"; in 'Unhappy Circumstances', of the "irreducible monad of the assertive rebellious will"; and in 'A Postscript on Modernist Poetics', of the 'monad of linguistic energy" (*Collected Critical Writings*, pp. 141, 187, 578).

65. This opening for this stanza is a kind of definition for the poem: it is made up of stanzas ("Fragments") which are themselves condensed, collapsed versions of a larger narrative ("short score"). These fragments tell a story (though not necessarily of a linear nature) through a kind of poetic shorthand. For the poet, they are "inspirational", each containing a little epiphany ("Visionary insights") which shines through the complexity and difficulty of comprehension ("Clouds of dark discernment"). Collectively, the "Fragments" of the poem attempt to display the "full spectrum" of human experience, from "wrath" to "thankfulness", even though the "rainbow" of their final resolution (an implied covenant) is yet to be wrought. Hill is talking to himself – the "yoú" is that part of his being (the 'Ariel' or spiritual quality, as opposed to the material being) that has refused or forgotten to respond thus. So, setting aside "nature" in favour of "nurture", he articulates the problem of what he calls "redemption" in terms of the power of the written word ("Any sentence") to ratify existence ("have / life") or to approach the condition of music (see stanza 20), even as he accepts the 'life sentence' that is his more prosaic lot.

65.1 short score A condensed orchestra score omitting some of the less important instruments and often combining several parts on one staff; such fragments may offer, nevertheless, "Visionary insights", however incomplete ("still to be / fully wrought") they may be.

65.2 the rainbow still to be fully wrought For the rainbow as God's covenant to man (and so "fully wrought" only at Judgement) see Genesis 9:12-13: "This is the token of the covenant which I make between me and you and every living creature that is with you, for perpetual generations: I do set my bow in the cloud, and it shall be for a token of a covenant between me and the earth."

65.3 I HAVE FORGOTTEN MORE THAN YOU KNOW The tone is of an older man addressing a younger upstart; cf. Zoe (of Stephen) in Joyce's *Ulysses*: "God help your head, he knows more than you have forgotten" (p. 475). But it is also the poet chiding his ancient persona, only to be rebuffed. John Lyon cites the question-and-answer exchange of lines 6-7 as reminiscent of the "intensely linguistic comedienne" Hylda Baker, whose later career in the 1970s was plagued by forgetfulness and the "increasing and debilitating symptoms of Alzheimer's disease" ('What are you incinerating?', pp. 90-91). Hill has stated that "fraught mime" is for him as significant as the "history and contexts of etymology" and that he has "learnt as much from Daumier, Hylda Baker and Frankie Howerd as from ... John Donne and Gerard Manley Hopkins" ('A Matter of Timing').

65.4 not nature but nurture 'Nature vs. nurture' concerns the debate about the relative importance of inborn, 'natural' qualities as compared to those acquired via environment and upbringing (nurture) to differences in human behaviour. Here, Hill makes the distinction between revealed religion, which must be taught ('brought to mind'), and natural religion, which is innate (in the "nature").

65.5 *Mein Ariel, / hast du, der Luft, nur ist...?* See stanza 54 for an explication of this Frank Martin refrain, stanzas 79 and 91 for its verbatim repetition, and stanza 115 for its appearance in an altered form.

65.6 So name your own / sentence. Any sentence The syntax recalls the challenge of the card player or magician: 'Pick a card. Any card'; here, "sentence" denotes both the unit of syntactical structure and the punishment meted out by a court of law (cf. "life" and "appeal" in line 12).

65.7 appeal to music To appeal is to make request (to a higher court) for the alteration of the decision of a lower court; here, "music" is the higher court, that to which all art aspires.

66. The poet details the "delusion" he harbours: he believes himself to be the "secret keeper" of the enigma of the Lilith-like character introduced in stanza 8; he identifies in this stanza and in himself the provenance of this vampiric, yet sexually arousing, potent force. In 'Dolores (Notre-Dame des Sept Douleurs)', Swinburne holds the titular figure at a close distance, his leash taut, his exacting control over the poem ("each turn immaculate") symptomatic of the tension between poet and subject. Though not explicit ("nothing spoken"), the poem has a palpable physicality ("crouch and spatter"); the reader is forced to confront desire in its basest form ("deferring to the mirror"). With what appears at first to be a banal interjection, Hill announces that he is not, like Swinburne, a "hair / fetishist", something which he is "ashamed / to confess" as it proves his love of and commitment to Dolores is not absolute. Now, the Dolores figure is identified in the work of Füssli, and Hill employs the artist as an example of "self-mastery of abasement", of one who gave himself over entirely (in a way that Hill does not) to the idea of the female demon. What are we to make of these lusty, grotesque works which celebrate the dark and the vampiric? Is there nothing between "lust and friendship"? Are we to accept Swinburne's 'Dolores' – filled with purple verse, wallowing in wilful grotesquery – as part of the poetic canon? Is Füssli's *Nightmare* (for instance) – with its goblin and gratuitous nude – to be taken seriously? The answer is given by way of analogy: in the time of Louis XIII, the King's public use of a commode was accepted, even considered regal; in the times of Swinburne and Füssli, the grotesquely sexual was an allowed, received artistic trope. Tastes, like

"ETIQUETTE", change: what was art becomes obscenity, and vice versa.

66.1 Dolores In Swinburne's 'Dolores (Notre-Dame des Sept Douleurs)' (1866), the vampiric, titular *femme fatale* both tempts and repels: "By the ravenous teeth that have smitten / Through the kisses that blossom and bud, / By the lips intertwisted and bitten / Till the foam has a savour of blood, / By the pulse as it rises and falters, / By the hands as they slacken and strain, / I adjure thee, respond from thine altars, / Our Lady of Pain." Her "engorged smile" suggests Pater's description of da Vinci's 'Mona Lisa': "She is older than the rocks upon which she sits; like the vampire, she has been dead many times, and learned the secrets of the grave" (*The Renaissance*, p. 131). See also stanza 67; and "Lilith / we háve met" in stanza 8.

66.2 sign-language A system of communication using gestures rather than writing or speech, especially the highly-developed system of hand signs used by or for the hearing-impaired. Here, "sign-language" refers to the Victorian conventions – manifest in Swinburne's 'Dolores' – which connoted sexual acts through a widely-understood code.

66.3 *bouts-rimés* The French term for 'end rhymes', lines closing with rhyme, as in Swinburne's 'Dolores'. In the game of *bouts-rimés*, rhymes are artificially supplied to the poet in advance.

66.4 Never a hair fetishist [...] ashamed to confess Unlike Swinburne: "Though obscure be the god, and though nameless / The eyes and the hair that we kiss: / Low fires that love sits by and forges / Fresh heads for his arrows and thine; / Hair loosened and soiled in mid orgies / With kisses and wine" ('Dolores', stanza 36).

66.5 Füssli's Henri Füssli (1741-1825), also known as Johann Heinrich Fuessli or Henri Fuseli, an Anglo-Swiss painter and draftsman who c.1763 travelled to London to study, where he was befriended by Joshua Reynolds. Füssli exhibited works of a grotesque and visionary type, including the celebrated *Nightmare* (1781; see Appendix, fig. 6), in which a naked sleeping woman asprawl a bed is watched by goblin-like figures, one of which perches upon her. Many of his drawings, too, reveal his romantic fascination with the terrifying and the weird.

66.6 auto-erotic pencil Here, "pencil" is used in its archaic sense of the artist's fine brush; it shares its etymology (Latin 'tail') with 'penis', hence the pencil is "auto-erotic", and an agent of "self-mastery of abasement".

66.7 Nothing between lust and friendship | one gibed Nietzsche made this 'gibe' in *Thus Spake Zarathustra*: "woman is not yet capable of friendship: she knows only love [...] women are still cats, and birds. Or at best, cows" (p. 43).

66.8 OBSCENITY'S ETIQUETTE The 'etiquette' here is of the court of Louis XIII: happy to give audience while sitting on the toilet, the French King – in what must be deemed an excess of decadence – had a commode fitted to his throne. Cf. Hill's reference to the "performance / of sacral baseness, like kings at stool" in *The Triumph of Love* (LIV).

67. In a casual voice ("Can't do"), Hill announces that he is unable to produce dialogue, even when the narrative of the poem (or the implied editor, the "dramaturge") demands multiple voices. Instead, he admits to providing the reader with "Snatched asides" only; these are the phrases made distinct from the main body of the text by capitalization, or italics, or in parentheses. Hill cannot "do dialogue"; at best, he has been able only to snatch the odd perfect word "in mid-flight" – that is, with reference to the French phrase, *esprit de l'escalier*, only when it is too late. This poem is a response to the contemporary world, and so the "clinching" phrases and the "snatched asides" respond to "public claims"; the examples given (each introduced by the demotic "like") are: when to use laughter for gain ("when to act entitled by a laugh"); bracing yourself for a fight ("kick yourself for courage"); laughing and (humourously) standing in for your own deceased other self ("doubling up as / your dead stand-in"); and regaining popularity at very much the wrong moment ("to go under / only to be | insensately revived"). Hill has described himself as a kind of music-hall clown, a stand-up (doubled-up) comic; for which sin against the soul he asks pardon of the Dolores or Lilith figure within (see stanza 66). To request such forgiveness is to reject the triviality described – but if nothing done was real, then how can such a request for pardon be entertained seriously? Hence both the unrelenting pun on "Check", and the sense of the tears as "prosthetic". The stanza thus succeeds in dramatizing its rhetoric of failure; Hill has moved, by insincere supplication to his dark muse (in whom he does not place his faith – see stanza 66), from an inability to "do dialogue" to a commanding enactment of the demotic performative.

67.1 dramaturge The "dramaturge" (either the dramatist, who is surely the poet himself, rather than his editor) aims for "confrontation", which is the essence of drama. The self-reflexive nature of the lines recall "recensions" in stanza 57; the recurring editorial voice is found in stanzas 18, 47, 48, 104 and 114.

67.2 *mots de l'escalier* An adaptation of Fr. '*esprit de l'escalier*', referring to the things one wishes one had said only after it is too late ("mid-flight" of the ascent or descent of the staircase). Cf. Eliot's 'Ash-Wednesday' (III) in which the speaker narrates the "turning" from stair to stair.

67.3 besieged privities That is, private sentiments "besieged" as public items; poems for performance. There may also be the innuendo of 'private parts'; the public has him, as it were, 'by the balls'.

67.4 doubling up / as your dead stand-in There is a paradox in this phrase, as one's stand-in is already one's double; here, "doubling up" also suggests doubled up with laughter.

67.5 go under Either a) to sink below the surface; or b) to be administered an anaesthetic.

67.6 insensately Without sense or understanding, foolish.

67.7 LILITH Here, "Dolores" and "LILITH" refer again to Swinburne's poem 'Dolores (Notre-Dame des Sept Douleurs)' (see stanza 66), in which a Lilith-like figure (Liliith being, in Hebrew scripture, the evil child-killing first wife of Adam) is conflated with the Virgin Mary and addressed as "Dolores, Our Lady of Pain".

67.8 nothing we did was real That is to say, we were acting, posing, like the "stand-in" of line 8.

67.9 I ask / your pardon Here, not the demotic 'I beg your pardon', but "I ask / your pardon", which invites a legal interpretation. The phrasing recalls the suddenly deliberate sotto voce "for grief of no known cause, excuse me" of stanza 56.

67.10 prosthetic tears That is, unreal tears, manufactured for the occasion, and standing in for real tears (see line 8); "Check" here functions both in the sense of 'verify' and 'stop'.

68.
The stanza opens with a premise: in this scene, justice is "not in order"; the uncommon, prefixed antonyms throughout

the stanza – unreason, unforgetting, uncomprehending, unsorrowed – attest to this. The "ex-captives" – the remnants of Burmese hill tribes (see line 8), displaced, dispersed and brought into the sudden light of the twentieth century; not hypochondriacs or fashionable malingerers ("Valetudinarian") but completely abject, chewing dirt. Unable to forget their pasts, they are isolated from their own culture and from us ("in alien unforgetting"); their religion is "grief and indignation" and, unable to move beyond this state, they remain a "lost tribe", gathered together ("sequestered") but inexorably separate. A wilfully cultured voice speaks of these refugees from humanity with disdain: their speech is "primitive", they neither understand nor can be understood ("uncomprehending; / incomprehensible"). If they were dead, the finality and gravitas of death might allow us to see them as eloquent; living – but dying – they receive none of our sorrow: a shabby state. This stanza is one of their few threnodies, and yet its eloquence is questionable ("unless you call thís eloquence"). Urging himself to a conclusion ("GO ON"), Hill affirms the cleansing power of the fire of justice ("transparent bale-fire"): like the final eschatological things, it is "massive, shimmering", and purifies a path through the "incoherence" of the afflicted, like the City of God towering above the storm sewers in stanza 15. Yet how can this principle be reconciled with the abjection and misery just presented? Justice – elemental, although unspeaking – frames the stanza: the first and penultimate lines culminate in the esoteric power of the last, but the eloquence of the image and the vision of justice it entails is at best imponderable.

68.1 order In a judicial context, "order" is the established procedure of the court (as in 'come to order'), procedure here not being followed. Cf. "INORDINATE | wording of Common Prayer" in stanza 51.

68.2 Valetudinarian Hypochondriac, or fashionably malingering; an ornate word provocatively at odds with the abject misery to follow.

68.3 sequestered Here, "sequestered" denotes isolation, gathered in a group but separated from their natural environment; in a judicial context, the term refers specifically to the removal of the jury from outside influence during the course of a trial.

68.4 lost tribe Although the phrase is resonant of the Ten Lost Tribes of Israel (see 2 Kings 17:6-9), the meaning here is not

ANNOTATIONS

Hebraic but secular, suggesting the anthropological 'discoveries' by intrepid explorers of tribes entirely removed from general society, photographed as curiosities.

68.5 loanwords / scavenged from Burmese dialects A loanword is a word from one language which has become part of the everyday lexicon of another; here, these "loan-words" are borrowed by the "lost tribe" of line 3 from "Burmese dialects". The specific suggestion is of the hill tribes of Burma (such as the Karen or Akha) whose languages are unique but threatened by exposure to the surrounding regions of Burma, Thailand and Laos; they face also physical threats, their subsistence farming lifestyle severely compromised by deforestation.

68.6 struck eloquent That is, the *image* of the dead and dying can 'speak volumes', more eloquently than anything they themselves can say. Cf. the more usual phrase, 'struck dumb', used to refer to one silenced by shock or surprise.

68.7 bale-fire of vanities A 'bale-fire' is a great open-air fire, especially one used to fuel a funeral pyre; there is a suggestion of Tom Wolfe's enormous novel, *The Bonfire of the Vanities* (1987), which catalogues the many foibles of 1980s New York (the novel takes its name from the ritual burning of objects of sin, especially Savonarola's 1497 razing of cosmetics and art).

69. Hill moves from the "alien" status of the lost tribe to the irrational ("unreason") concept of Oxbridge-style "Collegiality", the strange etiquette peculiar to the academic world, where processes are governed by academic rather than theological ritual, and where an élitist group practises an etiquette and defines ethics, all the while doing the general public no real good ("common disservice"). Hill pauses for a moment of reflection: having "come / so far" in the poem, he wonders ("Whát was I thinking"), and gives the possible answer of Bergman-style farce: showing up the horrors and absurdity of contemporary life by setting it against weighty symbolism. This may be fanciful, but there is "anarchy" in it; it involves that "bale-fire" of the previous stanza – the cleansing fire at both the beginning and the end of the world ("origin and survival") that threatens civilized life ("the silver | and private bride"). But is life really this dramatic? Is the end of the film the end of the world? No: there is no "final retribution", the vanities are not torched; instead, while the drama of the earth plays out, and while *The Seventh Seal* screens, a couple "sleeps through it", "innocent" and oblivious. There are mysteries which will remain mysterious until the apocalypse; all that can be said is that these images – of academia, of anarchy, of apocalypse – are Hill's, that all "THÍS" was his idea, ceremonies of innocence set against a backdrop of violence.

69.1 Collegiality The word has both an ecclesiastic and an academic meaning: in Roman Catholicism, it refers to the equal sharing of power by bishops; in academia, to the relationship between colleagues in a university.

69.2 Bergmanesque From Ingmar Bergman (1918-2007), the Swedish film and stage director whose two sets of film trilogies from the 1950s and 1960s demonstrate his growing disillusionment with the search for God, but with a thin veil of humour ("tragic farce", see 69.3).

69.3 tragic farce Hill offers 'tragic farce' as a description for the genre of *Speech! Speech!* in *Don't Ask Me What I Mean: Poets in their Own Words*: "In his essay on Christopher Marlowe, T.S. Eliot observes that a play such as *The Jew of Malta* is not so much a tragedy as it is a tragic farce. I have pondered that definition since my sixth-form days at Bromsgrove High School. To say that *Speech! Speech!* is an attempt to create the equivalent of that genre would be a fairly accurate suggestion" (p. 116).

69.3 I have come / so far That is, so far in life and also so far in the poem; cf. "how far is HOW FAR" in stanza 21.

69.4 flames ransacking the last scene Bergman's *The Seventh Seal* (1956) is a deeply symbolic fantasy set in plague-ridden medieval Sweden that explores the relationship between the individual and God. The film ends with a famous 'dance of death', with dancing figures in silhouette with the setting sun behind them. Its obscure philosophical and theological meanings have puzzled and intrigued many viewers. In *The Orchards of Syon*, Hill questions his preference for science fiction over heavy symbolism: "Re SEVENTH SEAL: prefer bright Connie / Willis to glum Ingmar? Pass" (L).

69.5 silver | and private bride The verticule allows two readings: in the first, a "silver" bride (silver because starring in a black-and-white Bergmanesque film) is imperilled; in the second, both the silver (the most valuable household objects) and the innocent maiden risk being stolen, vandalised.

69.6 THÍS / WAS MY IDEA An 'Idea', in the Platonic sense, is an image that yet stands for something more real beyond the

ANNOTATIONS

phenomenal world, as the meaning of *The Seventh Seal* may lie beyond the projected images and sensory experience.

70. Hill's next "idea" is of a more private kind, and occupies only an instant of time: sandwiched between its prosaic opening and prosaic close – "As the train curved into Groton I [woke and] looked oút for you" – are the kind of elevated thoughts and interviews that one might imagine and play out in one's mind while glancing out the window during a train journey…. The thoughts are at first personal and, it seems, romantic – Hill 'looks out' but "without desire" for a loved one; the poet's self-consciousness, however, is never distant, and he describes his use of the adjective "sadly" as "mawkish". The poet wonders if the "machine" – either the brain or the Dictaphone – is "turned on": are these thoughts to be eternized? Is he performing? Now in a fictional interview, Hill takes on the role of general sage and consultant: "The state" (presumably Massachusetts, where the ideals of the American Revolution were first expressed) is held to the character of its citizens (of which, in America, Hill is not one); he is in this stanza extraneous ("Surrogate") to the citizens of this state, foremost among those honoured for its civic and revolutionary ideas (indeed, as British, he may represent an authority against which they rebelled). The public can have his views (can take them, or leave them) on anything and everything: the fluorescent light debate ("fabrication / of natural light"), the perils posed to the natural world by industrialization ("the poison-runnels / greening with slick"). Hill then offers a brief, broad, political and social approbation in the form of a passing conceit: without "hierarchy" there is only anarchy (the "general dynamics" of mass movement); a curious link to the violence of the previous stanza is thus implied. And then the moment of reflection passes, the parentheses close almost as they opened, but now with the intimation of civic responsibility.

70.1 Groton Kenneth Haynes notes that while Groton has no special meaning in the poem, it happens to be Groton, Connecticut (rather than Groton, Massachusetts, as might be expected given Hill's time in Boston), through which Hill passed on a train "en route to New York to give a reading at the 92nd St Y in 1998" (personal correspondence, 7 Feb 2011).

70.2 poor / mawkish adverb The "mawkish adverb" is the feeble "sadly" of line 2, which should be either 'milked for all it's worth'; or 'clipped' as in cut, excised (like a used train ticket).

70.3 Is that machine turned on? The machine, ostensibly the device to 'clip' the ticket, is equally a Dictaphone recording the poet's musings, or a microphone he does not know is "turned on" when he was speaking frankly.

70.4 The state [...] its citizens That is, the whole is the sum of its parts, the state being necessarily reflective of ("held / to") the behaviours and beliefs of its constituents. Boston and the state of Massachusetts gave expression to many of the early revolutionary ideas of civic liberty.

70.5 Surrogate Here, the word seems to be used in its legal sense of a judge presiding over questions of guardianship; the poet as one who adjudicates on behalf of the citizens of the state. Also, one from outside the district, i.e., not a citizen proper.

70.6 They can have my views That is, the citizens of Boston are welcome to his views on all kinds of matters, ranging (here) from the fabrication of natural light (note the implied paradox) to environmental issues.

70.7 general dynamics In physics, if there were not the constraint and order imposed by hierarchical organization (into molecules, enzymes, etc.) then there would be only the ceaseless turmoil of quantum and atomic motion. Likewise, then, with social stratification.

70.8 As the train curved [...] But for "woke / and", the opening of the stanza is repeated at its close; the device urges the reader to perceive the lines between as consuming no more than a 'waking moment' (cf. "*augenblick*" in stanza 81). The repeated stress on "looked oút' redefines the casual act of looking through the train window in terms of civic responsibility.

71. The moment on the train having passed, Hill's thoughts return to the subject of Diana, introduced in stanza 36. She is now dead, and the physical causes of her death have been investigated (the autopsy presented as a "body / search"). She is at both a literal and a figurative Customs: the "*Quais*" representing both the processing of her body out of France at the Customs docks, and the crossing of the Styx ("restless limbo"). The embalming process is described in the terms of a woman's toilette ("depilatory", "ritual bath"); embalming is Diana's final act of make-up ("ultimate in cosmetics"). The

ANNOTATIONS

after-death appearances (at Customs, and the funeral) are her final public duties, and her quitting them is described by Hill as an escape from the hounding of the press, the untrue companions, from those who conspired to make her private life public ("betrayers / to public knowledge"). Hill can think of no other way to speak of her death other than that which is executed in this stanza: his desire to "commit" and "commend" her (the vocabulary of the funeral service) results only in a final – and impartial – description of her death as "a botched business", beyond the control of the public ("out of our hands"), not elevated, but paradoxically *reduced* (by removing life-supporting oxygen) "to the Sublime" (the vapourized spirit).

71.1 body / search Investigations conducted by customs officials when an individual is suspected of carrying illicit substances; a metaphor for the post-mortem treatment of Diana's body.

71.2 the *Quais* The "*Quais*" are the streets along the banks of the Seine in Paris; specifically those around the Pont de L'Alma, the site of Diana's fatal car accident. The "restless limbo", suggests the quays on the river Styx of Greek mythology, where those in transit wait to be ferried to Hades. 'Limbo' is the first circle of hell, the abode of those worthy neither of salvation nor damnation, the futile crowds.

71.3 the depilatory | and ritual bath The ritual, hair-removing bath is that of the embalmer preparing the body for viewing. Diana was embalmed, the controversial decision to do so taken by French embalmer Jean Monceau; the procedure clouded the results of the subsequent autopsy. The British inquest into Diana's death, concluded in April 2008, revealed that the princess's remains were decomposing so rapidly in the August heat that, if her body was to remain in viewable condition, the hospital had no choice but to embalm her. Justifying his decision at the inquest, Monceau explained: "Mr Chirac was going to come ... Prince Charles was going to come ... the body was not presentable" ('Coroner's Inquests', section 76).

71.4 vindictive protocol Here, *protocol* – vindictive because so spiteful as to be punitive – refers to the conventions of a royal funeral, the arrangements made between France and the United Kingdom for the transit of Diana's body, and the curious resentment of the royal family.

71.5 snarl-ups A British colloquialism for a hold-up, traffic jam, or general confusion; 'snarl' has angry and aggressive connotations.

71.6 commit, commend 'Commit' and 'commend' withstand two interpretations: in the first, the poet pledges devotion and formally praises; in the second, he buries the body (commits to earth), and entrusts the soul to the safe-keeping of God ('commend'). These words are also part of the Anglican funeral service: after Prayers, the minister leads the Commendation and Farewell, after which he performs the Committal at the graveside.

71.7 botched business Cf. "fuck-up as obligation" in stanza 61.

71.8 out of our hands That is, 'out of our control', beyond our sphere of influence.

71.9 the Sublime The phrase is unexpected: something is normally elevated, not "reduced" to the Sublime, that which (according to Kant) is 'absolutely great', 'boundless'. Chemically, 'sublime' refers to solids which vapourize when heated; to 'reduce' is to deoxidize.

72. Imitating "Prophet X" – a kind of cerebral hybrid of Malcolm X and Skelton ('Speke, Parrot') – Hill begins with a capitalized "ad lib" (as found elsewhere in the poem): "PRETTY BLOODY PRETTY BLOODY", a phrase belonging to a trained parrot: pretty in the senses of both 'rather' and 'comely'. The "BLOODY" here functions as both an intensifier (cf. 'damned') and a measure of brutality; its use leads Hill to "Those bloody Scots", persistently rebellious ("basted", like roasting chickens – or parrots – in their "contumacy") in that they continue to favour nationalism over total assimilation with Great Britain – it is, in some ways, like a "new Bannockburn". From the "bloody Scots" to the 'sullen pride' of the Welsh, then, who, like their emblematic "half-glimpsed" carp, are "unheld" by Britain. In the same way, the English treatment of Ireland ("our Irish trespass") is too terrible even to think of. "What phoenix", asks Hill, rises out of the fires of heartland English cathedral cities, ravaged by war and tawdry reconstruction – out of, even, the dysfunctional ("self-estranged") Althorp estate, seat of the Spencer family – what misery compounded ("grief's interest", which recalls "grief's thánksgiving" in stanza 52), what stately English timing ("Handelian measures"), what difficult, scant liberty ("freedom hardly won") characterizes the relationship

ANNOTATIONS

between England and her neighbours and charges? What was "forsaken in the act" of unification, what is lost by subsuming the nationalism of Scotland, Wales and Ireland in favour of one Great Britain? The question is rhetorical, and Hill leaves only one instruction: to "MAKE RESERVATIONS" – reserve a seat for the show ahead, and have doubts. When the parrot 'spekes' only English, and only of England, what is lost?

72.1 Parrot Prophet X Although there is an echo of Malcolm X and the Black Panther rebels, the reference here is Skelton's 'Speke, Parrot', a satire on the clergy and his age.

72.2 PRETTY BLOODY Like the talking parrot's 'Pretty Polly, Pretty Polly', originating in the traditional English ballad 'Pretty Polly', which tells the tale of a young woman lured into the forest, only to be slaughtered and buried in a shallow grave.

72.3 basted in contumacy 'Basted', meaning both a) a beating, or b) the cooking of meat in its own juices. Here, the Scots are "basted" in flagrant disobedience ("contumacy" in legal discourse refers to the persistent refusal to appear in court or obey its orders).

72.4 Bannockburn The site of the 1314 Battle of Bannockburn, at which a Scots army of 10,000 men defeated an English force more than twice its size; the battle is symbolic of the violence – and vehement nationalism – of the Scottish struggle for independence.

72.5 dereliction Intentional neglect of obligations; here, England's long-standing neglect of Scotland.

72.6 Sullen Welsh pride Cf. Welshman Dylan Thomas's 'In My Craft or Sullen Art': "Not for the proud man apart / From the raging moon I write ... But for the lovers, their arms / Round the griefs of the ages, Who pay no praise or wages / Nor heed my craft or art."

72.7 the carp A large fish with a single fin on its back, originally from Asia and now found worldwide in lakes and slow-moving rivers, widely bred for food.

72.8 Our Irish trespass That is, the 800 years of British intrusion into Irish affairs.

72.9 Coventry In 1940, during WWII, German bombers destroyed most of central Coventry, including the 600 year-old Gothic cathedral. The area was rebuilt after the war, with a now famous modern cathedral. Completed in 1962, the new cathedral stands next to the old, which is now kept as a memorial, an architectural phoenix rising out of the ashes. Hill describes the destruction of the city in *The Triumph of Love*:

"huge silent whumphs / of flame-shadow bronzing the nocturnal / cloud-base of her now legendary dust" (VII).

72.10 Brummagem A dialectic form of Birmingham, the city made "heartless" in WWII when the Birmingham Blitz 1940-1943 destroyed much of the inner city.

72.11 Worcester In the 1950s and 1960s large areas of the medieval centre of Worcester were demolished and rebuilt as a result of decisions by town planners.

72.12 Althorp The Northamptonshire seat of the Spencer family, resting place of Princess Diana (see stanza 22), and site of a memorial exhibition in her honour. In 1998, Charles Spencer, Diana's brother, published a history of the estate: *Althorp: The Story of an English House*.

72.13 Handelian measures Although born in Germany, George Frederick Handel (1685-1759) became a British citizen in 1710. His music ("measures") has come to represent a quintessential Englishness, hence his inclusion, here, in a collection of UK icons and symbols.

72.14 MAKE RESERVATIONS Cf. "MAKE ANSWER" in stanza 32.

73. Hill has a non-historical, even farcical conceit ("fancy"): Thomas Hobbes is doing "clogging dances" in the court of Charles II (the "dance-master"). Here, he is a character who by day functions as an agent of the Crown – dancing to its music (the "Handelian measures" of the previous stanza) before an unappreciative audience ("solemn cod mugshots"). His performance as the obedient citizen is in fact nothing more than a duplicitous ("self-artificious") act of playing along ("practised dumb-show"). For at night, the wholesome, energetic dancer ("kick and shuffle") was going home to write "BEHEMOTH" ("given" almost at the end of Hobbes's life, and so "almost in passing"), a work eventually banned by the Crown. The courtly ritual may have been performed for all to see, but the private act was subversive, an outlet for Hobbes to 'flex' his intellectual muscle while enduring the day-time control of the court ("under restraint"). "BEHEMOTH", unlike the public Hobbes, does not dance to the "music" of the crown, nor is it created in its language ("fróm music"); and, significantly, although written in private, it was nevertheless destined for publication – not "altogether" written "fór silence" despite the disapproval of Charles II. Hobbes would not dance

ANNOTATIONS

to the King's music; Hill's "fancy" is made of admiration and respect, the "anarchy" of stanza 69 having a presence in even the most seemingly conservative environs.

73.1 clogging dances Dances performed wearing clogs or hard-soled shoes of Lancashire origin made popular during the eighteenth century; here, the dances are "courtly" because they are performed (anachronistically) by Thomas Hobbes (the "him" of line 2 and identified in line 8) before a royal audience. Cf. Kemp's "nine days' wonder" in stanza 60 and Eliot's 'East Coker' I: "Earth feet, loam feet, lifted in country mirth". Cf. the 'Courtly Masquing Dances' which constitute the second section of *Scenes From Comus*, for which John Adson's 1621 book of chamber music, *Courtly Masquing Ayres*, was a source.

73.2 I / fancy him Here functioning both in the demotic sense of 'I imagine him', and in the poetic sense of 'My conceit is'.

73.3 up and doing A demotic phrase used to signify active, committed engagement; here, the sense is of the dancer performing with enthusiasm and drive. Cf. Longfellow's 'A Psalm of Life': "Let us, then, be up and doing, / With a heart for any fate; Still achieving, still pursuing, / Learn to labour and to wait."

73.4 kick and shuffle Both "kick" and "shuffle" are terms from the discourse of choreography: the 'kick' is the flail of the foot, the 'shuffle' its quick rhythmic dragging.

73.5 solemn cod mugshots Hobbes is imagined as performing before an unappreciative audience, whose lack of approval is reflected in their "solemn cod mugshots", that is, portraits painted faithfully but to the anachronistic eye resembling police photographs.

73.6 dumb-show That is, gestures as if in a pantomime. Here, the sense is of Hobbes successfully 'acting the part' (at clogging dances and suchlike) of one in full support of the Crown. Cf. "I / hear you are in dumb-show" in *The Triumph of Love* (CVIII).

73.7 almost in passing Both a) almost without calling attention to their significance; and b) almost in death, just at the point of death.

73.8 floor-chalks original / steps of memory The image is of a professional dance teacher ("dance-master") marking out his students' steps on the dance floor with chalk; the sense is of the mechanical and learned having – with sufficient practice – the appearance of the natural, innate, the "original".

73.9 BEHEMOTH The title of Thomas Hobbes's (1588-1679) history of the Long Parliament. While writing it Hobbes maintained good relationships with the court and publicly appeared to propound the Crown's message, but the text is subversive, an element not lost on the Crown: although written in 1668, the book was initially banned and published only in 1681, after Hobbes's death. Its title is taken from the Biblical name for a monstrous beast, mentioned in Psalms and Job 40:15: "Behold, Behemoth, / which I made as I made you; / he eats grass like an ox."

73.10 tó music […] fór silence Cf. Eliot's 'Burnt Norton' V: "Words move, music moves / Only in time; but that which is only living / Can only die. Words, after speech, reach / Into the silence."

74. This stanza – as Hill notes at its close – is a "scholastic / disputation" on the topic of the relationship between the church and state, as exemplified by reformer Martin Bucer's *De Regno Christi*, which proposes an England determined by the principles of Christianity, with its king governing all entities. The poet asserts that such a combination is inescapably problematic, and that the more a society or an age requires it as a solution, the more problematic it becomes, being an idea always unaligned ("out of true") with reality. Bucer, says the poet, "knew this" and yet remained a proponent of Christian democracy; the poet agrees, urging that one should "accept / no substitute" for a Christian democracy, despite its flaws and despite the inability of the material body to adhere to it ("immunity to reason"). The consequence is that Bucer's vision is not authenticated in daily life ('the body'), but affirmed only indirectly ("by proxy", like Christ dying for our sins or representing our suffering). The "scholastic / disputation" over, Hill now deliberately throws such earnestness into a state of mockery by writing stage directions for two characters in a pantomime or mystery play: a gross coupling of the body ("SCATOLOGY") dancing with Bucer's vision ("DESIRE"), and rendering it farcical.

74.1 *De Regno Christi* The title of the 1557 work in which Martin Bucer (see stanzas 60 and 95) proposed that the English Reformation extend beyond the Church and into Parliament: the nation was to become both ecclesiastically and civilly, as the title suggests, the kingdom of Christ.

74.2 not on That is, not acceptable, 'bad form'; or, never really likely to happen.

ANNOTATIONS

74.3 commonweal Hill expresses in *Style and Faith* ('Common Weal, Common Woe') his approval of the treatment of 'commonweal' in the *Oxford English Dictionary*, its authors' "succinct annotation" for him providing a contrast with other, less successful entries (*Collected Critical Writings*, p. 269).

74.4 out of true Not correctly aligned (here, as a picture 'skewed' in its frame).

74.5 accept / no substitute 'Accept No Substitute' was an advertising slogan coined by Glaswegian tea entrepreneur Thomas Lipton (see 'A Cup of Tea', *Icons: A Portrait of England*).

74.6 you máy suffer; / at best by proxy That is, you "máy suffer", in the sense of daily existence, rejecting this authentic truth; the body is in this sense immune to reason, and thus cannot accept, save by "proxy", Bucer's vision of a Kingdom of Christ, however 'rational' it might be. For the implication that one suffers in the image of Christ, see "soteriologies" in stanza 113 and the accompanying account of the argument which permits salvation through suffering.

74.7 scholastic / disputation In the scholastic system of education of the Middle Ages, scholastic disputations (or *quaestio disputata*) offered a formalized method of debate designed to uncover and establish truths in theology and the sciences. Fixed rules governed the process: they demanded dependence on traditional authorities and a thorough understanding of the arguments on both sides. See the discussion of the disputative literary form *laus et vituperatio* in the Introduction, pp. 7-9.

74.8 enter SCATOLOGY, dancing, with DESIRE The "theatricals" *enter* (in italics, the typeface of stage directions) as if characters on a stage (and in a pantomime or farce); "SCATOLOGY", the personification of excremental humour, is "*dancing*" with "DESIRE"; that is, the world of the body (in a gross coupling) flirting with "DESIRE" (the wish to experience Bucer's authentic vision).

75. After the theatricals of the previous stanza, Hill moves from abstract argument to visual description. Imagining himself as narrating a programme on the History Channel or a museum slideshow, Hill provides a voice-over ("taped commentary") to accompany documentary footage. The contemporary audience for the programme is viewing the scene from a great distance ("vantage", "latitude"); the place to which they "gaze across" from over the chasm of time is to them as foreign and incomprehensible as "ETRURIA", the ancient land and civilization about which we now know so little. Speaking on behalf of this Etruscan image, the narrator tries to communicate with his listeners, resorting in desperation to semaphore ("signal you", "miming in character"); his role is to "bear up" in this unfortunate position of representing the forgotten, but he is "nó goód" in this role. After the assertion that the machinations of time ("bearings") are "out" of synchronization, the poet finally provides a description of the scene and an instruction to "Look" at it. What the readers 'see' are scenes only "two generations" old, yet the vocabulary and 'props' are archaic and undecipherable to contemporary eyes; the smithies and drayhorses are "gone" (like Skelton in stanza 95). The poet/narrator shows this "noble" scene ("sorrowful" because forgotten) in recognition of its loss – his "taped commentary" narration is a personal testament both to the nobility of a bygone age (bygone, yet part of his own childhood) and to the short memories of those who can forget even the worlds of their own grandparents, who can 'pillage' and "erase" the files of history in only "one generation" (see stanza 1).

75.1 vantage A position of superiority and advantage, here with the specific geographical sense of a literal viewpoint.

75.2 latitude The pun is on "latitude" meaning both leeway for freedom, with the implication of permissiveness; and the geographical marker of points north or south of the equator.

75.3 taped commentary As one might find on a coach or tour bus excursion, drawing the passengers' attention to various sights along the journey, and providing historical information.

75.4 ETRURIA The region on the northwest coast of Italy in which the Etruscan civilization flourished in the first millennium BC, here capitalized like a road sign or a region on a map. Today, little is known about either the place or its civilization; Etruria remains ephemeral despite being vital to the spread of knowledge (the Etruscans introduced Greek culture and the alphabet into Rome), and only a few hundred words from its language survive. There is perhaps a suggestion of Napoleon's brief political fantasy, his 'Kingdom of Etruria' (1801-1807).

75.5 signal you [...] miming in character As one communicating by semaphore; also, in the sense of acting in the character of a part.

ANNOTATIONS

75.6 bear up To remain cheerful in the face of adversity. See also "make do" in stanza 32.

75.7 bearings must be out Cf. the "commonweal out of true" in stanza 74. Here, the "bearings" (which are "out", not in place) signify both a loss of direction (the bearings of a compass) and a kind of mechanical slippage ("slipped"), as from one car gear to another, skipping the one between.

75.8 slipped / two generations, perhaps three Cf. "files pillaged and erased / in one generation" in stanza 1.

75.9 stable- or smithy-yard With horses and iron no longer integral parts of contemporary existence, their lexica ("stable- or smithy-yard") have become obsolete.

75.10 clinker-rammel *Clinker* is the hard ash and partially fused coal residue found in a furnace; combined with *rammel*, the residue left – as litter – on the floor of the smith-yard.

75.11 snurring drayhorses 'Snur' is recorded in the *OED* as an obsolete verb meaning 'snort'; drayhorses are those large, strong horses which pull the carts (typically bearing the brewer's barrels) known as drays.

76. "Memory" (here personified, and addressed with the poetic 'O'), which in the previous stanza recalled a lost world, persists, but instead of childhood images, it now recalls (in a formal manner) those images that constitute his being – both those that can be recalled deliberately ("accidents / you can see coming"), and others ("floating perception") that are perhaps the product of luck. An image, inspired by Walton's *Compleat Angler*, presides over the last five lines: "LADY LUCK" watches over "PISCATOR". The art of poetry is analogous to that of fishing: the poet (the fisherman "PISCATOR") 'hooks' "perception" (like a fish in the water); having done so he must then process this perception ("gaffed and despatched"), all the while subject to chance ("curd-faced LADY LUCK"). This, says the poet, is how he has manipulated form ("worked" the "Italian locks"), how he turns the real and perceived into the poetical (continuing the conceit of fishing with "self-barbed" and "blind eyes"), by landing the image then making it into something more. The impossible conceit (piscatorial serendipity as an analogue of an intricate Italian lock) becomes itself a testament to poetical ingenuity, an image of the mind or memory working the "floating perception" into an "elaborate" device.

76.1 O CLEVER Memory Here, the poetic 'O' is used to directly address a personified Memory. Cf. "O bad luck" in stanza 82. The identical rhythm of the first two lines creates a sense of formality.
76.1 O CLEVER Memory Here, the poetic 'O' is used to directly address a personified Memory. Cf. "O bad luck" in stanza 82. The identical rhythm of the first two lines creates a sense of formality.
76.2 take my name As one blaspheming, 'taking the Lord's name in vain', or as a woman adopting her husband's name upon marriage.
76.3 true to type Both a) in keeping with the character; and b) consistent with the 'type' on the page.
76.4 slow motion As when the brain seems to slow down (at moments of crisis) the images it observes; "slow motion" is the term used in film and television discourses for images played at a speed slower than recorded, so that the action appears slower than in life.
76.5 *Ben trovato* A portion of the Italian saying, 'Se non è vero, è ben trovato' [Even if it is not true, it is well invented], which has come to mean, as it does here, 'well put'; the phrase is used in reference to an impressive piece of oratory which may not withstand close interrogation, here, the conceit of catching an image as one might a fish.
76.6 PISCATOR An angler, and as such suggestion of Saint Peter; cf. Izaak Walton's *The Compleat Angler*, a pastoral work written as a dialogue between the fisherman Piscator and his novice companion Viator (also Venator). Here, the capitalized "PISCATOR" vies with the "LADY LUCK" of line 9; a particular image is suggested (as if an illustration from *The Compleat Angler*), depicting fickle ("curd-faced") Fortune watching over a fisherman.
76.7 LADY LUCK Lady Luck, Lady Fortune, or the Roman goddess Fortuna, commonly believed to rule half of the life of man; his will is deemed to rule the other.
76.8 elaborate Italian locks [...] *concetti* of blind eyes 'Concetti' is the Italian term for literary conceits or examples of affected wit, often (as in the work of Petrarch), performing the function of a lock – the reader must find a key in order to gain access to the meaning of the poem. Eyes which read the poem without this key are therefore "blind" to its essence. This is the tradition of the *trobar clus*, the obscure and almost impenetrable troubadour verse open to only a select few. The

ANNOTATIONS

"blind eyes" may also be the unseeing eyes of the fisherman's fly.

77. The setting of this stanza is the seventeenth century, and in it Hill issues repeated instructions to his readers: they must "Revive", "Face", "reorder", "re-set" and "endorse". The imperative is to acknowledge the ugly, the suffering, the pain in life, rather than to ignore it. First, we must bring back ("Revive") the "antimasque" if we are to enjoy the fanciful masque – we must experience the grotesque as well as the playful. Then, acknowledge the physical reality of death – admit the "clownish" binding of the "corpse-jaw" and contemplate the "skeletal" appearance of old "geezers" approaching death. Donne is such a one: nearing death and composing his soul for it, he made himself up as his corpse ("*show-off!*") and is commemorated as such; this portrait stayed with him the rest of his days, not as a morbid reminder of things to come but as an instruction to instead focus on eternal things. The 'sermon' concludes with further imperatives: to "reorder" (or bring into cognizance) such themes as Donne's 'Meditations on Emergent Occasions' (his sermons); to affirm ("re-set") Burton's sense of life's melancholia; and (like Donne and Burton) to "endorse" in the face of life's grotesqueries the ultimate (beyond the "all but final degradation") reality of the Resurrection.

77.1 Revive the antimasque The antimasque played off against the seventeenth-century Jacobean masque at court often to subversive effect. Cf. Hill's 'revival' of the masque form in *Scenes from Comus*.

77.2 baroque / methane Methane is the gas that escapes from the body after death, here "baroque" because extravagantly grotesque. Cf. "baroque / ís beautiful" in stanza 78.

77.3 rot Both a) rottenness, the stench of death; and b) the demotic 'load of rubbish'.

77.4 Shakespearean girning Here, "girning" refers to the fixed grin of death, and to the common portrait of Shakespeare (the Droeshout Engraving) now known to be not a true portrait, a "fake".

77.5 smoke-ring To exhale a "perfect smoke-ring", the mouth is pursed into an 'O' shape; here, the painful moment of death exhales the soul thus.

77.6 bind the corpse-jaw Forceful closing of the jaw after death to avert the fixed grin.

77.7 skeletal geezers in the contemporary British sense of 'old man'; for etymological effect: 'guiser', one who pretends, as a mummer or pantomimist.

77.8 joke-book toothache Typical cartoon depictions of toothache sufferers show them with a bandage tied under the chin and knotted at the top of the head.

77.9 Dr Donne's top-knot shroud John Donne (1572-1631), metaphysical poet, preacher and Dean of St Paul's Cathedral, celebrated for his love poems and sermons (see line 11). Shortly before his death, Donne arranged for his portrait to be made. According to Isaak Walton, "he brought with him into [his study] his winding-sheet in his hand, and having put off all his clothes, had this sheet put on him, and so tied with knots at his head and feet, and his hands so placed as dead bodies are usually fitted, to be shrouded and put into their coffin, or grave" ('Life of John Donne', pp. 71-72). Donne appears emaciated, gaunt, skeletal; the funeral shroud sheet tied atop the head resembles a fabric crown or knotted muslin top of a boiled or steamed pudding (a "bag-pudding"). The 1631 Nicholas Stone effigy in St Paul's is modelled on this portrait. See Appendix, figs. 7 and 8.

77.10 FAMED / PILLAR OF THE CHURCH A STIFF An anachronistic imagining of the tabloid headline pronouncing Donne's death, with a grotesque pun on 'stiff'.

77.11 Jacobean Sermon The Jacobean sermon as "state-subsidised art" was an integral part of the political machine of Reformation England (Flynn, 'Review, *Purse-Proud Opulence*', p. 174). Here, "reorder" suggests both 'rearrange' (as for publication) and 'request more of'.

77.11-12 Burton's / *Anatomy* Robert Burton's *The Anatomy of Melancholy* (1621), is a medical handbook of 'melancholia', but its scope and idiosyncrasies make it a work of literature. Burton's depression (perhaps like Hill's) was abated by prolificacy: "I write of melancholy, by being busy to avoid melancholy. There is no greater cause of melancholy than idleness, no better cure than business" (*Anatomy*, p. 32) Here the anatomy is "re-set" as a drama re-staged in a different era, as a book reset in printer's type, and as a broken bone. See Hill's discussion of Burton in *Collected Critical Writings*, pp. 297-315.

ANNOTATIONS

78. The clichéd "That's great" is the response to the imperative "endorse the Resurrection" and is the voice of the poem's readers, who (like the preacher) have "come thís far" (nearly two-thirds) of the way into the poem. Sensing their frustration with the work's apparent lack of narrative drive, the poet essays an assurance that the complexity and ordered-disorder of the poem is its beguiling feature ("baroque / ís beautiful"). Further, like a Southern preacher embracing his congregation, he asserts that his readers "also have beauty"; that he and his audience are "meant for each other": he is their poet and they are his public. Such a partnership, he realizes, must be consensual: as freely-given sex requires willing parties, so successful oratory requires willing listeners. But to win "fresh auditors" (see stanza 92), Hill will not stoop to just anything: although "commerce" would suggest he abandon the "baroque" and "speak straightly", he refuses to do so, and instead images himself strangely as a slave upon the block, ogled by the monied classes yet retaining his dignity and self-respect. After this assertion, Hill closes the stanza with an image intended to prove his point: a relic, a Civil War bronze statue coated in green muck; a "Union trumpeter" in the Confederate South (and Hill, a white Englishman, adopting the voice of an evangelist preacher and imagining himself as a black slave): even this baroque artefact of the past is "less strange now than wé are". The baroque can indeed be beautiful, but to affirm this entails equally a recognition of our kinship with the "strange" within us all.

78.1 thís far At stanza 78 out of 120, "thís far" is nearly two-thirds of the way through the poem.

78.2 brothers and sisters The appeal to the "brothers and sisters" who are the poet's auditors suggests the preacher – specifically an evangelical preacher – delivering a sermon before his congregation. Cf. "Jacobean Sermon" in stanza 77.

78.3 baroque / ís beautiful The pun plays on the slogan from the 1960s African-American culture, 'Black is Beautiful'; here, it attests to the intricate beauty of life, despite the "baroque / methane" of the previous stanza; and, equally to the baroque beauty of Hill's own work.

78.4 we / were meant for each other The language is of Mills and Boon romance novels; the sentiment is that fate, the stars, or a kind of romantic predestination serve to unite lovers.

78.5 Consensual / the gifts [...] in both / unequalled The sense is of both sex and oratory as acts requiring (and to the same degree) consensual participants; in the case of oratory, a speaker and a listener.
78.6 reborn commerce The conceit is that of a plantation owner in the fundamentalist South ("reborn commerce"), ogling a black slave whom he may purchase.
78.7 abide / my chainhood on the block That is, both a) endure his sufferings like a slave exposed for sale; and b) accept the record of such exposure in print (the printer's engraved 'block').
78.8 bronze equestrian Union trumpeter One of the bronze statues which are monuments to Civil War heroes to be found in public parks and outside municipal buildings (and, en masse, at the Gettysburg National Military Park); a bronze of a United States cavalry officer who participated in the 1864 Battle of the Wilderness (an especially bloody conflict between Union and Confederate forces waged in the scrub of Virginia) bearing a bugle, its patina of oxidization over the years producing a green, swampy appearance. Hill may refer specifically to the soldiers' monument which stands at the front of the Brookline Public Library in Massachusetts; designed by Edward Clark Potter and matching Hill's description, it is inscribed "To the men of Brookline who heard the call of duty and offered their lives in the defense of the Union 1861-1865".

79. In this stanza, Hill uses a series of impossible, delicate metaphors to describe the relationship between the spirit and the flesh. He opens with a dictum on the subject of sleep, which for those nearing the end of life ("almost there") is required in ever-decreasing quantities (only "as and when you can"). "Captive" to their carnality, the sleepers will wake and return to the hold of their bodies ("immortality's incarnate lease") and must "Endure" this waking state ("vigil's identity") until released into death (from life, a state of "entrapment" in the mortal body). But, proclaims the poet, "There are worse obsessions" than that of detailing the relationship of the soul and the body. Like Ariel, the "free spirit" or impulse that lies behind the poem has been "shaped by captivity". Its incarnation in the poems ("forsaken" in the "telling") is the goal of the poet's "contemplation"; when the poem is complete, the poet will release the spirit, as Prospero did Ariel: "YOU HAVE MY LEAVE / GO NOW". The poetic impulse and the paradox of

ANNOTATIONS

"spirit" captured in poetic "vigil" is impossible to paraphrase; hence, the startling image of water turning ("self-making") into ice, as the image of poetic precipitation, "even as" the ice comes into being by virtue of the very act that calls it forth.

79.1 Write this. This instruction can be understood as either a) write this poem; or b) write what follows (take dictation).

79.2 We are almost there Almost at the two-thirds mark of the poem, here imagined as a long journey.

79.3 *Mein Ariel* [...] See other iterations of this refrain from *Der Sturm*; again, the image is that of the spirit entrapped ("incarnate") within the material body, and compelled to "Endure" its 'vigil'.

79.4 vigil's identity Here, 'vigil' suggests not only the watching, guarding, and praying of one keeping watch through the night, but also the sense of that which must be endured, specifically the spirit's "identity" within the flesh in which it is entrapped. The winter vigil (see the "ice") brings to mind Whitman's 'Vigil Strange I Kept on the Field' from *Leaves of Grass*, in which a soldier spends a night on the "chill ground" of an abandoned battlefield watching over the body of his fallen comrade. "Endure" (in the context of the soul entrapped within the body), suggests the words of Edgar in *King Lear*: "Men must endure / Their going hence, even as their coming hither; / Ripeness is all" (V.ii.9-10).

79.5 entrapment The word implies the spirit ("*Ariel*") made captive in the body, and thus identified with the flesh for a given time, before it can be set free.

79.6 YOU HAVE MY LEAVE, GO NOW The diction suggests Prospero's dismissal of the spirit Ariel in *The Tempest*: "then to the elements / Be free".

79.7 free spirit shaped by captivity In this context, the "free spirit" can be understood to be both Ariel (a spirit in "captivity"), and the human spirit, or soul, captive to the body.

79.8 forsaken in the telling, so to speak Here, "so to speak" functions idiomatically ('as one might say') and as an indication of direction: the poet ending his "contemplation" and turning instead to speech. The fancy or imagination (the "free spirit") is thus incarnated ("entrapment") in the body of the poem, its freedom betrayed ("forsaken") by the very act of giving it shape. The crystallization of water into ice in the following image further illustrates the paradox.

79.9 contemplation Cf. "Contemplation as love's estate" in stanza 54.

79.10 recognition 'Recognition' is employed not only in its demotic but also in its scientific sense: in the discourse of chemistry it refers to the ability of molecules with complementary shapes to attach to one another; here, as the ice spreading across the pond by exponentially and continually bonding with and adding to itself.

80. The "frail ice" of the previous stanza returns as the instantaneous change from one state to another. This instant – the "*augenblick*" – is pivotal in the experience of the artist, but the example of Beethoven is cautionary; his commissioned cantata *Der Glorreiche Augenblick* was "formed to obedience" in its worship of authority and was as such disordered and "unfocused". The editorial voice interjects: like that cantata by Beethoven, he claims, this work "MÁY BE INSUBSTANTIAL" and he advises the poet to "RESUBMIT" this section. The challenge to the poet is defined: "Even today", in his winter, his synapses failing, there is something "beautiful", a beauty one can neither deny nor avoid. Likewise, in the mind of the poet, bound to conform and compromise as he must, there is a fire burning (albeit "cold") and a "deepening visibility". The challenge is to translate the "*augenblick*" into image in such a way that (whatever the editor's fears) it captures the moment without being a "glorious" failure.

80.1 *augenblick* German, 'moment' or 'instant', as in the moment of "recognition" (see stanza 79) when water becomes ice. The reference is to Beethoven's cantata for the 1814-1815 Congress of Vienna, *Der Glorreiche Augenblick* (Opus 136). The cantata ('The Glorious Moment') is considered the nadir (see line 6) of Beethoven's career; William Kinderman describes it as "kitsch" and "an exercise in bathos" (*Beethoven*, p. 198), a jobbing piece of flattery for the four powers of Europe (France, Russia, Austria and Britain, with the addition of Prussia) who met (in a kind of forerunner to the United Nations) to determine their spheres of influence in an unstable Europe. The score demands four horns, which are sounded chordally; here, these 'speak' for the "mute powers" of Europe (see line 2).

80.2 grammar / of the centurion formed to obedience In ancient Rome, the "centurion" was an officer in charge of 100 foot soldiers (the century); here, Beethoven's musical command (his "grammar") being "formed" by his political masters. Cf. Luke 7:8, in which the centurion is described as "a man set under authority". Hill uses "centurion" in *The Mystery of the Charity of Charles Péguy*: "The sun-tanned earth is your centurion; / you are its tribune"; *The Triumph of Love*: "Did the centurion / see nothing irregular before the abnormal / light seared his eyeballs?"; and the first of the *Seven Hymns to Our Lady of Chartres* (2009): "Portrait of a centurion, haggard, shot / To glory".

80.3 pitched See stanza 9 for an account of Hill's use of pitch; cf. its use in stanzas 21, 90 and 109.

80.4 THIS MÁY BE INSUBSTANTIAL. RESUBMIT Cf. the similarly editorial, interjectory voice in stanza 48: "HAS BEEN | EDITED / NOT CLEARED FOR PUBLICATION".

80.5 nadir of your triumph That is, for Beethoven, the lowest point in a triumphant career, a "triumph" being also the processional entry into Rome of a general returning victorious from a campaign.

80.6 synapses Those junctions between nerve cells (especially in the brain) at which information is passed from one cell to the other; the sense here is of the nerve mechanisms being so eroded and worn that only an approximation of the signal is transmitted and received.

80.7 conflagration A great and destructive fire; here, oxymoronically, a "cold" inferno. Cf. the "auto-da-fé" of stanza 1 and "bale-fire of vanities" in stanza 68.

81. Out of the cold fire of the previous stanza comes the unforgiving littoral landscape of "the saltmarsh in winter", that becomes in turn an image of an old man, who sees himself as analogous to the bleak scene around him. The polluted drain-mouths ("yellow beards") compel the old man's "duty", that is, to respect as well as to observe the environment, however shabby it has become. He looks out onto a landscape of little islands of sewage, of wrecked boats, their "wormed ribs" visible above the salt marsh ("jutting through rime"). The landscape seems irretrievably bleak, and yet, with a shaft of sunlight ("Sun-glanced") it offers up – for a moment – a "striking" spectacle of uncertain beauty. This moment *appears* to be significant, it *seems* to move the landscape out of its bleak temporality and into the sublime, but it does not: it is tied to time and will endure for only a moment ("clock-shifts / of steady alignment"), it is an example not of lasting transcendence but rather of the fleeting Wordsworthian 'spot of time'. Experiencing it, the old man is not so much transported out of his position, but rather likens himself (a further analogy) to an obsolete relic ("decommissioned lighthouse"). Although (or because) he has experienced a "beautifully / primed" yet "immaterial reflection", he remains an anomaly in the world of time.

81.1 Again: the saltmarsh in winter The sense is of a cinematic retake: in the previous stanza, the saltmarsh was viewed through a clear, icy lens; now, it is viewed "Again", but reconceived as murky and polluted. Jeffrey Wainwright notes the relationship between the landscape in this stanza and that of stanza 102 ("A pale full sun, draining its winter light, / illuminates the brack and the bracken-coloured / leaves of stubborn oak"), adding that the "bleak" zones between water and land have for Hill an especial appeal: "The littoral has held a powerful place in Geoffrey Hill's poetic imagination right from the beginning" (*Acceptable Words*, pp. 136-137).

81.2 drain-mouths grow yellow beards Mosses, algae and other detritus gathering and multiplying at the mouths of drains.

81.3 decrepit analogues Examples from this stanza include "yellow beards" with the suggestion of an old man, and the "archipelagos", "collops" and "wormed ribs" that follow.

81.4 archipelagos, collops of sewage An 'analogue' is offered: "collops" (meaning greasy slices or chunks of meat) of sewage in the water are like chains of islands ("archipelagos"). Cf. "Why do I think – / urgently – of beach-sewage?" in *The Triumph of Love* (CXLII).

81.5 wormed ribs jutting through rime Rime is the thin coating of frost formed on cold objects exposed to fog or cloud; here, the salt marsh, with the exposed metal or timber beams of a boat – "wormed" as ravaged by pests and rust – that "jut" through this frost and catch the sun ("Sun-glanced"). Cf. the "tranche of frozen sunlight" in *The Triumph of Love* (XCII).

81.6 reflection beautifully / primed Cf. stanza 80: "the light / is beautiful – you can hardly avoid / seeing thát: shadows – reflections – on reeds / and grasses".

81.7 decommissioned lighthouse Developments in modern electronic navigational techniques have resulted in the decommissioning of almost all lighthouses and (as indicated in this stanza) of the people who once maintained and manned them.

ANNOTATIONS

82. The "clock shifts" of the previous stanza lead, inevitably, to the "End of a calendar year", the turning point (perhaps the end of 1999) at which the poet produces his own version of Plutarch's dual biographies, *The Parallel Lives*. The stories Hill chooses to tell in this modern remake of Plutarch are those of the "lost veterans" of the two World Wars, the "double / lives" of those whose histories "haunt" the poet (compare the "astronauts missing their stars" in stanza 7), and whose lost causes will be 'furthered' (by "How much", Hill cannot say) by the poem. But the poet knows that this account will not be heeded by a new breed of entrepreneurs ("openers of the new age"), intent on profit. Profit is their cause, and one they will further even at (like Hitler and his *Lebensraum*) the expense of the innocent. Such unscrupulous "winners" are "pitiless"; they care not for the ordinary people (Anna, Boris, Dmitri, Laika, the everymen and women of the free-market, the newly capitalized East) whom they exploit. But the poet does care and he (like the comet in stanza 105) will keep his appointment ("same time, same place") to retrench, to tell their stories, even if the theme is no more than oblivion and non-identity ("sháred únrecognition").

82.1 Plutarchan parallels The reference is to *The Parallel Lives*, a collection by ancient Greek essayist and biographer Plutarch. The *Lives* includes 46 pairs of biographies: the binary is that of one Greek life with its comparable Roman counterpart (see "double / lives" in lines 2-3); there are four additional unpaired biographies. The text provides unique information about the early Roman calendar (see "End of a calendar year" in line 2). Cf. two poems in *A Treatise of Civil Power*: 'Parallel Lives' I and II.

82.2 special order Special order' is a phrase from the discourse of commerce indicating that an item, although not immediately available, may be constructed or shipped at the request of the customer; here the "Plutarchan parallels" are commissioned of the poet.

82.3 double / lives One living a 'double life' has two identities, one secret and the other public; here, Hill employs the phrase in its Plutarchan sense, with the lives of "lost veterans" (presumably those of the two World Wars) seen as "double" – that which ended their deaths, and that which might have been had they not died.

82.4 openers of the new age Suggesting the twentieth-century 'New Age' movement, favouring spirituality over organized religion, holism over traditional medicine and mysticism over science. Equally, the sense of the new millennium.

82.5 fawning with sharp elbows That is, giving the appearance of slavish devotion while ruthlessly 'elbowing' through the crowd; thus, winning in "all ways". 'Winners' suggests its antonym, 'losers', the contemptuous contemporary expression for those left behind.

82.6 *lebensraum* The term *Lebensraum* [habitat; lit. 'living room'] was used by Germany during WWII to refer to the areas in the East which Hitler wanted to repopulate with native Germans as part of a geographical and cultural occupation. Here, it refers to Western speculators ("openers") capitalizing on the opportunities provided by an industrializing East.

82.7 resurrection men Those "pitiless" body-snatchers who rob graves for pecuniary gain, here a metaphor for those profiting from the entry of the former Eastern Bloc into the free market. Cf. "Begone you grave jewellers / and you spartan hoplites in masks of foil" in *Canaan* (p. 21).

82.8 O Cf. another use of the poetic 'O' in stanza 76: "O CLEVER Memory".

82.9 Anna [...] Boris [...] Dmitri, Laika The names are common in the Russian-speaking world but they invoke (vaguely) aspects of the Russian tradition: Anna (Karenina, or Kournikova, or Akhmatova); Boris (Pasternak, or Yeltsin); Dmitri (of the brothers Karamazov, or Shostakovitch); and Laika (the first dog in space). Here, the Russians initially "missed" the tide of Western capitalism which swept across much of the globe at the end of the 20th century, including locations formerly behind the Iron Curtain.

[1] **82.10 Let's all retrench** Meaning: a) gather together to consider our future actions; b) return to the trenches, the site of some of the greatest suffering of the last century; and c) (euphemistically) to be sacked from a job under the pretext of being surplus to requirements.

83. Hill was, at twenty, "Of an age to lapse or revert", to move either closer to or further from the Church. He is also now old enough to have collected "regrettable souvenirs", brought in to the poem are the tangible proof of his own 'artist guilt' ("*Künstlerschuld*") as one too young to have served, yet

ANNOTATIONS

willing to appropriate to himself the images of war. Just as time has for Hill brought out guilt and regret, eventually the "false / claims of veteran status" see the liars "hauled to account". Such folk have used the war for advantage, a crime comparable to the looting and hauling of sacked towns by Napoleon and his ilk, and during World War II by the Germans, who plundered and stole from Jewish households. Yet everyone ("*Jedermann*") is complicit, and there is a "seductive / pleasure" in the process. Rembrandts are misappropriated, and sold at random. This is a world in which survival and disaster ("bankrupts, timely / survivors") are matters of chance, a world in which "making" and "breaking" are everyday occurrences ("things familiar"). At the age of twenty, and with the moral confidence of inexperience, Hill was not able to comprehend such a world.

83.1 lapse or revert One lapses from and/or reverts to the Roman Catholic Church; in legal discourse, rights or privileges lapse when disused or when appropriate procedure is not followed, and property reverts when it is returned to its original owner.

83.2 bring back Both a) revive; b) return with something (as a souvenir, see line 2); or c) restore (as of pillaged art works) to their place of origin.

83.3 *Künstlerschuld* A German word meaning 'artist's guilt'; Paul Theroux has defined it as "the emotion a painter feels over his frivolity in a world in which people work in a rut that makes them gloomy" (*The Pillars of Hercules*, p. 121). Here, the term is employed in a literal sense, the artist guilty of having 'stolen' his subjects.

83.4 false / claims of veteran status Claims such as are made by those who fabricate stories of having endured the horrors of war; and are finally exposed. Cf. the "lost veterans" of stanza 82.

83.5 *Jedermann* German, 'everyman', but with an echo of the opening (the "strange mouthings") of *Moby Dick*, "Call me Ishmael". Here, it suggests Hugo von Hofmannsthal's 1912 play (with score by Sibelius) of this name, modelled on the fifteenth-century English morality play, *Everyman*; there is perhaps also a suggestion of the Frank Martin (see stanza 54) pieces for baritone and piano or orchestra, collectively known as the *Jedermann* monologues.

83.6 *den Haag* The Dutch name for The Hague, capital of the Netherlands and home of the International Court of Justice, the principal judicial organ of the United Nations; the city is also home to many of Rembrandt's self portraits in the *Mauritshuis* (see line 9).

83.7 old-gold The heavy, gilt frames favoured by the framers of Rembrandt, these "having the colour of old gold, of a dulled golden yellow with a brown-ish tinge" (*OED*, 'old-gold').

83.8 Rembrandts Paintings by Rembrandt Harmenszoon van Rijn (1606-1669) the Dutch painter and printmaker known especially for his self-portraits and observations of the "Dutch-Jewish" population of Amsterdam.

83.9 At twenty, ignorance was my judgement Cf. "Had none or made none" in stanza 84 and "with or without judgement" in stanza 87.

84. And what was Hill's judgement at twenty? Well, as the "ignorance" of the previous stanza suggests, he "Had none or made none." The poem, one stanza referring to another, as a relentless interrogation of its author's convictions, "may as well / tick over". In the previous stanza, the judgement and anticipated conviction was something similar to the war trials of Nuremberg, at which guilt and culpability were (like cheques) "Not transferrable." The setting is now the equally impressive international court of law in The Hague, invoked in the middle of a 'case', all of us complicit in the greater guilt. Hill, reverting to the role of the show-host, exclaims "WELCOME TO THE PEACE PALACE" to a peal of bells ("carillons en suite") – the tone is necessarily ironical (the more so if one associates "beggars in justice" with the absurd trial conducted by Mad Tom and King Lear during the storm). Hill can offer no better judgement than he could at stanza twenty-three, when he pronounced the (in this poem) hackneyed adage "The Dutch / are heroes...": justice is "Easier said" than it is done. Hill as judge is asked to speak to his findings, which are indeterminate ("A good question"). Finally, the show-host Hill invites the presumably vacant and equally useless opinions of the contemporary PEOPLE, typified by evangelical preachers ("BRER FIRE"), politicians ("SENATOR") and beauty queens ("MISS WORLD"). The conclusion is implied: nothing to be said, nothing worth saying.

ANNOTATIONS

84.1 Had none or made none. This opening sentence relates directly to the previous stanza; the play is on "judgement": first, the faculty thereof (discernment, of which the poet "Had none"); and second, the decisions made by exercising this faculty (of which the poet "made none").

84.2 tick over That is, take its natural course, or (like an engine 'ticking over') run idle. Cf. "clock-shifts / of steady alignment" in stanza 83.

84.3 asking for it Idiomatically, to be 'asking for it' is to be deserving of punishment or ill-treatment.

84.4 conviction Both a firmly held belief and a declaration of guilt with regard to a criminal offence.

84.5 Not transferrable As a cheque redeemable by the bearer only; cf. "PAYABLE TO BEARER", in stanza 40.

84.6 beggars in justice The destitute, picked up for vagrancy, awaiting the discretion of the court. The seat of the image may be that of the mock trial during the storm scene in *King Lear*.

84.7 there you háve me Meaning, idiomatically, 'You've caught me out', or, 'I don't know the answer'.

84.8 WELCOME TO THE PEACE PALACE The Peace Palace Library, owned by the Carnegie Foundation, is the seat of International Law. Sited in The Hague, it houses the principal judicial body of the United Nations, the International Court of Justice, and the Permanent Court of Arbitration.

84.9 carillons The sets of chromatically timed stationary bells hung in towers; here the echo is of bells being rung at a ceremonial visit to the Peace Palace – one large bell tower stands outside the Palace, and it houses a smaller set inside.

84.10 *supra* The literary instruction *supra* refers the reader to something at an earlier point in the same text; here to stanza 23: "The Dutch / are heroes | living as they have to". See reiterations and variants of the phrase in stanzas 38, 49, 94 and 103.

84.11 Easier said As in the proverbial 'Easier said than done'. Here, the vulgarity of the preceding sentence is confirmed; the two short sentences of line 10 are similarly clichéd.

84.12 Speak as you find Cf. *The Taming of the Shrew*: "Mistake me not; I speak but as I find" (II.i.66).

84.13 good question What the poet 'finds' (with the sense of a judge reaching a conclusion) is ambiguous: the question is a good one, but equally, an ambivalent one.

84.14 OVER / TO YOU Used on radio or television to invite a new speaker to opine; here, the media guests are "BRER FIRE",

Geoffrey Hill's *Speech! Speech!*

"SENATOR" and "MISS WORLD", would-be celebrities asked for their opinions on some aspect of justice. The tone may be that of the Fox News Channel, launched in 1996.

84.15 BRER FIRE Compare Joel Chandler Harris's *Uncle Remus* stories, with characters such as 'Brer [Brother] Rabbit' or 'Brer Fox'.

84.16 SENATOR Compare "wipe yo' smile" of stanza 53, as an echo of Clinton's near-impeachment by the US Senate.

84.17 MISS WORLD Since 1951, nations have selected their allegedly most attractive single women to compete in the Miss World beauty pageant; the winner is typically asked as part of the judging process for an opinion on world affairs.

85. The focus now shifts, for this and the next stanza, to the mechanics of this poem. Its obscurity is likened to a facetious anagram which one would have to "go psychic" to decipher; the tone and syntax is that of cryptic clues with teasing possibilities. As such, the poem reflects its times. It may be a "new age", but the "same old" quackery (a "dizzy spell" later emblematized by the futures market) is being peddled. Society is "near the edge" of 'breakdown'; breakdown as both psychological collapse, and a process of working "backwards" to its component parts to further understanding. The roles of the poet, the stockbroker and the cryptanalyst are combined in the oblique images of seeking "modern-demo" (an understanding), "memos to dawn-broker" (asking that action be taken), and "duty-savant" (identifying the person in charge, the one who knows how to implement the action arising from the new understanding. To this end, "CODEBREAKERS" are "our salvation", those who seek to decode and expose the modern din of words which make up the stock market rhetoric ("Logos of futures"), to expose it as a "world-scam" about to break. Our "Ultimate hope" is that we *can* decode and break to unbreak this logos: science is *not* "beyond reason". Democracy, for example, only just holds together, a bubble perpetually about to burst. It, too, is a kind of "world-scam", a "cryptic" but "convenient" word for social control.

85.1 Ruin […] small gin In cryptic crosswords, 'ruin' in a clue indicates that the solution is an anagram or a portion of that clue. One possible answer is 'ACUTE RINSING'. Cf. "frozen in time / before the first crossword" in stanza 2. Compare

ANNOTATIONS

"flowering currant that close-to stinks of cat" in Hill's *Without Title* (p. 4).

85.2 Develop the anagram Cf. the "cryptic but convenient acronym" of the final line and the "modern-demo" of line 6. 'Care to go' anagrammatically may be "grace too".

85.3 Psych a new age 'New age psychology', the science of a new age, is equally vertiginous, and vacuous. See also "openers of the new age" in stanza 82, and "profiles of the new age" in 26.

85.4 Force-field In physics (and science fiction) an invisible protective barrier around something; here, the precarious limits of mental stability.

85.5 Ruin smell [...] near the edge Adam Kirsch cites the first four lines of this stanza as an example of Hill "careening over the cliff of sense, so that all the reader can glean is mood" ('The Long-Cherished Anger of Geoffrey Hill', *New York Sun*, 1 August 2007).

85.6 CODEBREAKERS our salvation As the codebreakers at Bletchley Park, decoding of the Enigma contributed to the "salvation" of the allied forces. See stanza 7. The previous lines imitate the mind-games of one seeking to crack a code, when perhaps what is required is "psychic" insight.

85.7 Logos Either the Logos (Greek, singular), Jesus as the WORD of God; or the *logos* (English, plural) of the marketplace that adorn advertising material. The wisdom of the futures market is questioned; its icons are part of a "world-scam".

85.8 futures Financial exchanges in which specific quantities of a commodity (or commodified financial instrument) are sold at a specified price, with delivery for a specified time in the future. Because trading is done on anticipated rather than actual worth, such contracts are considered by many to be a "world-scam", particularly after the exposure of questionable practices on American markets during periods of worldwide financial crisis.

85.9 meniscus Although etymologically denoting the crescent moon, 'meniscus' refers to the convex surface of a liquid within a vessel or container, an effect caused by surface tension. A common example of meniscus is a glass filled by water to more than over-flowing; this state is fragile and easily destroyed by movement. Here, the sense is of the futures markets being at their peak, their surface tension "about to break". Cf. *Scenes from Comus*: "meniscus of desire" (3.1).

85.10 Ultimate hope The phrase echoes the commonplace that science and technology offer the only hope for modern humanity (cf. "ultimate in cosmetics" in stanza 71).

85.11 Take, / e.g., Democracy 'Take' functions both as an imperative, 'understand it', and as an instruction to 'use' (or try to use) democracy as a method for political organization. Cf. "Take it" in stanza 54. The initial letters of the last line read: ACBCA, echoing the near-palindromes of line 6.

86. The printer's 'blocks' of "twelve-line" stanzas are excreted by Hill, who is less a god-like Poseidon than "convulsively mortal", the swimmer in his goggles: each stanza a lap of the pool, the poet coming up for air ("head / solemnly breaking water") before disappearing again into his underwater world. The long-distance swimmer is tinged by chlorine, suggesting the Green Man of medieval romance, "spouting" (rather than 'sprouting') poetry. Hill rehearses ("Say again") the old questions: the invitation to go psychic (stanza 85); predicting the future ("hów múch?"); getting it right ("Is there ever a good time?"); and what is at stake ("What's on offer?"). The future is occluded, and any attempt to penetrate the obscurity ("Night and fog", as in stanza 88) is likely to prove but one "losing answer" out of the "thousands" considered; the loss, however, is not indicative of the heroics ("slapdash courage") implied. However futile, "Not all is ruin", as long as a "final salvo" can be offered in defiance. Here, that implies rousing the dead (Hipper, Jellicoe), honouring them with his "wreaths of iron", poems cast upon the "blóck", intended (like a floral wreath, cast into the sea to honour the dead) at least to float awhile, but (cast in iron) destined to sink without trace.

86.1 He voids each twelve-line blóck That is, the poet empties himself of each twelve-line stanza of the poem; the "blóck" is both the unit in which the poem is measured (the stanza) and the printer's block on which it is typeset. See "on the block" in stanza 78 and "Eight-block coda" in stanza 112.

86.2 head / solemnly breaking water As a swimmer coming to the surface after several strokes.

86.3 Poseidon The Greek god of the sea who, when furious, stamps his trident on the ground, causing earthquakes (of which he is also the god); here, the poet is "convulsively mortal".

ANNOTATIONS

86.4 green man The green man is a motif found especially in sculpture, both ecclesiastical and secular; he is normally depicted as round-headed, large-eyed, foliate, with leaves and tendrils or – when serving as a fountain – water "spouting" from his mouth. Here, the green man 'spouts' poetry, recalling the Middle English alliterative romance *Sir Gawain and the Green Knight*.

86.5 care to be psychic The phrase (in slight variation) is repeated from stanza 85: "care to go psychic".

86.6 NIGHT AND FOG See stanza 88 for a full account of the *Nacht und Nebel* decree and the 1955 film of the same name; here, the Anglicizing and capitalization suggests the title of Resnais's film rather than the Nazi decree.

86.7 losing answer / out of thousands submitted As in perhaps a crossword competition; but with the losing answer(s) announced.

86.8 final salvo Here, "salvo" is employed both in the sense of a volley of shots or clutch of bombs, and as the saving clause which preserves a reputation; the image is that of going down with one's guns still firing.

86.9 Jellicoe Hipper and Jellicoe were on opposing sides at the WWI Battle of Jutland (see stanza 6): Franz von Hipper (1863-1932) as Battlecruiser Commander of the German High Seas Fleet and John Jellicoe, later Earl Jellicoe (1859-1935), as Admiral of the British Fleet.

86.10 signal of requiem The image is that of 'signalling' at sea, the two commanders alerting the other to impending death.

86.11 cast wreaths of iron With the sense of throwing wreaths into the water (at a place of death), but also firing deadly shells, made of cast iron.

87. In another self-conscious, metatextual opening line, Hill states that, if he could, instead of straying tangentially around the globe and through time ("Rimbaud's career, Nigerian / careerists") instead "focus" on one thing "once", he might present a narrow but passionate (even if "plainly disordered") argument ("thesis") to his editors and critics ("examiners"). However, singularity of focus would not guarantee success: Hill's thesis might be received but still be rejected, his publishers ("drummers-up") having their eye on the wider markets rather than the niche audience that this thesis might hope to create. The various phrases ("Nigerian", "anomie", "disordered", "markets") coalesce in another cliché: "BIAFRA RULES", from which emerges an image of singular focus, that of Christopher Okigbo, the "young Igbo" schoolteacher ("master") and poet who (not unlike Rimbaud) exchanged an academic life not for the classical insignia of war ("panache", "command-flag"), nor for the Bond-like catchphrase of popular fiction ("POLITICS, ESPIONAGE, AND TRAVEL"), but for the brutal realities of the Biafran Civil War. The relative merit ("judgement") of this decision is left unconsidered (he sacrificed not only his career but his life), but his style – the courage of his acts – is "undisputed".

87.1 Rimbaud's career French symbolist poet Arthur Rimbaud (1854-1891) moved through France, Europe and North Africa engaging in poetical and entrepreneurial pursuits, duels and confessional autobiography; only his death in Marseilles at 37 ceased this whirlwind of activity.

87.2 Nigerian careerists The reference might be to Nigerians Major Nzeogwu (stanza 99) or Colonel Fajuyi (stanzas 19, 49, and 99), but poet Christopher Okigbo seems a more fitting choice: he gave up a Cambridge University Press position and an academic and poetic career to fight for Biafran independence (see lines 8-12 and note 7). Hill encountered Okigbo in 1967 in the Ibadan region of Nigeria, where he was visiting on leave from Leeds; Ezenue-Ohaeto attests to Okigbo having shown the English poet "a photo book of horrible injuries sustained by Northern Igbos" (*Chinua Achebe: A Biography*, p. 123). Okigbo is commemorated in the sequence "Ezekiel's Wheel" in Hill's *Canaan*; David Sherman notes the poet's search for a "mode of thinking that could bear the cost of witnessing Okigbo's life and death" ('Elegy under the Knife', p. 178). The two poets were born in the same year; but Okigbo was killed in action at 35.

87.3 anomie See also stanza 4. A sociological term referring to a distinct lack of norms in a society (and the resulting sense of alienation among the individuals within it); here, the centre of the self is anomic, the self alienated from itself.

87.4 thesis which they / must receive to reject The image is of a doctoral thesis submitted to big-name examiners who will reject it as "plainly disordered" but must "receive" it, have it brought to their attention and thus acknowledge responsibility.

87.5 BIAFRA RULES As if graffitied or shouted by a supporter of Biafra, the secessionist state of West Africa that survived from May 1967 to January 1970. See stanzas 19, 49 and 99 for accounts of the situation of the Biafran Igbos (line 8) and martyrs of the conflict.

87.6 long-dead young Igbo master Wainwright notes that this phrase is "redolent of Renaissance aestheticism" (*Acceptable Words*, p. 103); as such, it proffers an image of Okigbo as gallant crusader. 'Master' refers both to Okigbo's skill and to his having been a Latin 'master' at Fiditi Grammar School.

87.7 Ovid's *Amores* "Ovid's *Amores*", his elegiac studies of love and war; and "Latin eclogue", the genre of short, pastoral poetry, are invoked as emblems of Okigbo's life before the Biafran War, and as influences on his poetry.

87.8 with or without judgement That is, a) without a proper trial; and b) in support of a case perhaps insufficiently considered. The sense is of Okigbo as having "transferred" from academia and the politics of archaic war (the "panache", the plume atop the soldier's helmet, his "command flag" – all borrowed from "Latin eclogue" or from Ovid's love/war poems in *Amores*) for the 'real thing'; this authentic (rather than literary) war is represented by three capitalized words as the catchphrase for a Bond film, or the slogan on an army recruiting poster.

88. History is neither clear, nor kind nor just: the righteous are eliminated by military manoeuvres kept mum, and the heroism of women has only been recently "admitted" into the history books. Christ's death ("Ónce for all") should have been a final redemption ("cósts / of live demonstration waived"), but yet the contemporary, physical atrocity remains, as exemplified most horribly by the 1941 'Nacht und Nebel' decree. Other instances may be invoked, particularly (in Hill's poem, perhaps a little late) those heroines of World War II, Odette Sansom and Violette Szabo. Tortured victims are made to sign forced confessions with "broken / hands", are told to "Stand at ease" – though only in the soldier's sense – for execution ("against the wall"). Photographs of the soon-to-be-dead are taken, and for all their "cracked" and "stained" quality are all of what remains: the incontrovertible records of the horror of the actuality of the deaths – the "finest hour" in which the celebrated and heroic acts took place were also the darkest, the dawn executions at which suffering and evil were most obviously manifest. And yet Hill asks us to take his words with the proverbial grain of salt: the heroism of the Resistance fighters, of Odette and

Violette, should and must be celebrated, and yet are these not simply a few vignettes saved for posterity from the general panoroma of suffering, the "Night and fog" that enveloped an entire continent? Or, ignoring Hill's self-protective irony, his appropriation of such images, and the sentimentality of such films as *Carve Her Name with Pride* (1958), should we not accept these unflattering images for what they are: a true testament to heroism?

88.1 *Nacht / und Nebel* The 1941 *Nacht und Nebel* ('Night and Fog', see stanza 86) decree aimed to intimidate the public by arranging for those who opposed the Nazi regime to vanish without trace; not knowing the fate of loved ones inhibited resistance. The victims were imprisoned, tortured and executed, and forced to torture and execute each other. The italicized reference refers to the 1955 French film by director Alain Resnais, *Nuit et Brouillard* which depicts Holocaust atrocities via documentary footage; the film quite literally 'goes for the throat' (the idiom for an attack by a beast of prey). Hitler took the phrase from Scene III of Wagner's *Das Rheingold*, set in the dark realm of the Nibelungs, where the stunted dwarf Alberich (often depicted as Jewish) puts on the Tarnhelm to make himself invisible, and sings: "Nacht und Nebel, niemand gleich" [Night and Fog, like nobody].

88.2 Ónce for áll Suggesting both Christ's death (to redeem us all), and WWI (the war to end all wars), all rendered hollow by the cruelties of WWII.

88.3 dead women late admitted heroes 'Late' functions ambiguously: the "dead women" are admitted to the ranks of heroes only after death, and later than they rightfully should have been.

88.4 hands patched up for the occasion The forced signing of a confession after torture has mutilated the hands.

88.5 Odette Odette Marie Céline Sansom (1912-1995) whose work for the French Resistance led to her capture by the Gestapo in 1943. She was subjected to great cruelty (her back was seared with an iron, her nails pulled out), her torturers desperate to discover the location of a wireless operator and British officer. Sansom maintained her silence and endured two years of solitary confinement at Karlsruhr women's prison before being transferred to Ravensbrück, from whence she was freed at the end of the war. Awarded the George Cross in 1946, recognition for Sansom came not so "late" as for other war heroines.

ANNOTATIONS

88.6 Violette Violette Szabo (1921-1945), an English-French secret agent captured during a 1944 gunfight near Limoges. Szabo was incarcerated at Ravensbrück, but she fared worse there than Sansom, being interrogated, tortured, and finally executed in February 1945. She was posthumously awarded the George Cross (the second female recipient); the award was accepted on her behalf by her orphaned four-year-old daughter.
88.7 Stand at ease The military parade position 'stand at ease' is neither as alert as 'attention', nor as relaxed as 'easy'; here, it is the position in which prisoners are executed "against the wall" (see line 10).
88.8 Darkest at finest hour The sense is of the women's finest hours being also their darkest: *dark* because taking place at night (as Nazi executions commonly did), and because of the moment of death.
88.9 Add salt to taste This (culinary) version of the proverbial phrase, 'take with a grain of salt', adds to the pathos of the stanza; the Churchillian cliché ("finest hour") so inadequate in the face of such enormity.

89. In this stanza of clipped phrases and capitalized epithets (perhaps simulated crude talk in a pub), Hill applies medico-legal language to theological diagnosis. The instruction is to state a theme ("Write out a cause") and Hill's contention is that he has an "untreated / logomachic sarcoma" – a festering wound of, fittingly, epithetical tissue – *of contentious words*. The symptoms can be seen in this poem, in which he is unable to escape the equivocality of vocabulary. But who or what is to blame? It is a medical and ethical misadventure, a *grand mal* and a "grand malpractice" and all part of the "post-doctrinal foul-up"; in the modern era, theology and language are no longer one. Embarking on his statement of a "cause", Hill clinks glasses with "Augustine's fellow", Luther, who broke wind at such length as to be tuneful, an image which he can "Cross-reference" to the "ODOUR OF SANCTITY", whereby the sweet smell of saintly death is replaced by the stench of flatulence. Hill must "run" to escape the not unjust accusation that he is making jokes in bad taste. He has given himself a handicap, offering his cross-examiners and inquisitors (theological and legal) a head start ("ten yards"); he can do this and still win his case. But he must not be over-confident: he has friends, perhaps, but not "allies"; and his cause is phrased as a scatological continuation: "fart"; "odour"; "asshole". Redemption is not an emetic for the "post-doctrinal foul-up", and does not relieve us (he argues) of our responsibilities. But he must not overstate his case: he must not admit any possibility that time (rather than atonement) will absterge sin; nor should he invoke Anselm's detailed explanation of the reconciliation between man and God through the life and death of Jesus, as that may be wilfully misunderstood.

89.1 cause In legal discourse, the reason for bringing a lawsuit to court; here, the cause is cited after the colon.

89.2 crazed sanity Compare Joseph Heller's *Catch-22*: "Orr would be crazy to fly more missions and sane if he didn't, but if he was sane he had to fly them. If he flew them he was crazy and didn't have to; but if he didn't want to he was sane and had to" (pp. 56-57).

89.3 logomachic sarcoma *Logomachies* are lexical arguments (battles of words). Here, a *sarcoma*, or fleshy, malignant tumour, is described as being made of such; the lines read as self-diagnosis.

89.4 grand malpractice Malpractice is improper activity conducted by a professional ("untreated" and "sarcoma" suggest specifically a medical practitioner); "grand" is used in its legal sense of 'serious'.

89.5 post-doctrinal foul-up The sense of Christian doctrine (Augustine's *De Doctrina*) having been completely abandoned, with catastrophic results ("foul-up"): systematic doctrine is replaced by a view that natural sounds and impulses are just as worthy, for which Hill provides spurious justification (see the following 3 lines).

89.6 Augustine's fellow [...] angels' song The image is from the *City of God*, in which Augustine claims that some men "have such command of their bowels, that they can break wind continuously at pleasure, so as to produce the effect of singing" (XIV.24). Wind as song is also found in Luther: "I am of a different mind ten times in the course of a day, But I resist the devil, and often it is with a fart that I chase him away" (*The Wit of Martin Luther*, p. 74). Hill puns on "passing", which is both 'taken for', and the scatological 'emitting' ('passing wind'). Cf. 'Of Angels' Song', the title of a short tract by English Augustinian mystic Walter Hilton (d. 1396).

89.7 ODOUR OF SANCTITY The name from the Middle Ages for the fragrance given off by the bodies of saints; the "Cross-

ANNOTATIONS

reference" is to Luther's wind, a bad joke (and smell) from which one should "run".

89.8 cross-examination Questioning a witness from the opposing side in a trial, or any persistent, aggressive inquisition; the determined handicap: 'give you ten yards start'.

89.9 Don't overstretch it That is, 'don't labour your point'; in a scatological sense: 'don't overstretch the rectum'.

89.10 TIME / WIPES ALL THINGS CLEAN The sense is of sins needing to be actively atoned for rather than passively cleared by abstergent time.

89.11 CUR / DEUS HOMO The title (*Why God Became Man*) of Anselm of Canterbury's argument for the 'satisfaction view' of atonement. Hitherto, Christ's suffering on earth had been understood to be his paying (with his life) the penalty of human sin (known as penal substitution) or as a payment to Satan for the freedom of those under his bondage (the ransom theory). Anselm countered with Christ's suffering as his demonstration on behalf of all humanity of the debt of honour owed to God; Christ pays that debt and rectifies the imbalance of honour and sin.

89.12 filthy talk The misunderstanding of Anselm's title as degrading slang, as in the schoolboy humour that would translate the words as 'Why God is Queer'. Cf. "filthy" Latin in *The Triumph of Love:* "strong words of Christian hope, / *sub rosa*, the unmentionable graffiti" (LXXVII).

90. Now, when "Mediation" (in law, intervention for the purposes of reconciliation; in theology, the explaining of God to man) is a lucrative commercial exercise ("Mediation means business"), in an age which is itself mediatory between the Fall and redemption (the "business" end, the site of real action). The 'apostles' nevertheless prepare to launch themselves – as if by jet plane, with afterburners lit like burning cigars – upon the world. And in this world, mediation means war, and war in turns means commerce. The evangelists are wealthy; 'flying' with them is like holidaying with millionaires, their jets and cigars just two examples of the luxury of the lifestyle of the militant right. In this "galaxy / of voices", beset by static, the assurance of a right direction (a beam to "home on") it not easily discerned. For Hill, the "Animus", here embodied by the North American Christian evangelical Right, is what motivates him, what he – like a baseball player – "home[s]" on, even as he is pitched to (as he listens to their pitch). He is motivated, also, by a sense of urgency: he recognizes that he has but one split second of opportunity, and no second opportunity; he's in or he's out; the temple is standing, or its standing is destroyed. This is Apocalypse, if not Now, then Nearly; and its locus is the Unites States of the 1990s. Fittingly, the voice that emerges from the "galaxy" is that of Bill Clinton, but its lasting image may be that infamous "post-prandial" cigar.

90.1 apostles' jets The private aeroplanes of the super-rich preachers of the American far religious right, but by implication also that of the right wing military.

90.2 afterburners Auxiliary burners fitted to aeroplane exhausts to increase thrust, here "glowing" like the ends of affluent after-dinner ("post-prandial") cigars.

90.3 millionaires' playthings The sense is of a luxury holiday ("furlough / with millionaires' playthings") taking the place of any acceptance of responsibility ("duty").

90.4 galaxy / of voices Cf. "THEATRE OF VOICES" in stanza 104; but here with the suggestion of a babble of sound ("leaping | static") that confuses clear communication.

90.5 Animus Hostility or ill-feeling from without; the implicit contrast is with 'anima', the faculty of self-reflection. The image is one of seeking a radio beam to "home on", but encountering difficulties with "static" and "pitch".

90.6 pitch See also stanzas 9, 21 and 109; there is also a suggestion of the 'home run' which results from a 'pitch' in the game of baseball.

90.7 You can say that again A colloquialism indicating the listener's absolute agreement with the speaker.

90.8 Split second's chance allowed, no second chance That is, the barest instant to make a choice, with no opportunity to make another; in baseball terms, the difference between making it 'home' and being given 'out'.

90.9 pack it in To 'cram full', with reference to the 'mediation' of the 'apostles' (the crowds at religious festivals), but equally (perhaps) to the poet and poem.

90.10 its standing | here destroyed An aural ambiguity: the temple stands here but in a state of destruction; or, its status and reputation ruined.

90.11 Rum place for a cigar, *Herr Präsident*... "Rum" in the sense of unusual, a Britishism that disengages the speaker from the American scene. Hill refers to a sensational episode in which President Bill Clinton in his affair with Monica

ANNOTATIONS

Lewinsky used a cigar as a sex toy. See also stanza 53, where *"Herr Präsident"* is similarly invoked.

91. From one bad joke ("Rum place for a cigar") to another: now, Hill's poetic lay lays it on a shade a shade too thickly. Safe "in the arms" of his cloistering linguistics ("claustral love"), the poet resorts to elaborate punning, delineating the joke: "A pun" on *arms* is made, referencing the military arms of the previous stanza; another "on *lays*", this time sexual (Hill is "thát / sórt of a mind"); Hill then facetiously asks his readers if they are "still wíth" him. He is "Wandering again", cursed to pun; his words on the printer's block (and his fits of block capitals) are a "noose of twine" (like those hung around the neck of the criminal in his mugshot): even his own name is a joke, as he showed in stanza 60 ("Up the Hill"). He urges us, however, not to misunderstand his humour: it is not ingenuous delight of wordplay that fills his otherwise "vacant days"; such word games are not for him an "idyll" but an albatross. His "claustral love" such games may be, but do they bore his audience? An imagined child yawns at Hill's recital: both the child and we, the readers, have heard the *Der Sturm* refrain before; indeed we have already heard its reprise. But, evidently, patience is required. Hill makes a significant admission: he – perversely – requires "variant dolours" and sadnesses for his work: there is a perversity in the artist's desire for suffering. Dolores, the dark muse of the poem, is now a "FRÍGID BÍTCH", frigid because she – at times like this – offers no more than the finally fruitless, virtuosic play with language. Hill may not be the warring player of the previous stanza, but he is invoking here the "variant dolours" of his own straying, playing mind.

91.1 Thís lays it ón | a shade That is, the poem: a) attributes responsibility to a ghost; and b) effects a little bathos. To 'lay it on' is to exaggerate, or to place undue emphasis upon.

91.2 in the arms / of his claustral love The sense is both that of one in the close embrace of his love, and of that love being secluded, confined.

91.3 A pun, then The pun is on 'arms' as both weapons and limbs; there is a hint of the opening line of Virgil's *The Aeneid*: "Arms and the man" [*Arma virumque cano*].

91.4 Another one The pun is on 'lays' in its dual sense of poetic stanzas and the demotic 'have sex with'; the pun discovered, the opening lines of the stanza are repeated.

91.5 are yoú still wíth me? A demotic phrase meaning, 'Do you maintain your understanding?', 'Do you follow me?'.

91.6 blocked words hung around neck Like the Wandering Jew bearing his statement of penitence, or as one condemned, or like Coleridge's mariner with his albatross, Hill's "blocked words" (i.e., words on the printer's block) hang round his neck on a "noose of twine". Cf. "abide my chainhood on the block" in stanza 78, and "voids each twelve-line blóck" in stanza 86.

91.7 usual idyll Here, the sense is specifically that of a short piece of poetry in which a simple pastoral life is presented in idealized terms. There is a hint of the ironical: *Speech! Speech!* is unlikely to be construed as an idyll, unusual or otherwise.

91.8 yawning at the recital The child yawns at the recital of 'Mein Ariel...' from Frank Martin's *Der Sturm* (see stanzas 54, 65, 79 and 91); just as the child tires of the performance, so may the attention of Hill's audience wane as they hear yet again his refrain.

91.9 Teach patience Compare the reference to philosopher Simone Weil in stanza 31; "SISTER PERVERSITY", however, aligns this female image with Swinburne's vampiric Dolores.

91.10 DOLORES In this counterpointing of two clashing dictions, Hill conflates "dolours" (patient, passive, frigid lamentations), with "DOLORES" (the vampiric, sexually aggressive demon of stanzas 66, 67 and 109).

92. In this, the first of the four Rapmaster stanzas, Hill imagines himself as the inquisitor of the "RAPMASTER" (forcing him to declare his own *eppur se muove*) – a kind of poetic "evil twin" whose poetry of "trite violence" and improvisation (the "RAPMASTER" may be a rap musician) gives an illusion of mastery and "power" which Hill 'disclaims'. Leaving his questioning of the Rapmaster aside, Hill addresses his listeners ("auditors", "fresh" from the reprieve provided by Hill's interrogation), those who have "gone the full / distance" and remained attentive through the last 91 stanzas. These readers have work to do: the poet instructs them to "Take up" the printed page or the Internet page ("ón líne"), to audit the poem, to establish the "true nature / of this achievement", and determine how it has synthesized its disparate particulars into a comprehensive whole ("fixed / the manifold"), whatever the difficulty and lack of reward ("the non-appearance / of peculiar mercies"). Their task is to determine the authenticity of the

ANNOTATIONS

poem, and the poet argues that to do so they must "Presume", that is, have the audacity to get inside his head; only then can they "examine / the brain" and comprehend its prophetic potentialities ("regarding the Brazen Head"). Interrogation is the order of the day, it seems: just as the poet interrogates the Rapmaster, or the characters of *Friar Bungay* the Brazen Head, so the poet's readers must interrogate the poet's surrogate head or engine, the poem.

92.1 RAPMASTER That is, a master rapper (of rap music). This word is associated with John Skelton (see stanza 37), whose poetry – with its sharp, rhythmic iterations – has been described as a forerunner to rap music (see Baz Dreisinger's 'Def Poetry', p. BR.19).

92.2 Either the thing moves [...] or it does not The reference is to Galileo's '*eppur si muove*' [nevertheless, it moves], words the astronomer is said to have uttered sub voce at the end of his 1663 recantation to the Inquisition of his Copernican views. Consider, too, Eliot's *Burnt Norton*: "At the still point of the turning world. Neither flesh nor fleshless; / Neither from nor towards; at the still point, there the dance is, / But neither arrest nor movement." See also *The Triumph of Love*, in which Hill refers to his own "*eppur si muove*" (LXXV).

92.3 fake pindaric A form of ode with three-strophe sections, the first and second sharing one metrical form and the third having another.

92.4 evil twin Compare Salman Rushdie's *The Ground beneath her Feet* (2000) as a celebration of popular music and the evil twin (Elvis Presley's foetal twin). The evil twin is a pop-cultural take on Eros and Anteros, Cain and Abel, Jekyll and Hyde. Here, Hill uses it as a metaphor for his own battle with an opponent with whom he is in every way matched (see line 4) but who works for evil rather than good.

92.5 fresh auditors A play on 'fresh ears' meaning 'new listeners'; with a suggestion of auditors producing a systematic assessment of the poem, discerning the "true nature" of its "achievement". Cf. this emphasis of the auditory with "ón líne" in the following line.

92.6 gone the full / distance The sporting metaphor 'to go the (full) distance' is to do whatever is necessary to reach a goal; here, it refers to readers who have endured the poem through to its final quarter.

92.7 ón-líne That is, 'on the Internet', the "evil twin" of the printed page.

92.8 manifold The "manifold" is that part of the engine which relates to the head gasket; joining many connections into one. The image is of the brain – a hotbed of instability and strong emotions – as sitting within the "cauldron" of the skull; like the engine within the casing of the automobile. The manifold in Kantian philosophy is the term for the collection of individual particulars before they have been synthesized and understood; Hill discusses the term in its Kantian meaning in 'Our Word is Our Bond': "Greer's use of the Kantian 'manifold' is in part a technical gloss and in part an impressionistic tincture" (*Collected Critical Writings*, p. 159; see also pp. 139, 141 and 157).

92.9 Brazen Head The medieval Brazen Head was believed to possess prophetic powers; in Robert Greene's *Friar Bacon and Friar Bungay*, the head – man-made to surround England with a wall of brass – speaks three times before falling to the floor and shattering: "Time is", "Time was", and "Time is past".

93. Hill is again the inquisitor of the Rapmaster, but here concerns himself not with poetry but with the death of Diana. Just as in the previous stanza "the thing" either moved or did not move, so in this stanza forgiveness either is or is not required, and – asserts the poet – the scales of justice ("balance") determine that it is (emphatically) "nót". Joining the list (of processional mourners) and entering the lines of the page ("get in line") of those who are not to be forgiven are Prince Charles, Prince Philip and the Queen. They, like the hacks who proffer a journalism of "violence" and "miracle / confessions" are mourning England's daughter, but their speeches and articles do not get to the heart of the matter ("self-knowledge"). Diana, in death, is "beyond" the world of the tabloids ("spielers of abuse"); the public which mourns her may do so as her mother: the nation is Mother England mourning her dead daughter. Yet, on reflection ("Slów burn, slów double-táke"), this may not be appropriate: the nation's grief for the dead young mother ("grief matronal" in both senses) may better be understood in terms of Henry Moore's sculpted Virgin; having made this suggestion, the poet ends the stanza, promising to return to the discussion (as he will do in stanza 98).

ANNOTATIONS

93.1 Pardon is incumbent [...] ór it is nót That is, forgiveness is either necessary or unnecessary. The inclusion of "balance" in the following line suggests the emblematic 'scales of justice' that determine such decisions; the phrase "On balance" both reflects and denies the strict dichotomy of the opening line. The syntactical structure of the opening of stanza 92 is here repeated.

93.2 get in line The demotic 'wait your turn' acts as an instruction to become part of the lines of verse. A literal image is presented: having determined that those involved in the death of Princess Diana need not be pardoned (see 93.6 and 93.7), they must await justice.

93.3 SNÚFF MAN – with PRINCE OF FEATHERS – / PRATFALL his oppo Prince Philip (who grants royal warrants to cigarette companies); Prince Charles (whose heraldic badge features three white feathers); and the Queen, Philip's "oppo" (navy slang for 'opposite number'), whose "pratfalls" included her public address after Diana's death.

93.4 Persephone Cf. stanza 61, in which Diana is imaged as Proserpine, "Ceres' living child".

93.5 England's daughter The reference is to Diana, Princess of Wales: immensely popular with the public, Diana in her death became the daughter of all England. Hill refers to her death, along with companion and lover Dodi Al Fayed, in a car accident in Paris on August 31, 1997 (the public tributes appearing in September). See stanza 22 for Hill's first reference to Diana, and the accompanying biographical note.

93.6 Hack The verb "Hack" (cf. "spielers" in line 9) suggests journalists, whose hounding of Diana during her life and on the night of her death (her Mercedes chased by motorcycling paparazzi) was deemed by the public to be partly responsible for her unhappiness and death.

93.7 she is beyond it / and you are nowhere That is, Diana is dead, and beyond this commotion; while the "spielers of abuse" (the tabloid writers, the royal family) are as they were, nowhere.

93.8 spielers Glib, voluble speakers; those journalists who write for profit and tawdry effect, typically the tabloid papers.

93.9 The Northampton / MADONNA AND CHILD This sculpture, commissioned from Henry Moore (1898-1986) in 1943 by the Church of St Matthew in Northampton, was the artist's first major public work. The "grief matronal" refers both to Moore's sculpture (with its stylized vision of an infant Jesus atop his mother's lap) and the death of Diana, mother to the heirs to the throne and daughter of England (see line 5). Althorp, the stately home of the Spencer family and the resting place of Diana, who is buried on a small island in the middle of a lake on the estate, is located in the county of Northamptonshire. See also stanza 98, where Moore's sculpture is introduced with the filmic "TAKE TWO" (cf. "double-táke"). See Appendix, fig.9.

94. Leaving Diana aside, the poet can now "Hopefully" (Hill deliberately abuses the adverb) determine "how best" to beat his evil twin at his own game: "oút-ráp" the "RAPMASTER". He considers the manipulation of audiences ("work the crowd") – he could, "Like Herod" in the medieval mystery plays, get down from the stage and into the streets, to win the public appeal. But he is now too "short of puff" for such energetic performances; his vigour – dissipated, presumably, with age – can only be revived by such pharmaceuticals ("elixir") as Viagra ("revive the *membrum*"). The poet lacks not just Herod's physical energy but also the sexual potency of youth (unlike the sexy youths who 'rap'), and any "bonding" he enjoys will be "instant" and brought about by medical intervention (see stanza 3). Putting an end to this absurd question of how to beat the "RAPMASTER", the poet can only concede that it is "HÍS CÁLL" – and so change his tune, a way to opt out of an unequal struggle. At this, the midway point of the stanza, the tone and imagery shifts: Hill imagines British tourists, peddling their own brand of banal, xenophobic patriotism ("heroes / living as they háve to"). In these stock holiday destinations (places like the Algarve), as on coach tours of Europe ("mystery tour"), they reject the profound and mystical; in Lourdes, they resent even the forced comfort stop ("Pisses me off"). Their experience of religious fervour has been reduced to Diana's funeral; their comprehension to a veneration of Elton John, who performed at it a clichéd and recycled song. Divorced from the Church, the "Brits" use the lexicon of faith in vain ("CHRIST / ALMIGHTY") or in jest ("even the buses are kneeling!"). The mystery tour (with neither mystery nor magic) has replaced the mystery play: the "Brits" will never stop for Saint Bernadette, nor embrace Herod; their imaginative limit is 'Candle in the Wind'.

ANNOTATIONS

94.1 RAPMASTER The capitalized "RAPMASTER" is repeated in the first lines of stanzas 92, 93 and 95.
94.2 oút-ráp you For Peter Forbes, Hill's wish to "oút-ráp" is pitiful: "One section has Hill bragging that he can outrap the rappers. This is pathetic. Old men who quarrel with the innovations and fashions of their late years always cut a sorry figure" ('Poetry Wars', *The Guardian*, 2 Feb. 2002). This analysis ignores Hill's own sense of the absurdity of the comparison.
94.3 Herod / raging in the street pageants A stage instruction in the Coventry play, *The Shearman and Tailors' Pageant*, quoted in H. E. Marshall's *English Literature for Boys and Girls* (1909): "The movable stages were, of course, not very large, so sometimes more than one was needed for a play. At other times the players overflowed, as it were, into the audience. 'Here Herod rages on the pageant and in the street also' is one stage direction" (p. 195).
94.4 Swíg any óne / elixir to revive the *membrum* The use of performance-enhancing pharmaceuticals such as Viagra, which became available in 1998.
94.5 Squeeze / bóth tubes for instant bonding Cf. the instructions on epoxy glue packaging. Many epoxies come in two small tubes; an equal amount from each is mixed. There may be a suggestion of (youthful) glue-sniffing.
94.6 IT'S HÍS CÁLL A cliché with card-playing origins meaning: 'It is his responsibility to make the decision', i.e., the role of the RAPMASTER is to make the call (for the next dance, or song).
94.7 Algarve The Algarve region of Portugal is a popular holiday destination for Britons, one of several "places like that" which specifically cater to UK tourists, providing a (hotter) replica of home.
94.8 Lourdes A town in the Hautes-Pyrénées famous for the shrine where Our Lady of Lourdes is believed to have repeatedly appeared to Saint Bernadette during 1858. Millions of Christian pilgrims travel to Lourdes every year to partake of the waters of the grotto.
94.9 mystery tour Prosaically, a "mystery tour" entails buying a ticket for an unknown destination. However, the phrase has other connotations: first, the mystery of divine revelation, as in the tradition of English mystery plays (see 94.3) or for Saint Bernadette (see 94.8); second, the 1967 Beatles album, *Magical*

Mystery Tour, and the accompanying psychedelic film of the same name.
94.10 Whát do you meán | a break? English passengers on a European coach tour annoyed ("Pisses me off") at the compulsory short toilet break and/or on finding that the "mystery" destination is Lourdes.
94.11 Elton John Sir Elton Hercules John (né Reginald Kenneth Dwight) (1947-), English singer and songwriter; his 'Candle in the Wind', an homage to Marilyn Monroe, was promptly transformed in 1997 into a threnody and performed by John at Diana's funeral (see stanza 114). It was then released as a single ('Candle in the Wind 1997').
94.12 even the buses are kneeling Recent developments in suspension technology allow buses to 'kneel' to aid boarding and alighting of elderly, infirm or disabled passengers.

95. Now attempting to define the mystery of the previous stanza, the poet asserts – while addressing, again (and again in the first line), the "RAPMASTER" – that "Politics" must be "part" of the problem ("oúr conformable mystery"). Like the relationship between the poet and the "RAPMASTER", the relationship between the people and the "mystery" is one of polar opposites that are yet indissociable: loathing and solicitude – like good and evil twins who battle it out to the end. This eternal struggle is evidenced as "Tudor polity", when the powers and jurisdiction of state and church were being determined; Hill imagines Holbein and Skelton – its pictorial and typographical commentators – as those who (subversively) sought to expose the truths of their society (Skelton as a "rapper" in competition with the 'Master'). But society is not just, and does not always choose to remember the valiant efforts of such individuals: Holbein (here the "pettish / client" of his self-portrait) must be 're-gazed', his own "chalk-bloom" and "dust" having blown away; and Skelton – despite his ability to "outdance" even the "RAPMASTER" – is simply "gone", forgotten. Then, as now, the mercenary amoralists ("Moriscos", "hatchet-men") are so often the victors; Bucer's imagined England of churchly unison, to the extent that it became real, bred up in its Tudor stables "Eurostallions" of "good and ill" character. Politics, we are to understand, is a kind of (horse) race against time, in which the (equine) competitors are bred not for nobility but for the ruthlessness of

ANNOTATIONS

worldly success. And yet: "Skelton Laureate" has in the longer run 'outdanced' the 'right rappers' of his day; so, too, Hill implies, he may himself "oút-ráp" the RAPMASTER (see stanza 94).

95.1 true commonweal Cf. "true / commonweal out of true" in stanza 74; like an evil twin, politics are inseparable from faith.

95.2 Tudor polity The civil order of the House of Tudor, which held the English crown from 1485 to 1603; the "yoú" who haunts it is perhaps John Skelton.

95.3 the gaze of Holbein Hans Holbein the Younger (c 1497-1543), friend and illustrator of Erasmus, woodcutter for his own 'Dance of Death' series and for Luther's Bible, portraitist (hence the "drawn face"), fresco artist, oil painter, and worker of drawings in chalk (see line 6), and finally London plague victim. Holbein was an integral part of the Tudor court: in 1536, after settling permanently in England, he became court painter to Henry VIII and made numerous portraits and drawings of the King and his wives.

95.4 Skelton Laureate John Skelton, the unofficial Poet Laureate of that age (see stanza 37); Skelton endured a difficult relationship with the Crown, being both imprisoned by it (for reasons unknown) and appointed tutor to its Prince (Henry).

95.5 outdance yoú with your shádes The image is of sunglasses, worn for aesthetic effect, as well as a dance of death. Hill's sense is, however, that Skelton was something more than just a rapper.

95.6 Moriscos Moors who converted to Christianity after the Christian conquest of Spain; the sense is that of a lack of commitment to one's faith or values.

95.7 hatchet-men Those hired to do something nefarious, usually murder. Cf. "Enforcer" in stanza 5. The RAPMASTER and his like, Hill implies, would have been the Moriscos of Skelton's day, or the hatchet-men of his own time.

95.8 *De Regno Christi* [...] breaker of Eurostallions Martin Bucer's *De Regno Christi* (see stanza 60) is here employed as an emblem of Tudor and Reformation remaking, a vision that will "outdance" the rapping (or break-dancing) of these days. The metaphor of taming and training ('breaking') horses is here used to describe the grappling between independence from the Pope and the security of membership of a Europe united by Catholicism which typified England's position during the Tudor period. Hill uses similar equine imagery in *The Triumph* *of Love*: "Patriot Blood / is a great horse, so is Eurovista, / Kristallnacht is at stud" (CXI).

96. The Rapmaster is gone; the poet who created and named him has finally out-rapped him. But this is nothing new; the notion of creator ("name-broker") as destroyer ("carnifex") is "an old saw". Hill replaces the inquisition of his evil twin with more routine "Forms of enhanced / interrogation" which are manifested carefully ("by the book"). Placenames require explanatory "Footnotes": Birkenau, Buchenwald, Burnham Beeches and Dumbarton Oaks because they were sites of significance during World War II; Hollywood (added to this list of forests) because it creates images (however unreliable) of the past. Recovery of the bloody past is a slow and painful process: Hill envisages scholars ("Masters of arts") mordantly extracting from the dust ("foundry sand") the corrupt and unreliable evidence of atrocity. Such atrocities are evidence of the days of Sodom, and the search for them is a game of hide and seek – but one which involves "blood" and "fecal matter" and is something far removed from the days of childish play.

96.1 Tune up an old saw Proverbial, meaning 'revive an old iteration'; here, the record ("by the book") of butchery throughout the ages; but equally with reference to the curious skill of playing a saw as a musical instrument.

96.2 carnifex Latin, *carnifex*, butcher or executioner; as the Old Testament Jehovah, or even the poet who has named and dispatched the RAPMASTER. Cf. *Without Title*: "Truth's fatal vogue, / sad carnifex, self-styled of blood and wax" (p. 53).

96.3 BIRKENAU Formally known as Auschwitz II, Birkenau ('birch groves') was the largest of the Nazi extermination camps and the death site of more than 1,000,000 Holocaust victims during WWII. Given this enormity, a 'footnote' to explain the name seems an impertinence.

96.4 BUCHENWALD Buchenwald ('beech forest') was a WWII forced labour camp near Weimar. Unlike Birkenau, it was not strictly an extermination camp; nevertheless, some 57,000 of its prisoners were executed, fell victim to disease, or perished from starvation.

96.5 BURNHAM / BEECHES Burnham Beeches is a woodland near London, celebrated for its ancient beeches. During WWII, it was used as a Vehicle Reserve and military camp; vehicles

ANNOTATIONS

and other machinery were maintained and waterproofed there before the D-Day landings.

96.6 DUMBARTON OAKS A Georgetown (Washington, D.C.) mansion and gardens, in 1944 the site of the Dumbarton Oaks Conference, where representatives from the Republic of China, the UK, the Soviet Union and the USA negotiated the beginnings of the United Nations and the formulation of its Security Council.

96.7 HOLLYWOOD Hollywood is a district of Los Angeles, California, which has become synonymous with the world of film-making and television celebrity. Its inclusion in this list of dark forests is thus an impertinence. The structure and technique of lines 4-5 recalls *The Triumph of Love*: "We have already been sent to the dark / wood, by misdirection: Trônes, Montauban, / High Wood, Delville, Mametz" (CXXXV).

96.8 Masters of arts [...] praetorian bunkers The Roman god Saturn was associated with justice and with the humour of melancholy; "Saturn's justice" is ministered by gloomy, worthy scholars working in their privileged offices ("praetorian bunkers", the praetor being a high-ranking magistrate).

96.9 pourrying [...] their own fecal matter The sense here is of academics (those with MA degrees, "Masters of arts") as slow, gloomy figures ('saturnine' and so "bent" – with scholar's humps – to "Saturn's justice") sorting mechanically through the decomposing narratives of those war dead ("tortured figures"), figuratively drawing the rotting ("pourrying") corpses from their mass graves, where identity is confused ("suspect"), and the findings disgusting ("fecal matter").

96.10 the days of Sodom See stanza 55: "As many as the days that were | of SODOM."

96.11 then shriek / I'M COMING The image is of the game of hide-and-seek, in which the seeker, after a predetermined count (usually 100, here 120), then exclaims, 'Coming, ready or not!', here reduced to a single "shriek": "I'M COMING". Demotically, "I'M COMING" accompanies ejaculation.

97. With regard to what has been imaged in stanza 96 (Buchenwald, the days of Sodom), does the "radical powerlessness" of God need to be "reconceived"? How else to account for the endless iteration of atrocity (the new millennium promising only further doom), and the banal vacuity of the human condition ("backed-up inertia, ignorance")? Was it any different before the Creation (or evolution) of man, before Adam incestuously appeared from the red clay for which he was named (see stanza 16)? Original sin, the "ruination" of Eden, litters our corrupt world, the kingdom of Moloch and of Baal, the worshipping of false idols. Worse, we make a spectacle of it, the violence of our surroundings 'vomited' onto the cinema screen, thrown up for our enjoyment. The sense is of the poet summing up previous stanzas and coming to a conclusion which is also a question: given the debased, debauched and apocalyptic scenarios Hill has already presented, how he can reconcile existing ideas of God with such a show of "ruination"?

97.1 In re A phrase meaning 'with regard to' and with the specific legal sense, 'in the case of'. Given the enormity of what has just been considered (Buchenwald, the days of Sodom), and given the banal nature of what we are, should the powerlessness of God be reconceived? God is usually regarded as omnipotent, and so His reconception as 'powerless' is radical: Hill may be suggesting that after the horrors of the twentieth century (cf. "BUCHENWALD", "BIRKENAU" in stanza 96), God's inability to prevent atrocity ("powerlessness") needs to be thought of again and anew ("reconceived").

97.2 nihilism's palindrome "nihilism's palindrome", in addition to being a description of its preceding phrase, "doom-mood", is a pun on the Millennium Dome, the London landmark constructed to house an exhibition to commemorate transition into the third millennium. The exhibition was a costly financial flop (although a popular attraction throughout 2000, visitor numbers were far short of expectations), as the new millennium perhaps promises to be.

97.3 what it ís and we áre There is an echo of Rudyard Kipling's World War I poem, 'For All We Have and Are': "For all we have and are, / For all our children's fate, / Stand up and meet the war, / The Hun is at the gate!".

97.4 Adam made incest with the red earth Etymologically, 'Adam' is a confluence of *adamah* [earth] and *adom* or *admoni* [red or ruddy]. Thus the earth is Adam's 'mother' (the clay matrix), with which he "made incest" by the creation of Eve (from his rib).

97.5 matrix The matrix (from the Latin, *womb*) is that which is embedded or enclosed inside another. Here, the sense is threefold: first, as Adam is made of clay, and from that 'clay', Eve was fashioned; second, words as clay, moulded to sentences; third, the printer's mould in which his type is laid. The idea is of copies being made; even Adam, the first man and so the type of all, had as his matrix the "red earth".

97.6 cells / of Moloch, Baal's palaces The image is of contemporary communities having disobeyed the first commandment and taken up false idols, a fate of which the Bible warns first in Acts 7:43: "Yea, ye took up the tabernacle of Moloch, and the star of your god Remphan, figures which ye made to worship them: and I will carry you away beyond Babylon"; and then in Jeremiah 7:9: "Will ye steal, murder and commit adultery, and swear falsely, and burn incense unto Baal, and walk after other gods whom we know not." Both Moloch and Baal are figures of Canaan: Moloch a god to whom children were offered in sacrifice, Baal the name attributed to a variety of deities of the region. Cf. "Now it is / Moloch his ovens / and the dropped babes naked / swung by an arm / or a leg like flails" (*Canaan*, p. 12) and "They march at God's pleasure ... to topple Baal" (*Canaan*, p. 10).

97.7 violence filling the screen – projectile / vomiting The image is projected – 'thrown up' – onto the cinema screen, but the metaphor is that of projectile vomiting (not simple sickness but violent and sustained repulsion).

98. Moore's sculpture of the Virgin with Child, first mentioned in stanza 93, reappears as if a filmic shot ("TAKE TWO"). Made from quarried marble ("chalk ... risen to this"), like an ancient chalk 'sleeper' brought back to the surface, the sculpture is literally a "figure", to be documented in anatomical notation: the Virgin's "rt" hip-bone is "load-bearing". Laurie Smith points out the connection with Moore's detailed sketches of the homeless, some nursing mothers. Moore also "became a figure" in his own right, through the process of self-representation and self-making. But Moore's self-making seems to have found expression only in the Madonna, whose description catalogues the creative process itself; Hill transcribes the progression from the cerebral to the physical: "inward, understood, projected, wrought". The infant Jesus, on the other hand, is pleasing but lacking in depth of character, he is "prím, sweetened, incúrious". Yet the "unfocused selving" of the child – the "vacuity" that is the consequence of a lack of self-awareness – differentiates this image from those of Stanley Spencer, whose works transform the demotic and ordinary "truth of England" into an expression of religious energy which is "altogether | of our kind".

98.1 TAKE TWO The language is of the cinematic 're-take', Hill (the film director) having first imaged Henry Moore's 'Northampton Madonna and Child' in stanza 93.

98.2 deep surfaces 'Deep surfaces' is something of an oxymoron. It here refers to the undulations of sculpted stone, of the lustre and 'depth' of marble, the medium from which Moore's Madonna and Child is sculpted.

98.3 Moore also became a figure Moore's marble figures (both marble and chalk share the same limestone base) invoke ancient legends of sleeping figures buried in the chalk coming back to life; here, his 'Madonna and Child' has become a "figure" of the buried Diana. Laurie Smith notes Moore's sketches of the homeless (rough "sleepers"), but this observation leads her to mistakenly attribute the reference to Jacob Epstein, whose Madonna and Child is sited at the Convent of the Holy Child at Cavendish Square: "this refers to Epstein's Madonna and Child in St Matthew's Church, Northampton ... Epstein, like Moore ... sketched sleepers in the London underground" ('Subduing the Reader').

98.4 rt hip-bone The abbreviation of 'right' to "rt" suggests the impartiality of medical notes, or the preparatory anatomical notes made by sculptors. See stanza 98 for the abbreviation of 'right' and stanza 106 for the abbreviation of 'very'.

98.5 wrought 'Wrought' is the archaic past tense of work; here, it denotes the visible presence of the artist in that which he creates.

98.6 selving A word overlooked by the first editors of the *OED*, as Hill notes in *Style and Faith*: "For *self-being* the Second Edition adds Hopkins (retreat-notes of August 1880) to the original citations from Golding (1587), Fotherby (*ante* 1619) and Bishop Hall (*a* 1656), and the same meditation also serves to illustrate *selve / selving* (unknown to the original editors and overlooked or rejected by the 1933 *Supplement*)" (*Collected Critical Writings*, p.267).

98.7 Stanley Spencer's fixation –/ crazed-neighbourly In the work of Sir Stanley Spencer (1891-1959), a fellow student at Slade with Isaac Rosenberg (see stanza 27) and David Bomberg (see stanza 62), religious scenes are transplanted from their origins to the "crazed-neighbourly" landscape and cast of Spencer's birth village, Cookham in Berkshire. See, for example, Spencer's *The Resurrection, Cookham*, in which

ANNOTATIONS

Cookham village and its villagers are used to depict the Biblical scene, creating a sense of familiar, approachable chaos, and portraying – according to Hill – a "truth" of an altogether English kind (see Appendix, fig.10). According to Laurie Smith, the last lines of this stanza are a celebration of "near vacuity as a particularly English strength. The idea that near mindlessness is a strength is fascist, stemming from awareness that ignorant people are more malleable, and this stanza ... exposes the preoccupation that informs the whole of *Speech! Speech!* It is that 'high' culture should be accessible only to a small educated elite ... leaving the majority in vacuous ignorance, strong because obedient" ('Subduing the Reader').

99. The setting is that of a schoolroom, with an irate teacher berating his pupils, who cannot distinguish between cultural customs and political check-points (see stanza 49) and have no sense of the timeline of the last century ("Fajuyi was dead by then"). The teacher enunciates his frustration with scorn ("Hów many móre times?", "Can't you read English?", "I could weep", "Shall I hyphenate-for-you?"). Yet, simultaneously, the words invoke the unspeakable tragedy: gouged eyes that can no longer read, tears that need to be shed. Changing the metaphor, the teacher laments the fall from grace: tracing the "dead age" from "vintage" Brook Farm, through adulterated wine in a bin, to the "dregs" of society. His voice responds to the snide whimperings of the schoolboys (the *"faex Rómuli"*), by imagining such notions as "AUTHENTIC SELF" in terms of schoolboy slang ("stinker", "pass it on"), and tuning in to the schoolboys' "contagious" circle of slander and gossip (*"nasum in ano"*) as once again ("Hów many móre times?") the lessons of history and the betrayal of humanity fail to register.

99.1 Fajuyi [...] Major Nzeogwu For Major Nzeogwu, see stanza 49; for Fajuyi, see stanzas 19 and 49.

99.2 These are songs of praise Hill makes an explicit connection between Fajuyi's "praise-songs" (see stanza 19) and the Nigerian martyrs: "Fajuyi is for me the heart of the matter; he behaved nobly in the midst of total moral chaos. I'm fairly old-fashioned in the qualities I admire – simple courage, simple dignity. When I arrived in Nigeria in January '67, a month or two after the assassination of Fajuyi, the radio was broadcasting praise-songs for him. And I took very much to the idea, so certain sections of *Speech! Speech!* (and of *The Triumph of*

Love) are praise songs. And I wouldn't say that I meant much more than that; but I do seem to seize on figures who seem exemplary to me, and what I believe I know of Fajuyi is worth a praise-song or two ... Everyone says how negative I am, and I don't think I am, I think I'm very positive, and I love to praise, I love to admire" ('The Praise Singer', *The Guardian*, 10 Aug. 2002). Compare *Canaan*: "what do you mean / praise / lament / praise and lament / what do you mean / do you mean / beatitudes" (p. 39), and "Praise-song for oil drums, / a psalm of slippage" in the same poem (p. 57). 'Songs of Praise' is the title of a BBC programme which features hymns sung by church congregations across Britain.

99.3 Brook Farm Brook Farm was a utopian experiment in communal living established (1841-1847) in West Roxbury Boston, Massachusetts. The Farm was founded by George Ripley, a Unitarian minister, but most of the Farm's members had abandoned Unitarianism in favour of transcendentalism; they included Nathaniel Hawthorne, John S. Dwight, Charles A. Dana, and Isaac Hecker, while Ralph Waldo Emerson, W.E. Channing, Margaret Fuller, Horace Greeley and Orestes Brownson were visitors.

99.4 *faex Rómuli* The phrase used by Cicero in the first oration against Catiline to refer to 'the mob', the "dregs of a republic" (*Cicero*, W. Lucas Collins, p. 71); hence, recalcitrant public schoolboys in the lower classes.

99.5 AUTHENTIC SELF a stinker In British schoolboy slang, something unpleasant or foul-smelling. Cf. "I erased / WE, though I | is a shade too painful" in stanza 6.

99.6 pass it on As a secret message delivered in class from one pupil to a series of others.

99.7 *nasum in ano* L., 'nose in anus'; the travesty of the 'authentic self' passed from person to person via this unsavoury method. Wainwright observes a dichotomy: "We might see the Nigerian sections as in part at least authenticated by the poet's autobiographical involvement. But 'AUTHENTIC SELF a stinker', says the headlines, and the gossip is passed on in the manner of schoolboys' snide whispering" (*Acceptable Words*, pp. 103-104). Wainwright asserts that "The extent of our knowledge is not to be taken for granted, even if one can say 'I was there'" (103). Hill states: "A great deal of the work of the last forty years seems to me to spring from inadequate knowledge and self-knowledge, a naïve trust in the

ANNOTATIONS

unchallengeable authority of the authentic self' ('The Art of Poetry', pp. 282-283).

100. Having just announced that the poem is a "praise-song", Hill uses this stanza to praise his muses and predecessors. Even at this, the hundredth stanza, Hill is still introducing a performance: all the world's a stage, and on this dark and darkening world ("near-Stygian sets") the character of "the PEOPLE" (the "*faex Rómuli*" condensed to an everyman) is directed to enter to be unmasked ("discovered", as in a farce). Thanks to ("courtesy") the unforgiving, meticulous social satire of Balzac and Daumier the mob is placed in the limelight. As a poet, Hill owes fellow writer Balzac the greater acknowledgement; having cited Daumier as his muse (stanza 31), he owes him the greater apology. Hill could keep up (as if on Viagra) such thanks and acknowledgements "all night"; it is the kind of prevarication he deems necessary, and yet it defines the problematic of the poem: there are so many thanks to offer for what one has to say that one may never get around to saying it – "the PEOPLE" has entered the stage, but is yet to speak a line. A static image from one of Daumier's studies of travelling performers is presented instead of the promised drama: the father, a clown ("guignol") drums up business (as a "mountebank") for himself and his son, a fragile-looking acrobat ("coral-boned / tumbler"). Of the two, Hill 'suspects' that the father is the "better artist"; despite his seeming buffoonery. The clown is a "master of light and shade", a description which allies the "guignol" with Daumier, whose sculpted and etched faces (like those on the cover of *Speech! Speech!*) are keenly wrought and even in their often monochrome palette ("light and shade") betray the mix of dynamism and inertia ("torpor, avidity") which characterizes them. In this stanza, Hill's courtesies and stage directions have themselves become the drama; at the hundredth stanza, he is still acknowledging his predecessors.
100.1 near-Stygian sets That is, a theatre or film setting so unremittingly dark and frightening as the Styx, the river of Hades, or the underworld of Greek mythology.
100.2 discovered Written as a stage direction, with a character named "the PEOPLE" (see stanzas 1, 13, 22, 40) entering and being "discovered" as if a character revealed in a farce.

GEOFFREY HILL'S *SPEECH! SPEECH!*

100.3 Balzac Honoré de Balzac (1799-1850), the French novelist and playwright whose masterpieces of fiction, collectively known as *La Comédie humaine*, are a keenly detailed, realist reproduction of the social life of his era. Here, Balzac is named with Daumier as an antecedent to the stanza's opening trope (the PEOPLE, the *"faex Rómuli"* of the previous stanza, as staged before a public audience). Cf. stanza 12: "How is it you were clad – / Balzac, you said – in the wild ass's skin?".
100.4 Honoré Daumier Honoré Daumier (1808-1879), the French artist whose caricatures and other works commented on his social milieu, often with sharp satire. See stanza 31 for a fuller account of Daumier and the cover illustration of *Speech! Speech!*
100.5 keep this úp all night That is, the poet could continue making acknowledgements ad infinitum; in an age of Viagra (see stanza 94), the phrase invites and withstands a phallic interpretation, i.e., so exuberant as to be almost "rigid" with joy.
100.6 The mountebank [...] tumbler for a child As Michael Kooy notes, the images of the mountebank and his son are taken from sketches and paintings of travelling acrobats and clowns produced by Daumier during the 1850s and 1860s ('Word and Image', p. 203). See Appendix, fig.11, 'Les Saltimbanques', which depicts a mountebank (here used in its original sense of one whose job it is to attract crowds, from the Italian *'monta in banco'* [climb on the bench]) dressed in clown costume and resting his drum on a chair as he begins to 'drum up' business for himself and his acrobat son. His efforts are in vain: an indifferent crowd figures in the distance; his wife sits dejected, having given up any hope of success. In Hill's judgement, the "guignol" (the sharp-witted puppet of the French comedic tradition, here used as in French slang to describe one who is a buffoon or clown) has more gravitas than the acrobat and is – with his face-painting and mask-making talents – "the better artist". Hill's description of the child as "coral-boned" perhaps refers to medical research conducted in the late 1980s and early 1990s which experimented with the use of coral as a living, growing, replacement for bone grafts in children (see 'Coral Substituted for Bone Grafting in Posterior Verterbral Arthrodesis in Children'). Hill uses "guignol" in *The Mystery of the Charity of Charles Péguy*: "some guignol strutting at the window-frame" (section 4).

ANNOTATIONS

101. Virtue, like the comedy of the previous stanza is "all in timing"; the phrasing is similar to Hill's description of comedy as finally "a matter of timing and facial gesture" ('A Matter of Timing'). According to the poet – one accused of a constipating moral rectitude – we have no firm grasp, no certainty of virtue, only a sense of "instinctive balance" to keep ourselves (morally) upright. Following the first colon, Hill gives an image – alluding to the last picture of Captain Scott's party – to introduce a comparison which proves the importance of timing, of context: that between the heroics of Scott and the more ambiguous achievement of Shackleton who followed him. What stands between these two men and their expeditions – between the heroic sacrifice of Oates, for instance, and the safe return of Shackleton – is the Great War. It "did not / occur" to Scott's men, even as they estimated their "posthumous averages", but theirs was to be an heroic legacy, despite the elements of failure (reaching the Pole after Amundsen, not making it back). Shackleton, however, despite the epic qualities of his journey and the safe return of all his men, could not escape the public perception of an enterprise that might have been construed as an evasion of duty (hence "frozen out" and the "white feather"). What separated Shackleton from Scott's heroic legacy was simply the timing.

101.1 the group leans / into the camera A description of the last photograph taken at the South Pole of Scott and his men, made famous when published with other expedition photographs in the *New York Times* (see 'Scott's Own Story of His Terrible March to Death', 23 November 1913). See Appendix, fig.12.

101.2 Oates might have been found / dead on all fours behind the tent The words "tethered" and "on all fours" provide the comparison between Lawrence 'Titus' Edward Grace Oates (1880-1912), member of Captain Scott's second Antarctic expedition (see stanza 2), and the teams of huskies sometimes used as sledge-pullers in polar travel. (Scott was later criticized for not using these, he and his peers pulling their own sleds; see 'The Use and Abuse of Dogs in Scott's and Amundsen's South Pole Expeditions', pp. 303-310). Oates, aware that his physical condition was delaying his team and certain of his impending demise, walked out of the tent and to his death, after declaring (according to Scott's journal), "I am just going outside and may be some time" (Hill reiterates these words as "I may be gone some time" in *The Triumph of Love* [LXXIII]). Oates's selflessness has been received as one of the great acts of British history; however, the death of the entire Scott party means that his sacrifice was no more effectual than if he had died as a dog tethered behind the tent in which the party's frozen corpses were later found.

101.3 measuring posthumous averages / of bitter legend Those calculations of remaining life as found in Scott's journal (now a 'legendary' document); and the group's estimation of their legacy, the measure of fame and respect they might receive after death, given their only partially successful journey to the Pole.

101.4 The Great War did not / occur to them That is, they perished in 1912, before the outbreak of WWI; and so could not have entertained the possibility of the Great War.

101.5 Shackleton [...] was frozen out Sir Ernest Henry Shackleton (1874-1922) led the 1914 Imperial Trans-Antarctic Expedition, which proceeded despite the outbreak of WWI. The 'Endurance' was immobilised by the onset of ice and then crushed by the expansion of the spring thaw; the ensuing battle for survival and return of almost all crew members is one of the great stories of the heroic age of Antarctic exploration. Here, "frozen out" (which with "In time", recalls "frozen in time" in stanza 2) refers both to this literal freezing, and to the way that events of WWI eclipsed public interest in his experiences (colloquially, the phrase means 'social exclusion').

101.6 white feather The white feather is the symbol used to mark conscientious objectors as cowards; what is heroic in peacetime (Scott) might be considered cowardice during war (Shackleton): virtue, as the stanza observes, is all in the timing.

102. In this stanza, Hill uses a bleak, littoral landscape (the latter adjective is Wainwright's, who identifies Hill's preoccupation with such sites) as a metaphor for the winter of discontent. The landscape, which in its paleness recalls the colourlessness of the Pole (see stanza 101) is not lifeless: lit by a "pale" but "full" sun, the "wind spoórs" over it, offering traces of its different "zones". In stanza 61, winter was expected to bring with it the promise of spring, what Hill here describes as "apprehension's covenant"; but, he asks, could this littoral winter – forever "between the zones" – be our only landscape, a purgatory of human existence never to be ended by a *Paradiso*,

ANNOTATIONS

which must remain eternally "in prospect"? And, similarly, is the littoral landscape of this poem – still at stanza 102 in its winter – ever to be resolved in a final epiphany, or will the *"Paradiso"* remain out of reach ("in prospect"), unknown ("not accounted for") and unearned ("unaccountable")? There is beauty in this "vision" – this littoral landscape, this temporal life: it has its own 'bird of paradise', but the beauty and the bird can only be glimpsed: once sighted, it flees before either its name or its kind can be determined; we remain in the estuary ("between the zones"), with only the memory of the vision to get us through the winter.

102.1 A pale full sun, draining its winter light This colourless, frosted, wintry, yet 'illuminated' landscape appears at several points in the poem: see stanzas 57, 81, and 61.

102.2 stubborn oak The oak is symbolic of longevity and endurance; here, it may be "stubborn" because its leaves, rather than falling in the autumn, survive into the winter.

102.3 wínd spoórs That is, 'traces', the more familiar noun here used as a verb.

102.4 *Paradiso* The 'Paradiso' is the final section of Dante's *Divine Comedy*; see stanza 112 for Hill's reading of Dante "for the first time" and stanza 65 for his sense of "covenant". As Hill intimates, this littoral vision could be a suitable "end" for the poem.

102.5 heliograph A message sent by means of a movable mirror reflecting flashes of sunshine, here "blank" as without content, or because there is no sunshine.

102.6 lost estate The "lost estate" is Eden, perhaps to be regained in Paradise, but here fenced off by and from memory ("picketing"). Cf. stanza 54: "Contemplation as love's estate", and stanza 117, where the identical phrase, but italicized, refers to one of Charles Wesley's sermons.

102.7 unnamed Cf. the "unnamed god" in stanza 4, and the "TETRAGRAMMATON" in stanza 62.

102.8 estuaries The wide lower course of a river where the tide flows in, causing fresh and salt water to mix (see line 4). See stanza 81 for Hill's attraction to littoral zones.

103.
Purgatory is replaced by the torment of bad jokes: "BY AND LARGE" are two ringmasters of the big top, presiding over a "Cross-dressing" (positioned a-cross two lines and leotard-clad) acrobat who falls from a great height, only to be saved at

the last moment ("in mid-fall"). This is an image of last-minute salvation, but equally of the poet, who has "No better choice" than to perform. His performance takes place as the world watches and doubts his ability to finish the act – to catch the attention of a distracted public it must be the work of a daredevil showman. This element of virtuosic showmanship – of circus feats – is demonstrated by a display of linguistic facility, what Hill describes as "brave cockney rhyming / slang on an epic scale". In an attention-grabbing effort to demonstrate this semantic dexterity (his own brand of acrobatics), he japes on punctuation, quotes controversial television advertisements, answers absurd "true or false" questions. Hill plays with these kinds of language because the clichéd and the demotic rule (once again the "Brits are heroes"; the adage is now so familiar as to remain functional while unfinished): the "IN YOUR FACE" relentless display of English faux-masculinity ("twenty-four-hour / convenience machismo") rounds off a dextrously-wrought stanza which aims to prove that – in the midst of the Fall – the poet has "No better choice" to perform, to "Go for baroque".

103.1 BY AND LARGE A phrase of nautical origin (see "in full / rig" in stanza 112), 'by and large' – which has come to mean simply 'predominantly' – is here the name of an imaginary circus, the '*surname* and *surname*' construction being common in the discourse (e.g., Pepin and Breschard, Barnum and Bailey).

103.2 Cross- / dressing in mid-twist, salvation in mid-fall The image is of a male circus acrobat or trapeze artist clad in a leotard ("Cross- / dressing") and plunging to his death, only to be 'saved' (seemingly at the last moment) by his own agility. The emphasis is on the Catholic sense of 'choice' at the moment of death; cf. William Camden's "Betwixt the stirrup and the ground, / Mercy I asked; mercy I found", which Graham Greene employs as Pinkie's mantra in *Brighton Rock*.

103.3 Go for baroque Another pun on "baroque" (see "baroque / ís beautiful" in stanza 78); here, the wordplay is with the demotic 'go for broke', meaning 'do all possible'. The phrase also has a literal meaning: 'opt for a baroque style'.

103.4 Questions, questions. As spoken by one infuriated by the repeated queries of another: of course he (Hill) can make it (to the end of the 'show'), and, yes, he can "máke" (craft) the poem.

103.5 exclamation points Echoing the adage, 'Show me yours and I'll show you mine'; i.e., you query, and I'll exclaim.

ANNOTATIONS

Exclamation 'marks' (British usage) are known as 'points' (American usage).

103.6 Fly me! A 1971 advertising campaign for National Airlines featured an air hostess delivering the line "I'm Cheryl; Fly Me!". The advertisements were financially successful but enraged women's groups and prompted protest ('Fly Me Again',*Time*, 24 June 1974).

103.7 LOST THE PEACE / BY SUPERHUMAN SKIVING "LOST THE PEACE" is an inversion of 'won the war', and recalls William Bullitt's 1947 account of WWII, *How We Won the War and Lost the Peace*; here, the peace was lost by an evasion of duty ("skiving") of mammoth proportions, likely a reference to the treatment of Germany between the Wars, which served to antagonize as much as to appease.

103.8 cockney rhyming / slang In cockney rhyming slang one word is replaced by a pair, the latter of which rhymes with the initial word, but is then omitted; thus 'going up the stairs' becomes not 'going up the apples and pears', but 'going up the apples'. Here, such obfuscating omissions are rendered on an "epic scale".

103.9 Across the board The phrase has horse-racing (and so cockney) origins: to bet across the board is to place a bet on the bookie's 'board' for a horse to win either first, second or third place.

103.10 twenty-four-hour / convenience machismo The relentless, banal nationalism of "the Brits", with its show of bravado and masculinity, is likened to American 24/7 convenience stores which (as their name suggests) never close; the comparison suggests that British 'machismo' is cheap and accessible. See stanzas 38, 40, 84, 94 for other 'x are heroes' constructions.

103.11 IN YOUR FACE! A colloquial phrase, meaning forthright, perhaps offensively so.

104. In this disjointed stanza, the virtuosic playing with clichés and colloquialisms which typified the previous stanza is displaced by the poet's musings on the difficulty of using language accurately. As if taking notes or scribbling marginalia, Hill describes Freud as a "V. poór linguist" then cogitates on his term "*unheimlich*"; is there, the poet wonders, a better alternative in Latin (or even Inuit)? German, above all ("*über alles*") other languages, has a vocabulary most fit for metaphysics; this affords the awkward link between Freud's uncanny and Schubert's Romanticism. As if again in a littoral purgatory (see stanza 102), the poet, like Schubert's wanderer, nears the end, but seeks a guiding light. In another unwieldy shift, Hill now moves away from Schubert to the "nóble" "THEATRE OF VOICES", apparently some kind of heavenly community, shouting to Hill through the clouds. However, their efforts to communicate are muffled by the "acoustic din", by other voices, and the poet's partial deafness (see stanza 25), which means that he hears only the equivocal "EQUITY, ELIGIBILTY, CULPABILITY": as so often in the poem, the signal is interrupted, the message not received. The final lines make clear the poet's predicament: any attempt to hear the "VOICES" is necessarily doomed. Language will always be *unheimlich*; lost in the telling, scattered across the seas. An editorial voice intrudes (like that at the end of Goethe's *Faust*) to order that the stanza remain "UNFINISHED"; Hill's signal, like that which he attempts to receive, is interrupted.

104.1 V. Shorthand for 'very'. Cf. "yr" in stanza 106, and the quasi-medical "rt" in stanza 98.

104.2 *nota bene* Note (well) the disjunction between the unnecessary abbreviation of 'very' and the uncommon expansion of 'n.b.'.

104.3 *unheimlich* *Unheimlich* (German, 'unhomely'; 'uncanny'), that which is at once familiar and foreign, with unsettling effect. Freud addressed its etymology; his linguistic assertions have been questioned (see 'Dreamwork as Etymology'); hence he is a "V. poor linguist". Hill uses *unheimlich* in his criticism (*Collected Critical Writings*, p. 504) and verse (*The Triumph of Love*, CXVII).

104.4 What's weird in Latin The closest Latin equivalent (its inexactitude may be the point) is *alienus* ('strange').

104.5 Inuit / not too secure (official) Either, the Inuit language of northern Canada is endangered, as the number of native speakers declines (an "OFFICIAL" finding); or, one's own command of the tongue is shaky. Cf. "Syntax / is a dead language" in stanza 99.

104.6 Stubborn metaphysics [...] *über alles* The discipline of metaphysics ("Stubborn" because – especially in its Kantian form – dealing in absolutes) calls for "German above all", a phrase originating from the 1841 song 'Deutschland Uber Alles' which in 1922 became the German national anthem.

ANNOTATIONS

104.7 Leiermann *Leiermann* (German, 'hurdy-gurdy man'), the closing piece in Schubert's 1827 song cycle *Winterreise* [Winter's Journey], where the lonely wanderer on his way to death (Hill's "Where do I gó?") finds in the organ-grinder a fellow outcast. His final lines address the musician: "Wunderlicher Alter, soll ich mit dir geh'n? / Willst zu meinen Liedern deine Leier dreh'n?" [Strange old man, shall I go with you? / Will you play your organ to my songs?]. Cf. "Hurdy-gurdy the starter / handle" in stanza 53.

104.8 Like a Southern evangelical preacher, Hill echoes song 19 of Schubert's *Winterreise*: "Ein Licht tanzt freundlich vor mir her, / Ich folg' ihm nach die Kreuz und Quer; / Ich folg' ihm gern und seh's ihm an, / Dass es verlockt den Wandersmann" [A light does a friendly dance before me, I follow it here and there; I like to follow it and watch / The way it lures the wanderer]. Cf. "EASY NOW, SOUL-BROTHER!" in stanza 115. *The Orchards of Syon* offers a variation: "Oh, my sole / sister, you, little sister-my-soul" (VII).

104.9 Soul-brother, show a light! Echoing (and mocking) the motto of modern France, ('*Liberté, égalité, fraternité*') which originated in the Revolution.

104.10 THEATRE OF VOICES For Hill's deafness, see stanza 25; John Lyon notes that in *Speech! Speech!* "Hill's 'THEATRE OF VOICES' proves hard of hearing" ('What are you incinerating?', p. 94).

104.11 pelagic diasporas That is, dispersions across the oceans.

104.12 [LEAVE UNFINISHED] The square brackets indicate the intrusion of an editorial voice (see also stanza 114: "[EDIT TAPE]") and *The Triumph of Love* (the "ED"). The stanza is unfinished: there is no full stop.

105. The broadcast is resumed, but injustice remains: Hill in this stanza presents the case of code-breaking mathematician Alan Turing, once "indispensable" to the war effort, a magician with numbers ("*thaumaturge*") whose miraculous cracking of the Enigma code was a major boon for the Allied war effort. Yet such clear and indubitable virtue did not prevent Turing from being first "dispensed with" by Government officials and then – according to those who believe his suicide was in fact a murder (Hill's strident "THÁT RÍGHT?" rehearses this debate) – "disposed of". Would those privy to the truth of such questions ("those who know"), asks Hill, do the same today? Would we even be here today if Churchill had not refused to conclude a "Vichy peace"? Such questions are difficult to determine ("hard to say"), and yet, it seems, one must try, if only out of respect to "Daventry and Droitwich" – the public voice of WWII – who cry out in simultaneous "disbelief" and "recognizance" at the present-day repetition of injustices such as those meted out to Turing. And such evasions of justice return with the regularity of comets.

105.1 thaumaturge A *thaumaturge* is a master of magic, a magus. The tribute is to Alan Turing (1912-1954), the Hut 8, Bletchley Park code-breaker (see stanza 7) who believed himself to be immune ("untouched" by the "contingent", that is, by worldly concerns that impinge upon or compromise the absolute) from persecution by authorities, but who was first "dispensed with" by Government Code headquarters after his 1952 conviction for homosexuality and then "disposed of" by semi-enforced chemical castration (he was offered only the alternative of incarceration). Hill refers to his death by suicide in the Clutag *A Treatise of Civil Power* ('A Treatise of Civil Power', XIII): "And Turing died (really) like Snow White", i.e., by biting a poisoned apple. After a 2009 Internet-led petition, UK Prime Minister Gordon Brown made a posthumous public apology to Turing for his ill-treatment by British authorities. See also *The Triumph of Love* (XVI); and 'A Cloud in Aquila' in the Penguin *A Treatise of Civil Power*.

105.2 THÁT RÍGHT? A colloquialism meaning, 'You don't say'; the tone is sceptical.

105.3 among those who know Compare Dante's "*maestro di color che sanno*" [the master of those who know], his tribute to Aristotle in canto IV of the *Inferno*, that treatise of divine justice.

105.4 Would we [...] have concluded a Vichy peace? This sentence can be read in two ways: without the leadership of Churchill throughout WWII, would the Nazi administration established in France in 1940, known as the Vichy regime, ever have been brought to a close ("concluded"); second, without Churchill, would not we [England] have been in danger of 'concluding' a similar compromise?

105.5 hard to say Both: a) uncomfortable to utter; and b) difficult to determine.

105.6 Daventry and Droitwich Daventry was the site of the first BBC high power AM (long wave) station 5XX which opened on

27 July 1925 and brought good reception of the National Programme to almost all of the UK population. The Daventry station broadcast Third Programme and BBC Europe to most of England and parts of Western Europe until 1978. Droitwich took over from Daventry in 1934; it is located near Hill's birthplace of Bromsgrove, Worcestershire (see John Phillips's 'Droitwich Calling').

105.7 recognizance A formal agreement made by somebody before a judge or magistrate to do something, for example, to appear in court at a set date. Cf. "bulk recognizance" in stanza 32.

105.8 a comet's faithfulness of assignation That is, with the regularity of the comets, their 'appointments' as visible from earth being always kept.

106.
The controlling metaphor is still that of a winter scene, a landscape of death ("DE MORTUIS"), a frozen railway line from which the ice will not be burnt or chipped. These are the remembered train journeys of Hill's boyhood, through a countryside afflicted by the hardship of war; but also of the railways taking Jews to concentration camps, though Hill, in the innocence of childhood, did not then know the meaning of words such as "*Arbeit*" and "*heraús*". Almost as if addressing the Zeitgeist (the "you" of line 9), he recalls the fears ("terror-stricken") and ignorance ("unteachable") of childhood; then, using the metaphor of baptism, of vows undertaken on his behalf, faces the issue (now) of his own complicity and/or responsibility, given that these are memories or associations that he did not have (but now must confirm). "*Sadly*", he concedes, the joke (the "lást laúgh") is on him: like it or not, he is complicit; however reluctantly, he may need to accept ("show up in time for") the responsibilities that the image (the train journeys, the winter landscape, death) entails.

106.1 DE MORTUIS The first words of the Latin phrase, 'De mortuis nil nisi bonum dicendum est' [Let nothing be said of the dead but what is good]. In a legal context, the phrase is (somewhat oddly) used to indicate that defamation can only be actioned on behalf of the living. Cf. Hill's use of this same truncating device in stanza 34: "PER / ARDUA" (ad astra).

106.2 arms tilting to the right of way The image is of that of trains: the ice on the rails is thawed by gas-fuelled burners ("acetylene") and coke fires ("braziers"); the cold has frozen the rail indicators in one position and they must be "chipped-free" of ice to allow them to function ("tílting to right of way"). The suggestion is that of the Holocaust: the sounds and images represent, in an abbreviated way, the unspeakable bitterness of what Hill refers to in line 1 as "those journeys".

106.3 *Arbeit / heraús* A conflation of: a) 'Arbeit macht frei' [work makes freedom], the slogan wrought in metal and hung over the entrances of a number of concentration camps, including Dachau and Auschwitz; and b) 'Juden, heraus!' [Jews, Out!], shouted by Nazi troops as they forcibly removed Jews from their homes.

106.4 eight-coupled / coal engines The specification of engines as "eight-coupled" also indicates wartime England, in all likelihood the kind of journey taken by the author in his innocent childhood on one of the London, Midland and Scotland (LMS) coal engines.

106.5 viaducts That is, those bridge-like structures carrying rail lines across valleys, here "shaken" by the vibrations of the heavy engines as much as by German bombing.

106.6 smoke of manufacture and destruction Cf. "Making, breaking | things familiar" in stanza 83.

106.7 put me down / as That is, 'write my name on the list of those who were'; more simply, 'record me'.

106.8 my first promise The image is that of baptism, of vows and promises made on his behalf which, when he has come of age, he must renew (confirm) for himself.

106.9 *Sadly* An italicized reiteration of the "poor / mawkish adverb" of stanza 70.

106.10 show up Colloquially, to "show up" is to make an appearance, or arrive.

106.11 yr An abbreviation of 'your'; see also "rt" in stanza 98 and "V." in stanza 104.

107. The problems continue: even if one knows what one wants to say, and has discovered a way of doing so, there may be no one who wishes to listen to what you have to say. Conceiving of himself as in this predicament, and instructed by an uncomprehending audience ("WHÁDDYA – WHÁDDYA – / call thís") to not be didactic ("script or prescription") but instead "Look on the bright side" (a response to recent grim stanzas), Hill imagines his future. The poet tries out a "Dysfunctional" Charles Williams-esque use of language achieving perplexity but not profundity, so instead the poet will "Act through" mimed gestures, playing the role of one not 'going places', but instead (contemplating being a "stiff") must nominate a price for his life. In order to vindicate himself before this uncomprehending audience, he could resort to its own methods: "Become vindictive". But in doing so, he would (despite being victorious) only "Fall" victim to their own diseased modus operandi ("infections"). Hill expatiates, imagining the write-up of his "Fall": he is the latest virtuoso poet ("pastmaster"), but, while still writing ("mid-stride"), he has been struck by strokes ("grand infarctions") and rendered speechless. In this state he may pray to Mary, but she – like his audience – may not be listening: "YOU THÉRE, LÁDY?"

107.1 Look on the bright side 'Always Look on the Bright Side of Life', which closed the 1979 film *Monty Python's Life of Brian*, is here imagined as sung by a crowd. The song is often sung at football matches, and was ranked third in a UK poll of preferred funeral music ('Angels "Favourite Funeral Song"'). Cf. "why are we waiting?" in stanza 53.

107.2 WHÁDDYA A contraction of 'what do you' (here followed by "call thís"), capitalized to indicate a demotic voice.

107.3 script or prescription That is, either something read by an actor or written by a doctor (in notoriously bad handwriting); the dichotomy here is between recording history, or prescribing its cure.

107.4 Cite your own / stiff going-price Obliquely imitating something like 'stick it up your whatever'; this poem, says the PEOPLE, is "Dysfunctional". There is a disjunction between the slang of "WHÁDDYA" and the scholarly "Cite".

107.5 THIS / ALSO IS THOU, NEITHER IS THÍS THOÚ A phrase (of unknown origin) often used by literary figure and mystic Charles Williams (1886-1945), included in his compilation *The New Christian Year* to suggest the paradoxical view of God to which Christians must hold. According to Bernadette Boksy, the phrase has an instrumental faculty: "Reading the sentence, and encompassing the two statements as factual, enacts a mental process basic to Williams's Romantic theology: to fully keep in mind, at the same time, the ways in which mental or physical creations reveal God's nature and the ways in which they do not and cannot" (*The Rhetoric of Vision*, pp. 64-65). The phrase was central to Williams's thought and he occasionally manipulated it into variations (see

"This is not He, yet also is this He" in *The Figure of Beatrice*, p. 181).

107.6 secondary infections An infection acquired during the course of a separate initial infection. To 'fall victor' to secondary infections is thus an achievement of limited heroism, an unprovable assertion of mastery in a context of failure.

107.7 pastmaster One (especially in the role of master of a guild) especially adept in a particular skill; but also with the sense of being out of touch with the times.

107.8 infarctions Those deaths of tissues caused by a block in blood supply, as in the phrase 'myocardial infarction', medical terminology for 'heart attack'. Hill has suffered two heart attacks, one in the late 1980s, another while writing *The Orchards of Syon*.

107.9 mid-stride Compare the opening of stanza 111; there is a suggestion of the heart attack, an acute assault on the body which takes many sufferers entirely by surprise.

107.10 Pray for us sinners An echo of the litany: "Holy Mary, Mother of God, pray for us sinners, now and at the hour of our death. Amen." These words are echoed in Eliot's 'Ash-Wednesday' (I).

107.10 YOU THÉRE, LÁDY? Supplication (to the Madonna, the "LILITH" of stanza 8, or the "DOLORES" of stanzas 66, 67, 91 and 109), but expressed in the demotic, in the voice of the PEOPLE.

108. The theme of this stanza is the persistence of the erotic impulse (if not the ability to enact it) into old age (but what would the young know of this?). The emphasis is (perhaps recalling Yeats's 'Sailing to Byzantium') of the old man contemplating the young and their sexual energy ("Not lóve"). The conceit is of the poet (with romantic intent) inviting a young woman into his home under the auspices of looking at a Rembrandt picture book. Unable to empathize with his younger companion, the poet instead offers to "Share" (but "nót múch") his appreciation and knowledge of art ("THE POLISH / RIDER"), and, especially, of the erotic as embodied within the painting of the Shunammite woman, however uncertain his erotic response to that might be. The response to the non-erotic 'Polish Rider' is "wonderful" and uncanny (see stanza 104), but he is (even as an old man) stirred uncertainly by the implicit eroticism of the other picture, yet not easily able to react. Rembrandt's 'Polish Rider' is for Hill (following the banal cliché) "wonderful"; the poet's sceptical response ("When was he / ever in Poland?") marks the end of the self-portrait: the poet can think of no more games to play, and conceives of an end to all games ("No more games | / I can imagine"). Whether unwise or innocent ("Responsible / or not") Hill desires not the faux intimacy created by these petty debates, but the plain comfort of physical closeness: to "hóld" as he wishes to be "held".

108.1 aírhead A late twentieth-century insult of American origin, one whose skull is filled only with air.

108.2 Whát do you knów! The stresses emphasize the ignorance of age contemplating the sexual activities of youth, and being told that it's not love (stupid), but something else.

108.3 THE POLISH / RIDER 'The Polish Rider' is a 1655 oil painting, one of several works attributed to Rembrandt which have had their attribution called into question in critical discourses (the "late / colloquies" of lines 6-7) during the second half of the twentieth century. In the case of 'The Polish Rider', the debate was fuelled in large part by the certainty that Rembrandt was never in Poland (see lines 5-6). However, more recent scholarship has argued for attribution to remain with Rembrandt; Simon Schama attests it was "certainly painted by Rembrandt" and "likely that a family of Lithuanian nobles commissioned Rembrandt to make a portrait of one of their young sons then studying in the Dutch Republic" (*Rembrandt's Eyes*, p. 599). See Appendix, fig.13.

108.4 I will hóld you That is, hold you responsible, as Rembrandt is deemed 'responsible' for 'The Polish Rider'; "held ín you" in the following line, however, replaces this meaning with the physical sense of embrace, and emotional responsibility.

108.5 Shunammite woman In 2 Kings 4: the Shunammite woman is generous towards the king Elisha, offering him accommodation and food on his regular travels. Although she asks for neither payment nor thanks, the King promises her a child (she has none; her husband is old), and she becomes pregnant. Years later, her child suffers a head injury and dies in her arms; after seeking Elisha's assistance, the King – though not at the first attempt – raises the child from death. Hill refers directly to Rembrandt's *The Departure of the Shunammite Woman* (see Appendix, fig.14), which depicts its subject leaving her home, her faith such that she believes Elisha can resurrect her son. Although her husband and a stableboy are also figured in the composition, the Shunammite woman is the sole illuminated subject (see "nearer the light" in line 11).

109. The figure who comes "nearer the light" of Rembrandt's chiaroscuro turns out to be not the devoted Shunammite woman of stanza 108, nor the "LÁDY" of stanza 107, but – again, and to the poet's dismay – the vampiric "DOLORES", a metaphor, perhaps, for the unwanted resurgence of desire (see the end of stanza 110). The devout is mistaken for the debased; this reminds Hill of the contemporary habit of thought which aims – often via television programmes – to destroy the mystery of the saints by "knocking" their displays of devotion, which appear (to the secular, rational mind) "perverse". Such ignoble treatment betrays a lack of gratitude for those who, like Jesus, suffered on our behalf ("for ús beggars"). This "new / era" has replaced the saints with new heroes, with Ireland ("Erin", land of saints and sinners) identified as a possible exception: there, the traditional black comedy ("grave / setting of comedy") leaves room for the perverse and – even in films funded by Lotto – nationalists such as Seán Ó Riada seek to revive rather than destroy history. Such commitment to the old stories and their instruments ("*Bodhrans*"), Hill discloses, might pitch him "wild / with dancing excitement", were not the sentiment uttered confidentially ("in closed-círcuit confession"), as if in prayer.

109.1 DOLORES Not the "LÁDY" of stanza 107, but the sexually voracious, vampiric Dolores (aka Lilith) reappears; see also stanzas 8, 66, 67, and 91.

109.2 knocking Here, "knocking" is employed in its colloquial sense of 'criticizing'.

109.3 Did the socks / not rot on those feet Combining the WWI ANZAC digger slang of 'wouldn't it rot your socks' with the opening line of Blake's 'Jerusalem': "And did those feet in ancient time".

109.4 potsherds Potsherds, with fragments of broken pottery excavated by archaeologists, are a metaphor for all mankind, fashioned as we are from clay. Cf. Isaac 45:9: "Woe unto him that striveth with his maker! Let the potsherd strive with the potsherds of the earth. Shall the clay say to him that fashion it, What makest thou? or thy work, He hath no hands?"

ANNOTATIONS

109.5 new / era, new hero A take on the proverbial 'cometh the hour, cometh the man'.

109.6 Erin The poetic name for Ireland, and that used by nineteenth-century nationalists; here, it completes the alliterative pattern from "era" to "hero", "error" and "here". The broad reference is to the revival of Irish nationalism and literature in the nineteenth and early twentieth centuries, with perhaps a hint of James Joyce's 'comedy' *Finnegans Wake* (1940). The reflexive use of the pronoun "herself" is a locution particular to Irish English.

109.7 Lotto State-run lotteries, the proceeds of which are often donated to charities and worthy artistic ventures, for example, art-house films which celebrate national heritage. Note that the word "loot" can be derived from "Lotto". Cf. the 1998 film *Waking Ned Devine*, in which an Irish village unites to defraud a Lotto claim inspector after a fellow villager dies before redeeming his winning ticket.

109.8 *Bodhrans* An Irish hand-held frame-drum which enjoyed a revival during the 1960s and 1970s, in large part because of its use by traditional Irish band The Chieftains.

109.9 pitch Cf. Hill's use of "pitch" in stanzas 9, 21, and 90.

109.10 closed-círcuit confession In closed circuit television (CCTV), commonly used for surveillance purposes, the image is transmitted directly from the camera to selected monitors; it thus differs from broadcast television, which sends its signal indiscriminately. Here, Hill likens CCTV to the confession, where admission of sin is communicated to a single monitor, the priest.

109.11 John Reedy | otherwise Seán Ó Riada John Reidy (commonly misspelled as Reedy, as here) was the birth name of Seán Ó Riada (1931-1971), the Cork-born musician and folklorist who become a figurehead for the renaissance of traditional Irish music. In the 1960s, Ó Riáda was almost solely responsible for the revival of the bodhran (see line 9). "ÁND práy / for" reiterates the ritual: "And pray for us sinners, now and at the hour of our death."

110. While in the previous stanza Hill was concerned with the fate of history, he is in this stanza concerned with his own fate and his own history. He is uneasy ("discomfited") even thinking about (or, being unable to think about) the "prospect" of his "own dying". Sensing his authoritative mode to be the pose of an unwarranted, unsanctioned ("unwitnessed") arbiter of justice (only "faux-legalisms"), Hill attests that many things – abstract ideas like justice or faith – can be indicated but not shown: requests for proof and evidence of authority can never be satisfied. What Hill *can* show, he argues, is what he 'sees', which he presents "here" in the second half of the stanza: an image from his childhood, the language of which is now arcane, forgotten. In presenting this image, Hill imagines that his readers "see" it "also": by looking through the poet's eyes, this vision – otherwise lost to unremembering – is preserved. Hill manipulates an eternizing conceit: the poet, unable to conceive of his own death and dissolution, in memory, preserves his "flare" of "desire" forever in poetic recollection.

110.1 My faux legalisms […] I could indicate but not show The image provided is of Hill's "faux-legalisms" gaining a guarantor despite being unwitnessed documents.

110.2 Whát I see / here […] the chapel wind-vane's blistery fake gold The language of lines 7-10 is deliberately archaic, poetical, rustic, and specifically located in English and northern England: the fierce winds ("fell-gusts", blasting down from the 'fells' or hills; "unfixable" in the sense of 'volatile' and 'unpredictable') are described as "ratching" (an obsoletism meaning 'lifting up') the "chimney-cowls" (the metal hoods on chimneys which prevent downdrafts); the gale swings the wind-vane, alternately shading and shining light upon its surface of weathered, "blistery" gilt. Cf. the "intricately / graceful wind-vane's confected silver" in *The Triumph of Love* (XLIX).

110.3 I imagine | yoú see this also The verticule produces a distinct ambiguity: Hill imagines that his readers see the image just described, but he is the imaginer of such images (which are in turn witnessed – unlike his "faux-legalisms" – by his readers).

110.4 the flare through memory of desire Cf. the opening lines of 'The Burial of the Dead' from Eliot's *The Waste Land*: "April is the cruellest month, breeding / Lilacs out of the dead land, mixing / Memory and desire, stirring / Dull roots with spring rain."

111. Still apprehending his own death, Hill considers (using the demotic, supposing "sáy") the moment when without notice ("Míd-stride") the rapture takes his spirit from this

ANNOTATIONS

familiar earthly world (in which he is "fully housebroken"). Now a lifeless "dead weight", Hill's mortifying body is left on earth to rot; his spirit, on the other hand, ascends, catapulted into the milky way and a poetical landscape of stars as depicted by Ivor Gurney – a landscape immortalized in verse and music and so unchanged, unchangeable, constant. The metaphor continues: the spirit journeys "way out" (the pun is a compliment to an unidentified beloved, for whose "sake" it is made) through and past the constellations of Orion, Andromeda, Cassiopeia (the 'stars' of the stars), to a "small / unnamed constellation" which Hill can 'bring to light' through the act of naming: he 'gets' to name it *"Constellation Kreisau"*. His allegiance is to a tiny, overlooked pocket of resistance, to the sacrifice of the just when faced with evil, to those martyrs who go only half-remembered: Hill would like to see a small light burning for them.

111.1 (*encore!*) The traditional call for more from an appreciative audience echoes the poem's title, but the French word equally denotes that the poet is "still" en route ("Mídstride"). Cf. "mid-stride" (107.9).

111.2 eject from the planet Compare Luke 17:34-36: "I tell you, in that night there shall be two men in one bed; the one shall be taken, and the other shall be left. Two women shall be grinding together; the one shall be taken, and the other left. Two men shall be in the field; the one shall be taken, and the other left." The suggestion of sudden death, of one leaving the earth and (in imagination) going out to the constellations, recalls the "infarctions" of stanza 107.

111.3 housebroken as a pet trained to urinate and defecate outside, or in a litter tray.

111.4 dead / weight An inert weight; in context, the word has scatological implications, and again suggests sudden death ('to drop dead').

111.5 *pudor* An expression of due shame; a veil drawn over something unacceptable. Here, "let it lie" means both 'let it be', and 'leave it' (the droppings) where they lie.

111.6 Orion A constellation on the celestial equator said to resemble a hunter with club and shield.

111.7 way out The pun is on "way out" meaning both 'distant' (as in ejected from the planet) and 'irreverent'.

111.8 Andromeda in full / rig A moderately bright constellation of the northern sky, named after the queen of Greek mythology.

The nautical phrase "in full / rig" likens Andromeda's 'fancy dress' (she appears as if in chains) to the rigging of a ship.

111.9 as GURNEY last saw her Ivor Gurney (1890–1937), poet, musician, WWI veteran, and sufferer from manic depression. In his F.W. Bateson Memorial Lecture, 'Gurney's "Hobby"', Hill refers to Gurney's synaesthetic description of Orion in 'Severn & Somme' ("the song Orion sings"), and to his use of Andromeda in 'Tewkesbury' to compare earthly construction and the "great cosmic architecture visible in the night sky": "Square tower, carved upward by the laboured thought... Queenly Andromeda not so exalted often" (*Collected Critical Writings*, pp. 443-444). The sense is of Gurney and Hill as separated by time but united by the "constancy" of the constellations. Cf. the faithful "assignations" of comets in stanza 105.

111.10 Cassiopeia A northern hemisphere constellation shaped like the letter 'W'; said to represent the queen of that name of Greek mythology, mother of Andromeda.

111.11 *Constellation Kreisau* The Kreisau Circle was the name given by the Gestapo to the anti-Nazi group centred around the Kreisau estate of Helmut James, Count of Moltke. A rare example of German *Widerstand*, the members included Peter Yorck, Count of Wartenburg and Adam von Trott zu Solz. In 1943, the group planned an active political coup; in January 1944, Moltke was arrested and the group began to dissolve. Many of the group were executed after their involvement in the July 1944 failed assassination attempt on Hitler. Cf. Hill's 'De Jure Belli ac Pacis' *(Canaan)*, dedicated to the memory of Werner von Haeften, hero of the German Resistance.

112. The end of the poem is nigh: it is now time for the "Eight-block coda" and the reader is forced to wonder at the explicit reference to order in what has seemed to be – structurally – a chaotic poem. Hill's temptation (like Dante in his *Paradiso*) is to 'overreach' in his efforts to find a high note on which to end his poem. Here, this temptation is personified as the Tempter, a morality play-like figure who encourages vanity and pomposity, one who should not be admitted, especially if he uses the poet's own voice, and so offers a genuine temptation. Hill made a pact that his "topos" (*topic*, but also literal *place*, as the *bolge* in the *Inferno*) would be "SODOM", for him the contemporary word and its horrors; he admits that this topic is overblown ("grandiose / unoriginal"). As if stuck in another of Dante's metaphorical ditches (perhaps that of prodigality, or fraudulent rhetoric), he can not remember what promises he made, nor even what promises are – he is a "damned liar" and a liar damned for his tricks: pretending when younger to have read Dante, adopting voices other than his own while striking a pose. Having rejected (as Dante did) the temptation of the high note, instead reasserting his theme of "SODOM", Hill now invokes the "standard" treatments of that theme, even if they are not entirely successful. If he is treating his self himself – with literature, perhaps, as the laws of poetical catharsis demand – then not 'so much the better', but "só much the worse": the suggestion is that the pharmaceutical 'tuning' of stanza 3 is a more successful course of treatment than the (in literary terms) more orthodox 'remedy' (compare Eliot's 'Little Gidding') prescribed by Dante.

112.1 Eight-block coda to the CITY OF GOD The word "to" in this line produces an ambiguity: the following, final eight stanzas are either a coda coming after ("to") the bulk of the poem (here entitled "CITY OF GOD"); or they may be dedicated "to" Augustine's *City of God*, of which the whole poem may be an interpretation. See also stanzas 15 ("the City of God / riding her storm sewers"), 115 ("Where coda to the City of God") and 117 ("Unapproachable City of God"). By the time of writing *The Orchards of Syon* Hill could only attest: "City of God not likely" (XXX).

112.2 Tempter As a threat to one who has aggravated the speaker so greatly that further aggravation would elicit an extreme, often violent, response. Here, addressed to Satan, the medieval "Tempter", the temptation being to 'reach' a celestial climax.

112.3 my topos is SODOM An author's *topos* (Greek, 'place') is his theme; here, Sodom, the city the name of which has become a byword for depravity.

112.4 bolge In Dante's *Divine Comedy*, the *bolge* (literally 'ditches') are the concentric circular grooves on the inverted funnel of the descent into hell; the sense here is of the poet being guilty of a particular offence and as such doomed to be trapped in one or "some other" of Dante's *bolge*, that is, "other" than the *bolgia* for sodomites (the seventh in Dante's order). Hill may consider himself trapped in the eighth *bolgia* (for fraudulent rhetoricians); hence "damned liar".

112.5 broken accents As one speaking in a foreign language and with limited competence.

112.6 Dante Dante Alighieri (1265-1321), Italian poet and author of the *Divine Comedy*, his vision of the Christian afterlife. The *Divine Comedy* is essential to world literature, and so to be a literary luminary and yet admit to not having read it amounts – for the dedicated canonist, at least – to a shameful admission. Cf. "a *Paradiso* / not accounted for" in stanza 102.

113. In this stanza, the legacy of the Holocaust is invoked via the art of Joseph Beuys and Anselm Kiefer. Kiefer is introduced via his teacher Beuys, whose 'Auschwitz Demonstration' represents the "disassembly" (sometimes literal, as with the broken glass of the *Kristallnacht*) of the Jews; the poet asks if what "we", civilization, have "cóme to" is nothing more than Beuys's boxed mishmash of decomposing rodents ("dead-centres") and "ash". In Kiefer's 'Breaking of the Vessels', the collected knowledge of civilization (represented by the books in a glass-fronted case) is shattered, the leaden tomes ("metals") tumbling to the floor. Through images of "violent / disassembly", the works of Beuys and Kiefer bring the physical disassembly of the Jews "back into being"; their memorials offer a kind of salvation via memory. Obscure 'scraps' raise the questions of salvation with reference to the eternal rhythms of making and breaking, creation and destruction. Salvation is achieved by "obscure / soteriologies", by a "vital" line of faith. The dead are raised (as if for "Auction"); we can – through these *vitrines* – eyewitness the horror of Holocaust and its aftermath ("Autopsy", auto-psy); and the "Scrap" of broken things and broken bodies ("avatar").

113.1 vitrine A vitrine (French, 'glass pane') is a glass case used to house curios or collections; alternatively, a shop window.

113.2 how does it connect / with the world of ANSELM KIEFER Most simply, via the work of Joseph Beuys, whose 'Auschwitz Demonstration' (1968; see Appendix, fig.14), a seminal work of German and specifically Holocaust art, consisted of collected objects housed within a museum-style vitrine; Kiefer (1945-), the German artist whose oeuvre betrays inescapable ties to the Holocaust, studied with Beuys during the 1970s and, though he is primarily a pictorial artist rather than a sculptor, Kiefer is viewed as Beuys's successor. The mention of a vitrine within a post-Holocaust context suggests the *Kristallnacht* [Night of the Broken Glass] of 9-10 November 1938, when a Nazi mob, spurred on by a speech by Goebbels, rampaged through German cities, smashing the shop windows of Jewish businesses.

113.3 ash and shivered / glass While many of Kiefer's works use ash or ashen palette, the shivered glass suggests one work in particular: the 1990 sculpture 'The Breaking of the Vessels', in which a bookcase (the receptacle of collective and collected knowledge) is shown in disarray, its glass front reduced to shards. The books – weathered, torn and haphazard; some about to tumble from the shelves – are made of lead. See Appendix, fig.16.

113.4 Memorialized dead-centres without / focus Holocaust art of the kind produced by Beuys and Kiefer: their productions are "dead-centres" in that they are accurate, 'on-target' memorials (despite being "without / focus"), and in that they have death as their topos.

113.5 pulled / back into being The imagery returns to Beuys's vitrine, the disassembly of which demands that the reader attempting to make sense of the work forcibly 'pull' the Holocaust experience "back into being".

113.6 soteriologies The name given to the various theories of how man achieves salvation; here obscure because complex and no longer the subject of contentious debate.

113.7 Auction Bueys's 'Auschwitz Demonstration' was sold 'on the block' before its first exhibition ('Representation and Event', p. 11); but the etymology of 'auction' (from Latin *augere*, to increase) is recalled: it is as if the "things" of line 10 have been exaggerated for inspection, as a photo enlarged to make detail visible.

113.8 Autopsy Like "auction", "autopsy" is employed in its literal sense of looking into the dead.

113.9 Scrap-avatar The implied equation functions in two ways: a) as a linguistic description of the contents of Beuys's vitrine (a path to salvation through throwaway scraps); and b) as an instruction to 'scrap avatars', to toss out the incarnate. The paradox is of something being both dead-centre and without focus, i.e., without an explicit allegory or theme. 'Avatar' has recently acquired an additional meaning: it is used to represent individuals in cyberspace, especially players in an online game.

114. The "Autopsy" of Holocaust art is re-jigged as an investigation into the aftermath of Diana's death, and the cliché "When all else fails" is used to signify the death of the individual. Televised, and with celebrity performers (see stanza 94), her funeral was a staged operation – as much an exercise in public relations as a memorial service. But, according to Hill, those who scripted the performance could not control the power of the liturgy or the authentic grief of the masses; he offers examples as proof. 1 Corinthians 13, so well known as to be commonplace, was read at the funeral by Tony Blair ("a man in too-tight shoes"); neither his inappropriate showmanship nor the familiarity of the verse could entirely ("beyond redemption") "degrade or debauch" its subject ('redeemed' by Diana in life): "LOVE". The gates of Buckingham Palace may be vulgar, and its mass of cellophane-wrapped bouquets equally so, but the poet has joined the masses in their pilgrimage "Six times" during this poem. The Thames, the artery of England, can "take over" his and the people's grief – this is genuine national mourning. The camera ("EDIT TAPE") catches pious "high prelates" acting inappropriately during the ceremony, but even this does not destroy its grandeur: the uniform guardsmen, "heroic" pallbearers, make recompense. Even the Queen, with her artificial "SORRY" televised mourning (so poor an "act" that she appeared a "Comedienne") could not debase the occasion; a genuinely grieving public, sensing her insincerity, became a "hostile nation". Through these images, Hill aims to demonstrate that the funeral may have been reduced to a theatrical performance ("CURTAINS. CREDITS"), but – because of the authenticity of the service and of the grief – it could (as in stanza 71) only be "reduced to the Sublime".

114.1 CORINTHIANS 'The Love Chapter', 1 Corinthians 13, the first Pauline Epistle, is one of the best-known passages of the Bible. Many of its expressions have passed into idiom, including, "through a glass darkly", and "the greatest of these is love".

114.2 read / by a man in too-tight shoes As was 1 Corinthians 13 (see 114.1) by a visibly uncomfortable then-Prime Minister Tony Blair in Westminster Abbey at the 1997 funeral of Princess Diana.

114.3 degrade or debauch the word LOVE In the King James, the Greek *agape*, meaning 'sacrificial love' is translated as 'charity', but in more modern versions (as in that read by Blair),

ANNOTATIONS

it is translated as 'love'. Philip Stephens writes of Blair's ability to use his "theatrical gifts" for political effect, noting that his performance of Corinthians and his televised response to Diana's death were "the most brilliantly accomplished of the many performances that marked out Blair's political ascent" and that "the death of Diana offered a moment to bring the entire nation into the New Labour tent. If that required a few dramatic flourishes for the television cameras, so be it" (*Tony Blair*, p. 8). Corinthians is at risk of being degraded by the mass public as by Blair: Hill has said (in language markedly similar) that while he does not believe in any Golden Age of civilization, in the contemporary world, "the tempo of the degradation, the intensity of the debauch, have certainly increased" ('Meaningful Speech', p. 198).

114.4 vulgar gates The many bunches and wreaths of flowers left at the gates of Buckingham and Kensington Palaces after Diana's death, and the "Six times" already in this poem ("trip") that Hill has 'visited' this theme (see stanzas 22, 35, 36, 61, 71, 93). The palace gates, where the 'vulgar' masses collected to mourn, are gilt and ornate.

114.5 Thames England's principal river invoked as the symbol of London; it rhetorically relieves the burden of grief ("take over") from the mourning masses ("plebeian").

114.6 Evangelical high prelates caught / spitting out plum stones George Carey, the Archbishop of Canterbury (1991-2002) who presided over Diana's funeral, and who is identified with the evangelical wing of the Church. There is a suggestion of adopting democratic accents, rather than the 'plummy' accents of the British upper class. Cf. Stephen's story in *Ulysses* of crones on Nelson's Pillar "spitting the plumstones slowly out between the railings" (p. 97).

114.7 [EDIT TAPE] Cf. "[LEAVE UNFINISHED]" in stanza 104; square brackets indicate an editorial voice.

114.8 Guardsmen Diana's casket was carried by an Honour Guard of British soldiers, their trained uniformity ("alignment") and matching red jackets adding to the gravity of the occasion.

114.9 Comedienne to act / SORRY for hostile nation Hill refers to the live public address made by the Queen before the BBC 6pm news on the eve of Diana's funeral, in which she made a personal tribute to Diana, thanked the public for their flowers and well-wishes, gave thoughts to Diana's family and those who had died with her, and urged the importance of a collective grieving on the morrow, when a united Britain would be presented. Hill's sense, however, is that this apology was rehearsed and insincere, an act, and as such criticized by a "hostile nation".

115. If stanza 114 were a return to Diana, has Hill lost track of his plans? What happened, he wonders (without a definite article, giving a sense of telegraphese), to the planned "CODA to the CITY OF GOD", introduced in stanza 112? Hill admits he "has a mind" (meaning both the mental capacity and the inclination) to improvise, and offers this as an explanation for his abandonment of his planned coda; the refrain "*dú, mein Ariel*" is included to remind us of his tendency to wander and to repeat himself. But Prospero has lost the dignity and solemnity Hill gave him earlier; in response to the question of improvisation, he now utters, with language most prosaic, "Shove off, there's a love". With another shift in tone and matter, Hill offers (another) winter landscape of pruned wisteria, cut back to expose both its lifeless appearance and the snail trails on its supporting lintel – this pre-Spring, pre-life landscape is, Hill assures us, not bad as an "aubade", a beginning: the poet is not yet (though "not quite") at the end of his life, nor at the end of his poem ("final gasp"). He must turn the end into the beginning and the beginning into the end: his winter scene is not fitting; the "LAST POST" must become the "reveille". But the play on words is irresistible: "reveille" becomes first "Re evil", then "relive", then "revile", and then "revalue", which leads him (so easily led) to the more problematic "self- / revelation", a phrase sufficiently troublesome as to cause him to call a halt to the game using, fittingly, the jazz idiom, "EASY NOW, SOUL-BROTHER!" Hill needs to stick to his plans and finish the poem, not improvise in free-language. As he predicted, his "mind / to improvise" has prevented him from furthering his coda; at this stanza's close we are no closer to the "CITY OF GOD".

115.1 Where CODA to the CITY OF GOD? The opening of this stanza refers to the first lines of stanza 112, which announced the "Eight-block coda to the CITY OF GOD". See also stanzas 15 and 117.

115.2 Restore / what decrepit organ? A reference to the late twentieth-century practice of restoring non-functioning or otherwise "decrepit" church and town hall organs to their former glory, an exercise financed by donation, fund-raising

ANNOTATIONS

and bequests; here, "organ" may also refer to a particular faculty of the brain or to a medium for expression such as poetry.

115.3 *dú, mein Ariel* Literally, 'you, my Ariel', the phrase is a variation of the Frank Martin refrain repeated throughout the poem (see stanzas 54, 65, 79 and 91).

115.4 Shove off, there's a love Shove off' is a slang instruction to 'be gone!' 'Love' is a friendly address to a woman or child. Here, a compressed iteration of Prospero's first instructions to Ariel ("Go take this shape / And hither come in't: go, hence with diligence!") and final dismissal ("to the elements / Be free, and fare thee well!").

115.5 Under half-dead / wisteria [...] The purple-flowering, fragrant climber wisteria (here trained against a stone support, or "lintel"), is commonly pruned in winter, when it is without leaves and flowers; pruning thus leaves it apparently "half-dead".

115.6 glitters / with their mucilage The secretions ("mucilage") which mark the shiny ("glitters"), criss-cross tracks of the snails on the cobbled surface of the stone lintel onto which the wisteria is trained.

115.7 aubade A piece of music or a poem written to be heard at or appropriate to dawn, or, as here, at the revelation of the City of God.

115.8 final gasp One's final breath, or one's last – often vain – efforts towards achieving a goal.

115.9 Extrapolate / LAST POST into reveille That is, extend the 'last post' (at this, the conclusion of the poem), the military bugle call (indicating 'lights out') played at military funerals and memorial services, so that it becomes the 'reveille', the soldier's bugle-sounded wake-up call. The two calls are often played together at funerals and commemorative services to symbolize death and resurrection; here, the sense is that of making a beginning out of an end.

115.10 Re-evil [...] revelation The shift from good to evil is followed by the transformation – through a set of anagrams and homonyms – from 'evil' to 'revelation'. The wordplay acts as an instruction: with regard to ("Re") evil, first "relive" it, then denounce it ("revile"), then take stock of and reconsider ("revalue") the worth of self-investigation ("self- / revelation").

115.11 EASY NOW, SOUL-BROTHER! See also stanza 104 ("Soul-brother, show a light!"); and "RIDE IT, PREACHER!" in stanza 116.

116. Still unable to focus on his coda, Hill's dialogue in this stanza is between the everyday self and the 'you' of the imagined self ('the poet', what Yeats called the 'Dialogue of Self and Soul'). He imagines an interviewer, or the reader (or even his wife) asking how he could have lived through his muse (the previous stanza's "SOUL-BROTHER") for "so long", how it is that he seems to write as if in his sleep, like an automaton ("as if sleep-walking"). 'Soul' argues with 'self' and the effect is comic: the poet denies walking in sleep and Hill asserts that the quite the opposite is true – he falls off chairs while awake. Interrupting his own wandering ("But – / yes") he notes that finishing a 120-stanza poem is a significant undertaking, it is "a lengthy haul to the diploma", the reward for all the hard work. He's got his licence; he imagines himself publishing a volume for poets entitled "Self-correction without tears", and confidently boasts that, while the coda may appear to have wandered off the road, he has the skill to steer the poem – large and unwieldy as it is – to its destination ("see me reverse / tango this juggernaut onto the road"). Like Isaiah, he can turn back time ("TEN DEGREES BACKWARD"); he can perform miracles. The more celebrated vision is Ezekiel's, of the throne chariot of God and its mighty wheels (Ezekiel is "the better mechanic"), but Hill prefers the more "beautiful" vision of Isaiah. The beauty of Isaiah's manoeuvre is his showmanship of the articulation of his vehicle, the sight of "Áll eighteen / wheels engaging the hardtop", with "no / body-damage to speak of". The conceit is of Hill as the frenzied driver of his own chariot: driving this juggernaut of a poem to its conclusion, he rides the brake during this, the coda, the pacificatory "EASY NOW, SOUL-BROTHER!" of the previous stanza is replaced by the determined, the undaunted matching syntax of "RIDE IT, PREACHER!"

116.1 lived throúgh him The sense of one living "through" another refers to the model in Christianity, but equally to the muse, and, potentially (and in the Yeatsian sense) to the dialogue of 'self' and 'soul', image of the self wrought in and by art.

116.2 I fall off chairs Hill wrote, in an article in *The Guardian*, of his own physical clumsiness, and its relationship with his thinking: "The physical is important to me although – or because – I'm a physically awkward person. The irruption of spoken questions and demands breaks into my thinking self

Annotations

like a physical blow" ('A Matter of Timing'). Note the implied dialogue, self accusing 'soul' of sleepwalking, and receiving an indignant reply.

116.3 juggernaut The British term for a very large, long truck used to transport goods in bulk; an extension of the Hindu Jaggernath, the large monument of Krishna which in Puri, Eastern India, is dragged through the streets on a heavy chariot, under the wheels of which people once threw themselves in order to become martyrs. Here, Hill imagines the poem as this unwieldy vehicle, which he is nevertheless able skilfully and artfully to manoeuvre ("reverse / tango") back onto the road.

116.4 TEN DEGREES BACKWARD, Isaiah says The quotation is from Isaiah 38:8, and describes Isaiah's response to Hezekiah, who did not believe the prophet's assertion that he would survive his illness. To prove his power, Isaiah performs the miraculous feat of turning back time: "Behold, I will bring again the shadow of the degrees, which is gone down in the sun dial of Ahaz, ten degrees backward. So the sun returned ten degrees, by which degrees it was gone down."

116.5 Ezekiel's the better mechanic Continuing the automotive metaphor, the Old Testament prophet is imagined as a "mechanic", though one less "beautiful" than Isaiah. In Isaiah 1-3, the prophet has a vision of God in his chariot, a vehicle of which the superior manoeuvrability and generally spectacular appearance defies mechanical norms. Ezekiel's vision of the throne chariot of God with its "four wheels by the cherubims" (Ezekiel 10:9) is a staple of esoteric thought; hence, here, he is the "better mechanic".

116.6 hardtop The metal surface of the road.

116.7 RIDE IT When driving, to 'ride it' is keep either the clutch or brake partially depressed; here, the poet as prophet ("PREACHER"), likened to the 'driver' of the Chariot of Isaiah or Ezekiel.

117. Hill, by his own rueful admission, has not made progress with his coda; he is "No nearer Jerusalem". Returning to the quandary of stanza 107 (whether to "Become vindictive in self- / vindication"), Hill argues than any justification of his 'self-hatred' and its resulting poetry would be equally unjust as the self-hatred itself; he has weighed the arguments "for and against". Rather than be forced into self-justification (by those, for instance, who might say that he procrastinates), Hill will embrace a "Poetics of self-rule"; he will follow the example of Luther who – in the face of scorn – proceeded with his own convictions. In this poem, Hill's "self-rule" is indicated on the page by his rule-breaking use of capitals (which he belatedly identifies as indicating "STAGE DIRECTIONS AND OTHER / FORMS OF SUBPOENA") and italics (which, for reasons undisclosed, "surprise" even the poet). Three stanzas from the poem's promised end, Hill's inability to reach his Jerusalem is not proof of its non-existence, something the poet explains via a double-negative: the City of God is "Unapproachable"; it probably is real, "*not*" a mirage, with a strangeness not imaginative but awesomely material.

117.1 No nearer Jerusalem As in Blake's 'Jerusalem', the establishment on earth of the Heavenly City: "I will not cease from mental fight / Nor shall my sword sleep in my hand / Til we have built Jerusalem / In England's green and pleasant land." See also stanza 35.

117.2 Júst as únjust There is a dual sense of 'just versus unjust' and 'equally as unjust'; with an echo of Matthew 5:45: "for he maketh his sun to rise on the evil and on the good, and sendeth rain on the just and the unjust", or Acts 24:15: "there shall be a resurrection of the dead, both of the just and unjust."

117.3 Why nót twist Luther The (rhetorical) question seems to be as follows: why not twist the text "*Ich kann nicht anders*", Martin Luther's proclamation (see stanza 20). Hill conceives of the shaping of language as 'twists' of manipulation: in this poem, he uses the phrases "usual twist" (5), "twist my text" (26), "mid-twist" (103); in *A Treatise of Civil Power* he identifies criticism of his own poetic 'twists': "But what are we accused of, twist by twist? / Varieties of things though laissez-faire / is not among them" ('A Treatise of Civil Power', VI).

117.4 list price A published or advertised retail price of an item which is often discounted by the seller.

117.5 CAPITALS [...] surprise *myself* Lines 7-9 are unmistakably metatextual: Hill (finally) provides some explanation for some of the typographical devices he has employed throughout the poem: capitals and stage directions are described as a literary version of the evidence provided witnesses under summons ("SUBPOENA"), while italics are surprising. See Introduction, pp. 37-41 for a full account of these and other typographical aspects of the poem.

117.6 City of God See references to the City of God in stanzas 15, 112, and 115.

ANNOTATIONS

117.7 Lost / estate (WESLEY?) Charles Wesley, (1707-1788) English evangelist and founder of Methodism. The phrase is found in several hymns by Wesley and his brother John, and appears in Charles Wesley's sermon 'Awake, Thou That Sleepest': "Now awake thou that sleepest in spiritual death, that thou sleep not in death eternal! Feel thy lost estate and 'arise from the dead.' Leave thine old companions in sin and death. Follow thou Jesus, and 'let the dead bury their dead.' 'Save thyself from this untoward generation.' 'Come out from among them, and be thou separate, and touch not the unclean thing; and the Lord shall receive thee'" (*The Sermons of Charles Wesley*, p. 219).

117.8 probably *not* a mirage Cf. Eliot's vision in Part V of *The Waste Land*: "And upside down in air were towers / tolling reminiscent bells". Mirages are the result either of superior images (in which the imagined shapes lie above the line of vision) or inferior images (in which they lie below, appearing upside-down, "wróng / way úp"); the inferior is the more common, and so Hill's assertion that the inverted towers are "probably *not*" a mirage emphasizes the horrifying reality of the falling towers of the City of God, a vision Eliot describes as "Unreal", meaning that it is so strange as to *appear* imaginary.

118. Even at the poem's crucial closing, when its message ought to be clarified and emphasized ("dead / heart of the matter"), Hill is "Inconstant": although there is frivolity in his laughter there is no joy, and nor does his laughter give joy. He is nearing the end, about to publish his poem, to offer it up to the public at auction for bids (despite risking accusations of "libel"), *to determine its worth*. Again, he voices imagined criticisms: everyone says (obscured in German) that Hill and his poem are "wantonly obscure" – Hill provides his answer in the third person, as if imagining his broadcast voice: the accessible (the supposed opposite of 'obscure') is today "traded" as democratic. The implication is that obscurity is not to be equated with élitism. Hill answers questions such as these with a new casualness, the veracity of his answers less important to him, and his confidence in their veracity stronger than in the past. Hill describes himself as open in all other aspects of life than his verse; he is for instance "shaken by others' weeping" (recalling his reaction to Diana's funeral, but also suggesting that he is not shaken by his own), he defines himself (humbly) as "duty's memorialist", as the rememberer of and for the "known-unknown", those heroes who missed their stars in stanza 7, those "servants of Empire" who died with their spirits intact, impenetrable and everlasting, even as their bodies (buried under the far-off veldt) were cut through by lilies, the new shoots now growing through the rib-cages.

118.1 heart of the matter Cf. Graham Greene's *The Heart of the Matter*, in which an "Inconstant", adulterous Major Scobie negotiates his relationship with his wife and with his Catholicism.

118.2 Thin veil of libel The phrase withstands two interpretations: in the first, the poet's poorly disguised ("Thin veil"), malicious attacks are up for auction ("bids"); in the second, libel – itself a "Thin veil" over the truth – is "úp" on the auctioneer's block.

118.3 *man sagt* German, 'they say'; the poet nonchalantly responding to his critics. In *The Triumph of Love*, Hill employs pseudonyms to indicate the criticisms of his poetry – his scorn is heaped on them and what he considers their wilfully complex arguments, their "defunct pomp": "So – Croker, MacSikker, O'Shem – I ask you: / what are poems for? They are to console us / with their own gift, which is like perfect pitch" (CXLVIII).

118.4 ACCESSIBLE / traded as DEMOCRATIC That is, that which is understood without difficulty ("ACCESSIBLE") is marketed to the public as inherently enfranchising, equitable ("DEMOCRATIC"). This is a sentiment with which Hill takes umbrage; cf. *The Triumph of Love*: "Take accessible to mean / acceptable, accommodating, openly servile" (XL). See also Hill's discussion of a modern-spelling edition of Tyndale's *New Testament*, in which he describes Tyndale's world as "so beyond comprehension that the ambition to render it 'accessible', 'available to today's reader', is in every sense vain" (*Collected Critical Writings*, p. 290).

118.5 duty's memorialist One who writes historical memorials, or delivers a memorial address; here, doing so in service of "duty".

118.6 unburied That is, for the anonymous multitude who worked – thanklessly – for the benefit and glory of expansionist nation-building (especially that of the British Empire); in "known-unknown" and "unburied" there is a suggestion of the Tomb of the Unknown Soldier, the name, since WWI, for the graves used to house (either physically or symbolically) the unidentified bodies of soldiers.

118.7 veldt Dutch, 'grassland'; specifically, that of South Africa which became the setting of the Boer War (1899-1902), where thousands of "servants of Empire" died. Their bodies are imagined as buried beneath the veldt, with lilies (like Zulu spears) growing through the rib cage. The line echoes Matthew 6:28-29: "Consider the lilies of the field, how they grow; they toil not, neither do they spin: and yet I say unto you, that even Solomon in all his glory, was not arrayed like one of these"; but compare Joyce's *Finnegans Wake*: "I considered the lilies on the veldt" (p. 543).

119. The rhetoric of the stanza is the move from rejection and mockery to affirmation of the poet's method. Hill casts his judgement on his poem: it has been a "Shambles" of inversions and reversals ("peripeteia") which has failed even to "discover" history, let alone "make it". Its comic moments ("Loud laughter / track"), the odd forced joke here and there, have been no real "compensation" for its failure (expressed with the upper-class, "bád shów"). The poem clearly "needs working on", but is there any point in working on it if nobody "needs it"? Is the poet's inner voice – his "AMICUS" – to be heard if there is no court to bear witness to it? The best way to proceed, argues Hill, is to "Make a good / ending", one that will exemplify the "good life", one which is easy to adopt ("teár throúgh it"). But there are subtle distinctions – between status (social acceptance) and real authority, for instance, or between the gratifyingly *sensual* and the sensorily *sensuous* – how can these subtleties be reconciled with the need to persist, to proceed, to act, to speak? As an answer, Hill offers Catullus as a model: he parodied and imitated but was finally right and successful, "sure- / foóted" in his verse – a skilful imitator of the unskilful.

119.1 Shambles of peripeteia An apparent dismissal of the poem as messy (a "Shambles") and riddled with sudden shifts of circumstance ("peripeteia"), its attempts to reveal ("discover") history doomed to confuse, or make no impact.

119.2 laughter / track Pre-recorded laughter inserted into dismal television programmes ("bád shów") to encourage the audience to laugh along; "bád shów" (often followed by 'old boy') is an aristocratic reproof for a job not well done. See also "spools of applause" in stanza 8.

119.3 AMICUS An abbreviation of the Latin *amicus curiae* [friend of the court]; the *amicus* gives impartial advice to the court, bearing witness rather than giving evidence.

119.4 Make a good / ending To die well, with honour; but also to make a good ending for the poem (in this the penultimate stanza).

119.5 the good life Aristotle's recipe for 'the good life' included just action towards one's friends and community, and the ability to determine the best course of action by drawing on the ethical fundamentals instilled during upbringing.

119.6 teár throúgh it To 'tear through it' is to rip it up or (of a book) to read it quickly; here, the sense is also to live life richly, without unnecessary hesitation, but also to do this without reflection.

119.7 Dissever sensual / from sensuous *Sensual* describes the body and the senses (especially the physicality of sexual pleasure) as opposed to the mind or the intellect; *sensuous* refers to the pleasurable stimulation of the senses. Hill is attuned to the distinction, or perhaps indistinction, between the two words; he writes in *Style and Faith* of James Henry Augustus Murray, primary editor of the first *OED*: "Murray and his colleagues strike one as being finely attuned to English usages which are themselves reductive, collocative, analytical (as in the notes on Elyot's 'publike weal' vs 'commune weal', or on *sensuous*, 'Apparently invented by Milton, to avoid certain associations of the existing word *sensual*')" (*Collected Critical Writings*, p. 274).

119.8 the Límper The "Limper" is the *scazon* (or *choliambic*), Greek and Latin verse which ends with a spondee or trochee (rather than an iambus), and which effects a sense of lame, limping distortion (note the obvious pun on the metrical foot). The form, often used in longer pieces, was favoured by Roman love poet Catullus (c 84BC-c 54BC), most often in his poems of invective (see *Select Epigrams*, p. 28). Hill's conscious use of the meter (like Catullus's pursuit of Sappho of Lesbos; see stanza 120) is thus "sure- / foóted" despite its 'limping' quality; this intentionality gave Catullus's 'lame' poems their powerful invective. Peter McDonald notes that "The *OED* quotes Obadiah Walker in 1673, on 'Archilochus and Hipponax, two very bad poets' who 'invented these doggerel sorts of verses, Iambics and Scazons', and this citation is unlikely to have been lost on Hill" (*Serious Poetry*, p. 200).

ANNOTATIONS

120. The final stanza is what Hill admired in the last: a "sure- / foóted" foot-by-foot walk through a shambolic stanza. In a masterful display of manipulation of form and metatextuality, the "English" Hill (in English) follows a perfect Sapphic line with the scazon, the 'limping' "Thís", which literally "hás to be seen" at the end of a line in order for the line to function, to do as it claims. (The line also offers an image of the poet, limping in his old age, struggling to chase after a female object of desire.) Impressed by his own poetic virtuosity ("whát a way to go"), Hill puts forward as "supreme honours" the sculpted acts of protest ("effigies") made by his hero Daumier, whose unfired models ("goúged", "sagging clay") portray "corruption", but nevertheless are redemptive, offering abundant "purity". In literature, this purity is the result of masterful, responsible and attentive use of language, gouged and manipulated like so much clay, but written in the best "*English*", that of the RSC and the BBC ("the ALDWYCH") – an extravagant claim at best, given the wide range of voices listened to and echoed throughout the poem. And, for good measure, Hill follows the Aldwych with an apostrophe to the (American) "TIME-LIFE" magazine, before ending with a macaronic line of dog-Latin, infused with Greek, Hebrew and a pseudo-palindromic English. This final note is one of chaos: our linguistic cornerstones are debased to a kind of sputtering Creole; the capitalized babel of *cris de coeur* is symptomatic of a desperation to communicate, a final (if not altogether articulate) answer to the call for *Speech! Speech!*

120.1 English Limper | after the English Sapphic Metatextual references: the "Limper" is the distorting *scazon* of the previous stanza; "Sapphic" is the hendecasyllabic line, two trochees followed by a dactyl and another two trochees, of which this line (save the 'limping' "Thís") is a perfect example. Thus the "Limper" in line 1 comes "after" the "Sapphic". Both "Limper" and "Sapphic" are "English", like their creator (as opposed to 'Latin'); "Thís" at the end of the line "hás to be seen" (a phrase which invokes a demotic wonderment) in order for the scazon, the "Limper", to be witnessed. Greg Londe gives an excellent account in his blog *Name to Conjure* (11 November 2007); after suggesting that Hill may have come across the "Limper" in the work of William Carlos Williams, he notes that "the line is also a dirty little chase: limp old limper limping after Sappho".

120.2 whát a way to go A demotic phrase referring to a good death (the end to the "good life" of the previous stanza). The sense is of the artistry transforming what might appear deformed (the scazon) into a final flourish, a blaze of glory on which to go out.

120.3 Daumier's / effigies Michael Kooy identifies these "effigies" as those depicting corrupt legislators crafted "in unfired clay made by Daumier in the early part of his career" ('Word and Image', p. 199); here, they are invoked as satirical expressions of outrage, Daumier's modellings (sculpted from "sagging clay") lampooning the bourgeoisie (see stanza 31). Compare Catullus's angry love poems (stanza 119).

120.4 the ALDWYCH Aldwych is a crescent in the West End of London, invoked here for two of its addresses: the Aldwych Theatre, home from 1960 to 1982 to the Royal Shakespeare Company; and Bush House, the headquarters of the BBC, former bastion of received pronunciation.

120.5 whát cognómen Hill is probably referring to the *cognomen ex virtute*, the part of Roman nomenclature which could be awarded as an honorific e.g. Gnaeus Pompeius *Magnus* (the Great).

120.6 TIME-LIFE *Time-Life* (founded in 1961) is a publisher, known for selling books and music that are mailed to households on a monthly instalment. Cf. "PEOPLE" in stanzas 1, 13 and 22, 40, 100 and "VARIETY" in stanza 14. There is an echo of Shelley's 'A Lament': 'O world! O life! O time! / On whose last steps I climb, / Trembling at that where I had stood before; / When will return the glory of your prime?".

120.7 AMOR [...] AMEN "AMOR" is the Latin name for love gods Cupid or Eros, and means 'love' in many tongues; "MAN IN A COMA, MA'AM" is a near-palindrome, a last act of alliterative comedy recalling Malone, who "lived in a kind of coma" (as quoted in Ricks's *Beckett's Dying Words*, p. 2); the Latin "NEMO" [no man, no-one] recalls Verne's 'Captain Nemo', Dickens's 'Nemo' in *Bleak House*; and 'Little Nemo', the (anti-)hero of Windsor McCay's subversive 1904-1914 comic strips; "AMEN" (Latin, via Greek and Hebrew) is the assent of Christian worship (the 'last word') which translates to 'So be it'. Cf. the polyglottism ending *The Waste Land*, the linguistic "fragments" "shored" against the poet's "ruins" (V).

BIBLIOGRAPHY

Works by Hill

Hill, Geoffrey. 'Yes, Of Course I was Wired Weird'. Interview with Chris Woodhead. *Standpoint* (accessed 5 Dec. 2010) <http://standpointmag.co.uk/node/ 3154/full>.

— 'Trinity Sermon: Ash Wednesday 2008'. *Trinity College: Cambridge* (accessed 12 Jan. 2010) <www.trin.cam.ac.uk/show.php?dowid=520>.

— 'Confessio Amantis'. *The Record 2009*. Keble College: Oxford, 2009: 45-54 (accessed 13 Jan. 2010) <www.keble.ox.ac.uk/alumni/publications-2/Record09.pdf>.

— 'Strongholds of the Imagination'. Interview with Alexandra Bell, Rebecca Rosen and Edmund White. *The Oxonian Review* 9.4, 18 May 2009 (accessed 1 Mar. 2010) <http://www.oxonianreview.org/wp/geoffrey-hill>.

— *Collected Critical Writings of Geoffrey Hill*. Ed. Kenneth Haynes. Oxford: Oxford University Press, 2008.

— 'Civil Polity and the Confessing State'. *Warwick Review* 2.2 (2008): 7-20.

— *A Treatise of Civil Power*. London: Penguin, 2007.

— 'Sidney Keyes in Historical Perspective'. *The Oxford Handbook of British and Irish War Poetry*. Ed. Tim Kendall. Oxford: Oxford University Press, 2007.

— *Poetry Reading, Oxford, 1st February 2006*. Audio recording. Oxford: Clutag, 2006.

— *Selected Poems*. London: Penguin, 2006.

— *Without Title*. London: Penguin, 2006.

— *Scenes from Comus*. London: Penguin, 2005.

— *A Treatise of Civil Power*. Thame [England]: Clutag Press, 2005.

— *Style and Faith*. New York: Counterpoint, 2003.

— 'Geoffrey Hill'. *Don't Ask Me What I Mean: Poets in their Own Words*. Ed. Clare Brown and Don Paterson. London: Picador, 2003.

— 'A Matter of Timing'. *The Guardian* 21 Sept. 2002 (accessed 13 July 2003) <http://www.guardian.co.uk/books/2002/sep/21/featuresreviews.guardianreview28>.

— *The Orchards of Syon*. Washington DC: Counterpoint, 2002.
— 'The Art of Poetry LXXX'. Interview with Carl Phillips. *The Paris Review* 154 (2000): 272-299.
— *Speech! Speech!* London: Penguin, 2001.
— *Speech! Speech!* Washington DC: Counterpoint, 2000.
— *The Triumph of Love*. Boston: Houghton Mifflin, 1998.
— *Canaan*. London: Penguin, 1996.
— *New and Collected Poems, 1952-1992*. Boston: Houghton Mifflin, 1994.
— *The Enemy's Country: Words, Contexture, and other Circumstances of Language*. Oxford: Clarendon Press, 1991.
— *Collected Poems*. London: Penguin, 1985.
— *The Lords of Limit: Essays on Literature and Ideas*. London: André Deutsch, 1984.
— *The Mystery of the Charity of Charles Péguy*. London: Agenda/André Deutsch, 1983.
— 'Geoffrey Hill'. Interview with John Haffenden. *Viewpoints: Poets in Conversation*. London: Faber and Faber, 1981: 76-99.
— *Tenebrae*. London: André Deutsch, 1978.
— *Somewhere is Such a Kingdom: Poems 1952-1971*. Boston: Houghton Mifflin, 1975.
— *Mercian Hymns*. London: André Deutsch, 1971.
— *King Log*. London: André Deutsch, 1968.
— *Preghiere*. Leeds: Northern House Pamphlet Poets, 1964.
— '"I in Another Place": Homage to Keith Douglas'. *Stand*. 6.4 (1964/5): 7.
— *For the Unfallen: Poems 1952-1958*. London: André Deutsch, 1959.

Works about Hill

Alcobia-Murphy, Shane. '"Not Forgotten or Passed Over at the Proper Time": The Representation of Violent Events in Popular Culture'. *Culture, Language and Representation* 2 (2005): 19-40.
Anon. 'Books and Arts: Trust in Words'. Review of *Speech! Speech! The Economist* 21 June 2001: 81.

BIBLIOGRAPHY

Anon. 'Speech! Speech!'. Review of *Speech! Speech! Virginia Quarterly Review* 77:2 (2001): 65.

Anwin, David. *Inhabited Voices: Myth and History in the Poetry of Geoffrey Hill, Seamus Heaney and George Mackay Brown*. Somerset: Bran's Head Books, 1984.

Barber, David. 'The Orchards of Syon'. Review of *The Orchards of Syon*. *New York Times Book Review* 14 Apr. 2002: 20.

Barenblat, Rachel. 'Review of Speech! Speech!'. *Pif Magazine* 1 Feb. 2001 (accessed 10 June 2006) <http://www.pifmagazine.com/SID/662/>.

Birkan, Carole. 'Geoffrey Hill's "Collated" Poems and Criticism'. *Cahiers Charles V* 34 (2003): 139-154.

Blanton, C.D. 'Nominal Devolutions: Poetic Substance and the Critique of Political Economy'. *The Yale Journal of Criticism* 13.1 (2000): 129-151.

Bloom, Harold, ed. *Geoffrey Hill (Modern Critical Views)*. New York: Chelsea House, 1986.

Bolton, Jonathan. 'Empire and Atonement: Geoffrey Hill's "An Apology for the Revival of Christian Architecture in England"'. *Contemporary Literature* 38.2 (1997): 287-306.

Bourbon, Brett. 'The Remittance of Mistrust'. *Chicago Review* 53/54.4-1/2 (2008): 279-357.

Bromwich, David. 'Muse of Brimstone'. Review of *Speech! Speech! New York Times Book Review* 11 Mar. 2001: 28.

Bromwich, David. *Skeptical Music: Essays on Modern Poetry*. Chicago: University of Chicago Press, 2001.

Brownjohn, Alan. 'A Rush of Blood'. Review of *Scenes from Comus*. *The Sunday Times* 19 June 2005: 51.

Burt, Steven. 'Meaningful Speech'. Review of *The Orchards of Syon*. *Publishers Weekly* 8 Apr. 2002: 198.

Buxton, Rachel. 'Transaction and Transcendence: Geoffrey Hill's Vision of *Canaan*'. *The Cambridge Quarterly*. 34.4 (2005): 333-363.

Cavaliero, Glen. 'The Mysterious Charity of Geoffrey Hill'. *PN Review* 25.6/128 (1999): 10-12.

Christie, Tara. "For Isaac Rosenberg': Geoffrey Hill, Michael Longley, Cathal Ó Searcaigh'. *The Oxford Handook of British and Irish War Poetry*. Ed. Tim Kendall. Oxford: Oxford University Press, 2007: 542-563.

Clark, Steve and Mark Ford. *Something We Have That They Don't: British and American Poetic Relations since 1925*. Iowa City: University of Iowa Press, 2004.

Cook, Eleanor. *Against Coercion: Games Poets Play*. Stanford: Stanford University Press, 1998.

Davies, Paul. 'A Poem and its Context'. *Textual Practice* 22.4 (2008): 635-656.

Day, Thomas. 'Criticising the Critic'. *The Cambridge Quarterly* 38.2 (2009): 188-192.

— 'Geoffrey Hill's Finishing-Lines'. *Cahier Charles V* 34 (2003): 155-166.

— 'Sensuous Intelligence: T.S. Eliot and Geoffrey Hill'. *The Cambridge Quarterly* 35.3 (2003): 255-280.

De Gaynesford, Robert Maximilian. 'The Seriousness of Poetry'. *Essays in Criticism* 59.1 (2009): 1-21.

Dickey, James. *Classes on Modern Poets and the Art of Poetry*. Ed. Donald J. Greiner. Columbia: University of South Carolina Press, 2004.

Drexel, John. 'Geoffrey Hill: The Poet in Winter'. Review of *The Orchards of Syon*. *Contemporary Poetry Review* 7 Apr. 2003 (accessed 9 Aug. 2007) <http://www.cprw.com/geoffrey-hill-the-poet-in-winter/>.

Duncan, Andrew. *Centre and Periphery in Modern British Poetry*. Liverpool: Liverpool University Press, 2005.

Duncan, Andrew. *The Failure of Conservatism in Modern British Poetry*. Cambridge: Salt, 2003.

Ezenwa-Ohaeto. *Chinua Achebe: A Biography*. Oxford: James Currey, 1997.

Fitzgerald, Judith. 'Unfashionably Difficult'. Review of *Selected Poems*. *The Globe and Mail* 5 Apr. 2010 (accessed 10 Dec. 2010) <http://www.thegloabeandmail.com/ news/ arts/books/ article1523567.ece>.

Fogle, Andy. 'This Canon Fires'. *Popmatters* (accessed 10 Oct. 2008) <http://www.popmatters.com/books/reviews/s/speech-speech.shtml>.

Forbes, Peter, Sarah Maguire and Jamie McKendrick. 'Poetry Wars'. *The Guardian* 2 Feb. 2002 (accessed 10 Oct. 2004) <http://www.guardian.co.uk/books/2002/feb/02/ poetry.tseliotprizeforpoetry>.

Fordham, Finn. 'Mothers' Boys Brooding on Bubbles: Studies of Two Poems by Geoffrey Hill and Derek Walcott'. *Critical Quarterly* 44.1 (2002): 80-96.

Gervais, David. 'Geoffrey Hill: The Poet as Critic'. *PN Review* 31.4 2005, 63-64.

BIBLIOGRAPHY

— 'The Late Flowering of Geoffrey Hill'. *PN Review* 35.1 (2008): 32-36.

Gowrie, Gray. 'A Celebration with a Warning'. Review of *Scenes from Comus*, by Geoffrey Hill. *The Spectator* 5 Feb. 2005, 44.

Greenwell, Garth. '"The Pedagogy of Martyrdom": "Witness" in Geoffrey Hill's *The Triumph of Love*'. *Literary Imagination* 8.1 (2006): 91-108.

Hart, Henry. 'Geoffrey Hill: The Quest for Mystical Communion and Community'. *Religion and Literature* 39.1 (2007): 1-26.

Hart, Kevin. '"it / is true"'. *Words of Life: New Theological Turns in French Phenomenology*. Ed. Bruce Benson and Norman Wirzba. New York: Fordham University Press, 2010.

— 'Transcendence in Tears'. *Gazing Through a Prism Darkly: Reflections on Merold Westphal's Hermeneutical Epistemology*. Ed. B. Keith Putt. New York: Fordham University Press, 2009.

— 'Poetics and Power'. Review of *A Treatise of Civil Power*. *First Things* 182 (2008): 46-47.

— 'God's Little Mountains: Young Geoffrey Hill and the Problem of Religious Poetry'. *Sacred Worlds: Religion, Literature, and the Imagination*. Eds. Mark Knight and Louise Lee. London: Continuum, 2009: 23-36.

— 'Varieties of poetic sequence: Ted Hughes and Geoffrey Hill'. *The Cambridge Companion to Twentieth-Century English Poetry*. Ed. Neil Corcoran. Cambridge: Cambridge University Press, 2007: 187-199.

— 'Up and Dówn the | Hill'. Review of *Speech! Speech!* and *The Orchards of Syon*. *Notre Dame Review* 17 (2004): 157-161.

Hossack-Sime, Irene. 'Geoffrey Hill's "Annunciations"'. *Poetry and Reading* (accessed 1 Dec. 2008) <http://irenehossack.blogspot.com/2008/09/geoffry-hills-annunciations.html>.

Jeffers, Thomas L. 'That Which Sustains Us'. Review of *The Orchards of Syon*. *Commentary* 113.6 (2002): 56.

Johnson, Jeannine. *Why Write Poetry?: Modern Poets Defending Their Art*. Madison, NJ: Fairleigh Dickinson University Press, 2007.

Kendall, Tim. 'Geoffrey Hill's Debts'. *Modern English War Poetry*. Oxford: Oxford University Press, 2006.

Kilgore Jennifer, 'Seeking "The Root in Justice": Geoffrey Hill on Ezra Pound'. *Ezra Pound and Referentiality*. Paris: Presses Paris Sorbonne, 2003: 93-104.

— 'Peace it Together: Collage in the Recent Work of Geoffrey Hill'. *Cahiers Charles V* 24 (2003): 167-184.

Kirsch, Adam. 'The Long-Cherished Anger of Geoffrey Hill'. Review of *Without Title*. *The New York Sun* 28 Mar. 2007 (accessed 1 Aug. 2007) <http:// www.nysun.com/arts/long-cherished-anger-of-geoffrey-hill/51347/>.

Knottenbelt, Elizabeth M. *Passionate Intelligence: The Poetry of Geoffrey Hill*. Amsterdam; Atlanta, GA: Rodopi, 1990.

Kooy, Michael John. 'Word and Image in the Later Work of Geoffrey Hill'. *Word and Image* 20.3 (2004): 191-205.

Koppenfels, Werner Von. 'A Sad and Angry Consolation: Violence, Mourning and Memory in the Late Poetry of Ted Hughes and Geoffrey Hill'. *European Studies* 16 (2001): 227-249.

Laird, Martin. *Into the Silent Land: A Guide to the Christian Practice of Contemplation*. Oxford: Oxford University Press, 2006.

Logan, William. 'Author! Author!' Review of *Speech! Speech! The New Criterion* 19.4 (2000): 65.

— 'Falls the Shadow'. Review of *The Orchards of Syon*. *The New Criterion* 20.10 (2002): 75.

— 'The Absolute Unreasonableness of Geoffrey Hill'. *Conversant Essays: Contemporary Poets on Poetry*. Detroit, MI: Wayne State University Press, 1990.

— 'The Triumph of Geoffrey Hill'. *Parnassus: Poetry in Review* 24:2 (2000): 201.

— *Our Savage Art: Poetry and the Civil Tongue*. New York: Columbia University Press, 2009.

— *The Undiscovered Country: Poetry in the Age of Tin*. New York: Columbia University Press, 2005.

Londe, Gregory. *Name to Conjure: A Blog about the Poet Geoffrey Hill* 11 Nov. 2007 (accessed 1 Sep. 2010) <http://nametoconjure.blogspot.com/>.

Lyon, John. '"Pardon?": Our Problem with Difficulty (and Geoffrey Hill)'. *Thumbscrew* 13. (1999): 11-19.

— '"What Are You Incinerating?": Geoffrey Hill and Popular Culture'. *English* 54.209 (2005): 58-98.

BIBLIOGRAPHY

MacFarlane, Robert. 'Gravity and Grace in Geoffrey Hill'. *Essays in Criticism* 38.3 (2008): 237-256.

Mahan, David C. *An Unexpected Light: Theology and Witness in the Poetry and Thought of Charles Williams, Michael O'Siadhail, and Geoffrey Hill*. Eugene, OR: Pickwick Publications, 2009.

Mariani, Paul. 'The Limits of the Ineluctable'. Review of *The Orchards of Syon*. *America, The National Catholic Weekly* 9 Sep. 2002: 21.

McDonald, Peter. *Serious Poetry: Form and Authority from Yeats to Hill*. Oxford: Clarendon Press, 2004.

McHale, Brian. *The Obligation toward the Difficult Whole: Postmodernist Long Poems*. Tucaloosa & London: The University of Alabama Press, 2004.

Meiners, R. K. '"Upon the Slippery Place"; or, In the Shit: Geoffrey Hill's Writing and the Failures of Postmodern Memory'. *Contemporary British Poetry: Essays in Theory and Criticism*. Eds. James Acheson and Romana Huk. Albany: State University of New York Press, 1996: 221-240.

Merriman, Emily Taylor. 'Metamorphic Power: Geoffrey Hill and Gerard Manley Hopkins'. *Ecstasy and Understanding: Religious Awareness in English Poetry from the Late Victorian to the Modern Period*. Ed. Adrian Grafe. London: Continuum, 2008: 145-160.

Milne, W.S. 'Geoffrey Hill: *Speech! Speech!*' Review of *Speech! Speech! Agenda* 38.1-2 (2001): 139-143.

— *An Introduction to Geoffrey Hill*. London: Bellew, 1998.

Nicholas, Lezard. 'Hill Starts'. Review of *Speech! Speech! The Guardian* 17 Nov. 2001 (accessed 10 Feb. 2002) <http://www.guardian.co.uk/books/2001/nov/17/>.

Noel-Tod, Jeremy. 'Curious and Furious'. Review of *Speech! Speech! The Observer* 20 Jan. 2002: R.16.

O'Neill, Michael. *The All-Sustaining Air: Romantic Legacies and Renewals in British, American, and Irish Poetry since 1900*. Oxford: Oxford University Press, 2007.

Orchard, Christopher. 'Praxis Not Gnosis: Geoffrey Hill and the Anxiety of Polity'. *Poetry and Public Language*. Eds. Tony Lopez and Anthony Caleshu. Exeter: Shearsman Books, 2007.

Ozawa-de Silva, Brendan. 'Falls the Shadow'. Review of *The Orchards of Syon*. *Chicago Review* 49/50.3-4/1 (2004): 378.

Polonsky, Rachel. 'Puns, Puzzles and Dirty Jokes'. Review of *Speech! Speech!*. *The London Evening Standard* 12 Nov. 2001 (accessed 5 Jan. 2006) <http://www.thisislondon.co.uk/showbiz/article-368147-puns-puzzles-and-dirty-jokes.do>.

Potts, Robert. 'The Praise Singer'. *The Guardian* 10 Aug. 2002 (accessed 20 Jan. 2003) <http://www.guardian.co.uk/books/2002/aug/10/featuresreviews.guardianreview15>.

— 'A Change of Address'. Rev. of *Speech! Speech! Times Literary Supplement*. 25 Jan. 2002: 25.

— 'Theatre of Voices'. *The Guardian* 30 Nov. 2001 (accessed 23 Jan. 2005) <http://www.guardian.co.uk/books/2001/nov/30/bestbooksoftheyear.artsfeatures2>.

Pritchard, Daniel E. 'Geoffrey Hill: Unparalleled Atonement'. *Critical Flame* (accessed 1 May 2010) <http://criticalflame.org/verse/0509_pritchard.htm>.

Quinn, Justin. 'Geoffrey Hill in America'. *Yale Review* 89.4 (2001): 146-66.

Ratcliffe, Sophie. *On Sympathy*. Oxford: Clarendon Press; New York: Oxford University Press, 2008.

Ratner, Rochelle. 'Geoffrey Hill: *Speech! Speech!*' Review of *Speech! Speech! Library Journal* 125.18 (2000): 86.

Reeves, Gareth. 'This is Plenty. This is More than Enough'. *Oxford Handbook of British and Irish War Poetry*. Ed. Tim Kendall. Oxford: Oxford University Press, 2007.

Ricks, Christopher. *True Friendship: Geoffrey Hill, Anthony Hecht, and Robert Lowell Under the Sign of Eliot and Pound*. New Haven, CT: Yale University Press, 2010.

— *Allusion to the Poets*. Oxford & New York: Oxford University Press, 2002.

— *The Force of Poetry*. Oxford & New York: Clarendon Press, 1984.

Roberts, Andrew Michael. 'Error and Mistakes in Poetry: Geoffrey Hill and Tom Raworth'. *English* 56.216 (2007): 339-361.

— *Geoffrey Hill (Writers and their Work Series)*. Tavistock, Devon, UK: Northcote [British Council], 2004.

Rogers, David. 'Geoffrey Hill: Speech! Speech!' Review of *Speech! Speech! World Literature Today* 76.1 (2002): 152.

BIBLIOGRAPHY

Rowland, Antony. *Holocaust Poetry: Awkward Poetics in the Work of Sylvia Plath, Geoffrey Hill, Tony Harrison and Ted Hughes*. Edinburgh: Edinburgh University Press, 2005.

Schmidt, Michael. 'Editorial'. *PN Review* 32.4 (2006) (accessed 1 May 2010) <http://gateway.proquest.com/openurl?ctx_ver=Z39.88-2003&xri: pqil:res_ver=0.2&res_id=xri:lion-us&rft_id=xri:lion:ft:abell: R03863571:0.>.

— *Lives of the Poets*. London: Weidenfeld and Nicolson, 1998.

Sherman, David. 'Elegy under the Knife: Geoffrey Hill and the Ethics of Sacrifice'. *Twentieth Century Literature* 54.2 (2005): 166-192.

Smith, Laurie. 'Subduing the Reader'. Review of *Speech! Speech! Magma* 23 (2002) (accessed 12 May 2007) <http://www.poetrymagazines.org.uk/magazine/record.asp?id=14974>.

Thompson, N.S. 'Form and Function: IV, Form and Audience'. *PN Review* 30.2 (2003): 60-64.

Tuma, Keith. 'Who Needs Neo-Augustanism? On British Poetry'. *Contemporary Literature* 36.4 (1995): 718-726.

Wainwright, Jeffrey. *Acceptable Words: Essays on the Poetry of Geoffrey Hill*. Manchester: Manchester University Press, 2005.

— 'Geoffrey Hill: *The Triumph of Love*'. *PN Review* 26.5 (2000): 13-21.

Waithe, Marcus. '"The Slow Haul To Forgive Them": Geoffrey Hill and the Second World War'. *PN Review*. 31:1 (2004): 77-80.

Walker, P.K. '*The Triumph of Love*: Geoffrey Hill's Contexture of Grace'. *Sewanee Theological Review* 44.3 (2001): 275-298.

Ward, Jean. *Christian Poetry in the Post-Christian Day: Geoffrey Hill, R.S. Thomas, Elizabeth Jennings*. Frankfurt am Main: Peter Lang, 2009.

Williams, David Antoine. *Defending Poetry: Art and Ethics in Joseph Brodsky, Seamus Heaney, and Geoffrey Hill*. Oxford: Oxford University Press, 2010.

Wolfe, Gregory. 'Who's Afraid of Geoffrey Hill?' *Image* 66 (2010) (accessed 1 Oct. 2010) <http://imagejournal.org/page/journal/editorial-statements/whos-afraid-of-geoffrey-hill>.

Yezzi, David. 'Geoffrey Hill's Civil Tongue'. Review of *A Treatise of Civil Power*. *The New Criterion* 26 Mar. 2010: 22.

Works Consulted

Ackerley, Chris and Lawrence J. Clipper. *A Companion to Under the Volcano*. Vancouver: University of British Columbia Press, 1984.

Ackerley, Chris. 'Samuel Beckett and Annotation: The Horizon of Relevant Knowledge'. *Beckett and Phenomenology*. Ed. Matthew Feldman and Ulrika Maude. London: Continuum Books, 2009: 194-207.

Addis, Michael and Andrew Charlesworth. 'Memorialization and the Ecological Landcapes of Holocaust Sites: The Cases of Plaszow and Auschwitz-Birkenau'. *Landscape Research* 27.3 (2002): 229-251.

Alighieri, Dante. *The Divine Comedy of Dante Alighieri*. Trans. by Henry Wadsworth Longfellow. London: G. Routledge, 1900.

Anon. 'A Cup of Tea'. *Icons: A Portrait of England* (accessed 25 Nov. 2008) <http://www.icons.org.uk/theicons/collection/cupoftea/features/tea-advertising>.

Anon. 'Angels "Favourite Funeral Song"'. *BBC News* 10 Mar. 2005 (accessed 7 Sept. 2007) <http://news.bbc.co.uk/2/hi/entertainment/4336113.stm

Anon. 'Coroner's Inquests into the Deaths of Diana, Princess of Wales and Mr Dodi Al Fayed.' *The National Archives* (accessed 5 Jan. 2009) <http://webarchive.nationalarchives.gov.uk/20090607230718/http://www.scottbaker-inquests.gov.uk/role_coroner/index.htm>.

Anon. 'Fly Me Again'. *Time* 24 June 1974 (accessed 2 Oct. 2007) <http://www.time.com/time/magazine/article/0,9171,944906,00.html>.

Anon. 'Obituary: David Wright, 74, South African Poet'. *The New York Times* 5 Sept. 1994 (accessed 15 Apr. 2007) <http://www.nytimes.com/1994/09/05/ obituaries/david-wright-74-south-african-poet.html>.

Anon. 'Original Justice'. *New Catholic Dictionary (1910)* (accessed 8 July 2007) <http://saints.sqpn.com/ncd06177.htm>.

Anon. 'Pictures of Scott's Last Days'. *The New York Times* 7 June 1913 (accessed 1 May 2010) <http://article.archive.nytimes.com/100398252>.

Anon. 'Scott's Own Story of His Terrible March to Death'. *The New York Times* 23 Nov. 1913: 5.

BIBLIOGRAPHY

Anon. 'The Transmission Gallery: Daventry'. *UK Broadcast Transmission* (accessed 1 May 2008) <http://tx.mb21.co.uk/gallery/daventry/>.

Augarde, Tony. *Oxford Guide to Word Games*. Oxford: Oxford University Press, 2003.

Augustine. *The Confessions of St. Augustine*. Tr. E.B. Pusey. London: J.M. Dent and Co., 1907.

Ayto, John. *From the Horse's Mouth: Oxford Dictionary of English Idioms*. Oxford: Oxford University Press, 2009.

Balzac, Honoré de. *La Peau de chagrin ; Le Cure de Tours et Le Colonel Chabert*. Paris: Nelson, 1958.

Beattie, Geoffrie W. 'Truth and Lies in Body Language'. *New Scientist* 22 Oct. 1981: 230-232.

Bergman, Ingmar. *The Seventh Seal*. Motion picture. 1957. United Kingdom: Tartan Video, 2001.

Biro, Matthew. 'Representation and Event: Anselm Kiefer, Joseph Beuys, and the Memory of the Holocaust'. *The Yale Journal of Criticism* 16.1 (2003): 113-146.

Blake, William. *The Poems of William Blake*. Edited by W. H. Stevenson, text by David V. Erdman. Harlow, Longman, 1971.

Bosky, Bernadette Lynn. 'The Inner Lives of Characters and Readers: Affective Stylistics in Charles Williams's Fiction'. *The Rhetoric of Vision: Essays on Charles Williams*. Ed. Charles Huttar and Peter Schakel. London: Associated University Press, 1996: 59-75.

Brontë, Charlotte. *Shirley*. 1849. Oxford: Oxford University Press, 2007.

Broom, Sarah. *Contemporary British and Irish Poetry*. Houndmills, Basingstoke, and New York: Palgrave Macmillan, 2006.

Bunyan, John. *The Pilgrim's Progress : from this world to that which is, to come, delivered under the similitude of a dream*. 1678. New York: Pocket Books, 1957.

Burton, Robert. *The Anatomy of Melancholy, what it is: with all the kinds, causes, symptons, prognostics, and several cures of it, Volume 1*. 1621. Philadelphia, New York: J. W. Moore, J. Wiley, 1850.

Calverley, Charles Stuart. *Translations into English and Latin*. London: Bell and Daldy, 1866.

Cannon, Christopher. *Middle English Literature: A Cultural History*. Cambridge: Polity, 2008.

Clark, Tom. 'Subversive Histories'. *The American Poetry Review* 28:5 (1999): 7.
Cork, Richard, and Miles Richmond. *In Celebration of David Bomberg 1890-1957*. Exhibition catalogue. London: Daniel Katz Gallery, 2007.
Coward, Noel. *Private Lives*. London: Heinemann, 1930.
Cowell, Henry and Sidney Cowell. *Charles Ives and His Music*. New York: Oxford University Press, 1955.
Cowper, William. *The Poetical Works of William Cowper*. Ed. H. S. Milford. London: Oxford University Press, 1934.
De Quincey, Thomas. 'The Knocking at the Gate in *Macbeth*'. *The Oxford Book of Essays*. Ed. John Gross. Oxford: Oxford University Press, 1991: 131-136.
Dean, James, ed. *Richard the Redeless; and, Mum and the Sothsegger*. Kalamazoo, MI: Published for TEAMS (the Consortium for the Teaching of the Middle Ages) in association with the University of Rochester by Medieval Institute Publications, Western Michigan University, 2000.
Deutsches Worterbuch. Ed. Paul Hermann. Tubingen: Niemeyer, 1957-1966.
Dobson, Michael and Nicola J. Watson. *England's Elizabeth: An Afterlife in Fame and Fantasy*. Oxford & New York: Oxford University Press, 2002.
Dreisinger, Baz. 'Def Poetry'. Review of *Book of Rhymes: The Poetics of Hip Hop*, by Adam Bradley. *The New York Times* 8 Sep. 2009: BR.19.
Edwards, Michael. 'Quotidian Epic: Geoffrey Hill's *The Triumph of Love*'. *The Yale Journal of Criticism* 13.1 (2000): 167-176.
Eliot, T. S. *Collected Poems 1909-1962*. London: Faber and Faber, 1963.
— *The Sacred Wood: Essays on Poetry and Criticism*. 1920. London: Faber and Faber, 1997.
Ennius, Quintus. *The Annals of Quintus Ennius*. Ed. Otto Skutsch. Oxford: Clarendon Press, 1985.
'Examiner'. 'Is our Roman History Teaching Reactionary?' *Greece and Rome* 12.35-36 (1943): 57-61.
Fishlock, Michael. *The Great Fire at Hampton Court*. London: Herbert Press, 1992.
Fitz-Gerald, Shafto J. A. *Stories of Famous Songs*. General Books 2009 (accessed 1 Oct. 2010) <http://books.google.co.nz/books?id=wmk6X9_qm_4C>.

BIBLIOGRAPHY

Flynn, D. A. 'Purse-Proud Opulence'. Review of *John Donne and Conformity in Crisis in the Late Jacobean Pulpit*, by Jeanne Shami. *Essays in Criticism* 55.2 (2005): 173-177.
Fraser, Robert. Review of *Christopher Okigbo 1930-67*, by Obi Nwakanwa. *Times Literary Supplement*, 5 Nov. 2010: 29.
Gibbons, Brian. *Shakespeare and Multiplicity*. Cambridge & New York: Cambridge University Press, 1993.
Glennie, Evelyn. 'Beat of a Different Drummer'. *PBS Newshour* 14 June 1999 (accessed 25 Aug. 2007) <http://www.pbs.org/newshour/bb/entertainment/jan-june99/drummer_6-14.html>.
— 'Hearing Essay'. *Dame Evelyn Glennie Official Website* (accessed 21 May 2007) <http://www.evelyn.co.uk/live/hearing_essay.htm>.
Grass, Günter. *Selected Poems of Günter Grass*. Tr. Michael Hamburger and Christopher Middleton. Harmondsworth: Penguin, 1980.
Greene, Graham. *Brighton Rock*. 1938. London: Heinemann, 1970.
Gregorio, Barry E. 'Life on the Rocks'. *New Scientist* 13 Feb. 2010: 40-43.
Gritsch, Eric W. *The Wit of Martin Luther*. Minneapolis: Fortress Press, 2006.
Grovier, Kelly. 'Keats and the Holocaust: Notes Towards a Post-Temporalism'. *Literature and Theology* 17:4 (2003): 361.
Hale, Sarah Josepha Buell and John F. Addington. *A Complete Dictionary of Poetical Quotations*. Philadelphia: J. B. Lippincott and Co., 1855.
Hammer, Langdon. 'The American Poetry of Thom Gunn and Geoffrey Hill'. *Contemporary Literature* 43.4 (2002): 644-666.
— 'To the Dark Wood'. Review of *The Triumph of Love*, by Geoffrey Hill. *The New York Times Book Review* 17 Jan. 1999: 10.
Hanna, Ralph III. 'Annotation as Social Practice'. *Annotation and its* Texts. Ed. Stephen A. Barney. New York & Oxford: Oxford University Press, 1991.
Heller, Joseph. *Catch-22*. 1961. New York: Alfred A. Knopf, 1995.
Hoban, Russell. *Riddley Walker: A Novel*. New York: Summit Books, 1980.
Holmes, Paul. *Holst: His Life and Times*. London: Omnibus Press, 1998.

Hopkins, Gerard Manley. *Poems and Prose*. Ed. W. H. Gardner. Harmondsworth: Penguin, 1975.

Horner, Avril. *English Modernist or Postmodern European?* Salford: University of Salford European Studies Research Institute, 1994.

Huk, Romana. 'Poetry of the Committed Individual: Jon Silkin, Tony Harrison, Geoffrey Hill, and the Poets of Postwar Leeds'. *Contemporary British Poetry: Essays in Theory and Criticism*. Eds. James Acheson and Romana Huk. Albany: State University of New York Press, 1996: 175-220.

Ingelbein, Raphaël. *Misreading England: Poetry and Nationhood since the Second World War*. Amsterdam & New York: Editions Rodopi, 2002.

James, Stephen. 'The Smeared Vision'. *Poetry Review* 92.3 (2002): 97-100.

James, Stephen. *Shades of Authority: The Poetry of Lowell, Hill and Heaney*. Liverpool: Liverpool University Press, 2007.

Joyce, James. *Ulysses*. 1922. New York: Random House, 1934.

— *Finnegans Wake*. 1939. London: Penguin, 1999.

Kander, John. *Cabaret: Libretto (English)*. New York: Random House, 1967.

Kennedy, David. *New Relations: The Refashioning of British Poetry, 1980-1994*. Bridgend: Seren, 1996.

Kinderman, William. *Beethoven*. Oxford & New York: Oxford University Press, 1997.

Kipling, Rudyard. *Collected Poems*. Hertfordshire: Wordsworth, 1999.

Knowles, Elizabeth M., ed. *The Oxford Dictionary of Quotations*. Oxford: Oxford University Press, 2004.

Langland, William. *The Vision of Piers Plowman*. c.1360-1387. London: Dent, 1982.

Longfellow, Henry Wadsworth. *Complete Poetical Works*. Boston: Houghton Mifflin, 1950.

Lorca, Federico García. 'Theory and Function of the Duende'. *Toward the Open Field: Poets on the Art of Poetry, 1800-1950*. Ed. Melissa Kwasny. Middletown, CT: Wesleyan University Press, 2004: 197-208.

Lucas Collins, W. *Cicero: Ancient Classics for English Readers*. Middlesex: Echo Library, 2007.

Luther, Martin, tr. *Die Bibel oder Die ganze Heilige Schrift des Alten und Neuen Testaments. Nach der Übersetzung Martin Luthers*. 1534. Stuttgart: Württembergische Bibelanstalt, 1963.

BIBLIOGRAPHY

Marshall, H. E. *English Literature for Boys and Girls*. London: T. C. and E. C. Jack, 1909.

Martial. *Select Epigrams*. Eds. Lindsay and Patricia Watson. Cambridge & New York: Cambridge University Press, 2003.

Martin, Frank. *Suite from* Der Sturm, *Six Monologues from* Jedermann *and* Symphonie Concertante. Audio recording. MDG: 2010.

Munro, H. H. *The Complete Saki*. London: Penguin, 1982.

Murray, Carl. 'The Use and Abuse of Dogs in Scott's and Amundsen's South Pole Expeditions'. *Polar Record* 44.231 (2008): 303-310.

Nietzsche, Friedrich. *Thus Spake Zarathustra*. 1883-1885. New York: Algora Publishing, 2007.

Owen, Wilfred. *The Complete Poems and Fragments*. Ed. Jon Stallworthy. London: Chatto and Windus/Hogarth Press, 1983.

Partridge, Eric. *A Dictionary of Catch Phrases: British and American, from the Sixteenth Century to the Present Day*. London: Routledge, 1986.

Pater, Walter. *The Renaissance*. Cambridge: Chadwyck-Healey, 1999 (accessed 1 Mar. 2009) <http://gateway.proquest.com/openurl/openurl?ctx_ver=Z 39.88-2003&xri:pqil:res_ver=0.2&r es_id=xri:lion-us&rft_id=xri:lion:ft:pr:Z000728158:0>.

Paterson, Don. *The Blind Eye*. London: Faber and Faber, 2007.

Paulu, Burton. *Television and Radio in the United Kingdom*. Minneapolis, MN: University of Minnesota Press, 1981.

Phillips, John. 'Droitwich Calling'. *BBCeng.info: Recollections of BBC Engineering from 1922 to 1997* 1 Dec. 2006 (accessed 5 Oct. 2008) <http://www.bbceng.info/Operations/transmitter_ops/Reminiscences/Droitwich/droitwich_calling.htm>.

Phillips, John. *The Marquis de Sade: A Very Short Introduction*. Oxford; New York: Oxford University Press, 2005.

Porter, Darwin and Danforth Prince. *Frommer's London 2010*. Hoboken, NJ: Wiley, 2010.

Pouliquen J. C, Noat M, Verneret C, Guillemin G, and Patat J. L. 'Coral substituted for bone grafting in posterior vertebral arthrodesis in children'. *Revue de Chirurgie Orthopédique et Réparatrice de l'Appareil Moteur* 75.6 (1989): 360-369.

Reeves, Gareth. 'This is Plenty. This is More than Enough'. *Oxford Handbook of British and Irish War Poetry*. Ed. Tim Kendall. Oxford: Oxford University Press, 2007.

Resnais, Alain. *Nuit et Brouillard / Night and fog*. 1955. Motion Picture. Como Films: Criterion Collection, 2003.

Ricks, Christopher. *Beckett's Dying Words: The Clarendon Lectures, 1990 (Clarendon Lectures in English, 1990)*. Oxford: Clarendon Press; New York: Oxford University Press, 1993.

Rimbaud, Jean Nicholas Arthur. *Complete Works, Selected Letters (A Bilingual Edition)*. Eds. Wallace Fowlie and Seth Whidden. Chicago: University of Chicago Press, 2005.

Rosenberg, Isaac. *The Poems and Plays of Isaac Rosenberg*. Ed. Vivien Noakes. Oxford; New York: Oxford University Press, 2004.

Royle, Trevor, ed. *In Flanders Fields: Scottish Poetry and Prose of the First World War*. Edinburgh: Mainstream Publishing, 1990.

Sayers, Sean. 'The Concept of Labour: Marx and his Critics'. *Science and Society* 71.4 (2007): 431-454.

Scannell, Paddy. *Radio, Television, and Modern Life: A Phenomenological Approach*. Oxford: Wiley-Blackwell, 1996.

Schaff, Philip and Henry Wace, eds. *A Select Library of Nicene and Post-Nicene Fathers of the Christian Church. Second Series*. BiblioLife: 2009 (accessed 10 July 2010) <http://books.google.co.nz/books?id=ZFchZPQPUdgC>.

Schama, Simon. *Rembrandt's Eyes*. New York: Alfred A. Knopf, 1999.

Schubert, Franz. *Die Winterreise*. Musical score. New York: Kalmus, 1900.

Skelton, John. *John Skelton: The Complete English Poems*. Ed. John Scattergood. New Haven: Yale University Press, 1983.

Southey, Robert. *Poetical Works*. Eds. Lynda Pratt, Tim Fulford and Daniel Roberts. London: Pickering and Chatto, 2004.

Spencer, Charles. *Althorp: the Story of an English House*. New York: St. Martin's Press, 1999.

Stephens, Philip. *Tony Blair: The Making of a World Leader*. New York: Viking, 2004.

Street, Sean. *A Concise History of British Radio, 1922-2002*. Tiverton: Kelly Publications, 2002.

BIBLIOGRAPHY

Swinburne, Algernon Charles. *The Complete Works*. Eds. Sir Edmund Gosse and Thomas James Wise. London: Heinemann, 1927.

Theroux, Paul. *The Pillars of Hercules: A Grand Tour of the Mediterranean*. New York: Fawcett Columbine, 1996.

Thomas, Dylan. *The Poems of Dylan Thomas*. Ed. Daniel Jones. Oxford; New York: Oxford University Press, 2004.

Tiedemann, Rolf. *Can One Live after Auschwitz?: A Philosophical Reader*. Stanford CA: Stanford University Press, 2003.

Turing, Alan. *The Essential Turing: Seminal Writings in Computing, Logic, Philosophy, Artificial Intelligence, and Artificial Life, plus, the Secrets of Enigma*. Ed. B. Jack Copeland. Oxford: Clarendon Press, 2004.

Wale, Adebanwi. 'Death, National Memory and the Social Construction of Heroism'. *The Journal of African History* 49 (2008): 419-444.

Walton, Izaak. *The Lives of John Donne, Sir Henry Wotton, Mr. Richard Hooker, Mr. George Herbert*. 1675. Early English Books Online (accessed 1 Nov. 2009) <http://gateway.proquest.com/openurl?ctx_ver=Z39.88-2003&res_id=xri:eebo&rft_id=xri:eebo:image:102629:46>.

Weissmuller, Johnny Jr., and W. Craig Reed. *Tarzan, My Father*. Toronto: ECW Press, 2002.

Wesley, Charles. *The Sermons of Charles Wesley: A Critical Edition, with Introduction and Notes*. Ed. Kenneth G. C. Newport. Oxford & New York: Oxford University Press, 2001.

White, Sarah. 'Dreamwork as Etymology'. *Dreaming* 9.1 (1999): 11-21.

Whitman, Walt. *Selected Poems*. Ed. Stephen Spender. London: Grey Walls, 1950.

Wilde, Oscar. *The Importance of Being Earnest: A Trivial Comedy for Serious People*. Ed. Russell Jackson. London: Benn, 1980.

Williams, Charles. *The Figure of Beatrice: A Study in Dante*. London: Faber, 1943.

— Ed. *The New Christian Year*. London: Oxford University Press, 1941.

Wordsworth, William. *Complete Poetical Works*. Ed. Andrew J. George. Boston: Houghton Mifflin, 1960.

APPENDIX: IMAGES

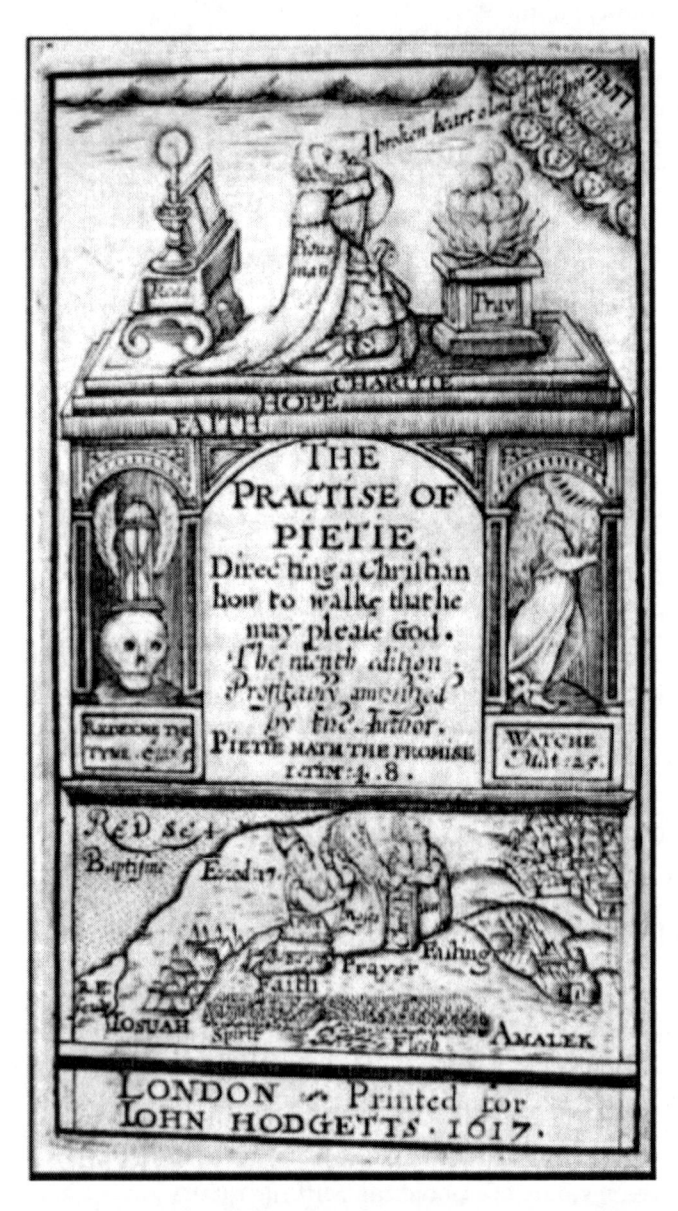

Fig. 1. Engraved title page of Lewis Bayly's *The Practise of Pietie*, 9th ed. (1617).

APPENDIX

Fig. 2. Dürer, 'Portrait of Maximilian I' (c 1519).

Fig. 3. Daumier, 'On Dit Que Les Parisiens...' (1864).

APPENDIX

Fig. 4. Caravaggio, 'The Flagellation of Christ' (c 1607).

Fig. 5. Bomberg, 'Portrait of Dinora' (1951).

APPENDIX

Fig. 6. Füssli, 'The Nightmare' (1781).

Fig. 7. Death portrait of Donne (1630).

APPENDIX

Fig. 8. Nicholas Stone effigy of Donne in St Paul's Cathedral, based on Donne's commissioned portrait (1631).

Fig. 9. Moore, 'Madonna and Child' (1943-44), Church of St Matthew in Northampton.

APPENDIX

Fig. 10. Spencer, 'The Resurrection, Cookham' (1924-1927).

Fig. 11. Daumier, 'Les Saltimbanques' (1866-67).

Fig. 12. The last photograph of the Scott party (1912).

APPENDIX

Fig. 13. Rembrandt, 'The Polish Rider' (1655).

Fig. 14. Rembrandt, 'The Departure of the Shunammite Woman' (1640).

APPENDIX

Fig. 15. Beuys, 'Auschwitz Demonstration' (1968).

Fig. 16. Kiefer, 'The Breaking of the Vessels' (1990).

A *GLOSSATOR* SPECIAL EDITION

Glossator publishes original commentaries, editions and translations of commentaries, and essays and articles relating to the theory and history of commentary, glossing, and marginalia. The journal aims to encourage the practice of commentary as a creative form of intellectual work and to provide a forum for dialogue and reflection on the past, present, and future of this ancient genre of writing. By aligning itself, not with any particular discipline, but with a particular mode of production, *Glossator* gives expression to the fact that praxis founds theory.

GLOSSATOR.ORG